Architecture and ekphrasis

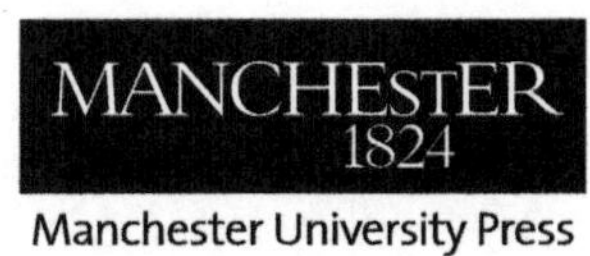
Manchester University Press

rethinking
art's histories

SERIES EDITORS
Amelia G. Jones, Marsha Meskimmon

Rethinking Art's Histories aims to open out art history from its most basic structures by foregrounding work that challenges the conventional periodisation and geographical subfields of traditional art history, and addressing a wide range of visual cultural forms from the early modern period to the present.

These books will acknowledge the impact of recent scholarship on our understanding of the complex temporalities and cartographies that have emerged through centuries of world-wide trade, political colonisation and the diasporic movement of people and ideas across national and continental borders.

Also available in the series
Colouring the Caribbean: Race and the art of Agostino Brunias Mia L. Bagneris
Bound together: Leather, sex, archives and contemporary art Andy Campbell
Staging art and Chineseness: The politics of trans/nationalism and global expositions
Jane Chin Davidson
Travelling images: Looking across the borderlands of art, media and visual culture
Anna Dahlgren
Empires of light: Vision, visibility and power in colonial India Niharika Dinkar
Art, Global Maoism and the Chinese Cultural Revolution Jacopo Galimberti,
Noemi de Haro-García and Victoria H. F. Scott (eds)
Addressing the other woman: Textual correspondences in feminist art and writing
Kimberly Lamm
Above sea: Contemporary art, urban culture, and the fashioning of global Shanghai
Jenny Lin
Engendering an avant-garde: The unsettled landscapes of Vancouver photo-conceptualism Leah Modigliani
The ecological eye: Assembling an ecocritical art history Andrew Patrizio
Migration into art: Transcultural identities and art-making in a globalised world
Anne Ring Petersen

Architecture and ekphrasis

Space, time and the embodied description of the past

Dana Arnold

Manchester University Press

Published by Manchester University Press
Altrincham Street, Manchester M1 7JA
www.manchesteruniversitypress.co.uk

British Library Cataloguing-in-Publication Data
A catalogue record for this book is available from the British Library

ISBN 978 0 7190 9949 6 hardback
ISBN 978 0 7190 9950 2 paperback

First published 2020

Typeset
by Sunrise Setting Ltd, Brixham
Printed in Great Britain
by TJ Books Limited, Padstow

For Nigel

Contents

Figures

Acknowledgements

My fascination with ekphrasis and the resonance between verbal and visual descriptions of architecture started almost as soon as I began to study art history. These concerns about how the practices and processes of recording influence our conception and understanding of the past have remained with me. Spatiality, temporality and the biographical trace have been predominant themes in my writing in recent years, where I have sought to question perceived, canonical norms and establish modes of enquiry that transcend a particular historical instance. Here I combine these preoccupations to explore how space, time and the notion of embodiment inflect on visual ekphrases of the architecture of the past.

The support of my editor, Emma Brennan, during the preparation of this book has been much appreciated. I am also greatly indebted to Dr Clare Barry who has given me invaluable assistance in the sourcing of the images and in compiling the index. Most of all, I wish to thank Nigel King. His strength and poise in recent years has been an inspiration, as has his invaluable enthusiasm for and confidence in my ability to complete this book.

Prolegomenon

DESCRIPTION [desciptio, Lat.]

1. The act of describing or making out any person or thing by perceptible properties.

Samuel Johnson, *A Dictionary of the English Language*, vol. I. London, 1755.

The long eighteenth century witnessed the emergence of new languages of architectural description, both verbal and visual. Here, I am concerned with the significance of graphic representation, as evident in drawings but more prevalently in prints, for the discovery of the ancient world and as a means of developing and disseminating architectural ideas in the eighteenth century. I wish to concentrate on the relationship between drawings and prints both in terms of their materiality and how they operate as engines of history. Fundamental to this are the ways in which the architecture of the past is described.

This book focuses on examples of graphic representations of architecture as they appear in architectural treatises, as well as publications of studies of particular antique buildings or sites, during the long eighteenth century. I argue that these images are in fact a form of writing, in the full sense of the word, as they have syntactical and linguistic qualities that convey both ideas and experience. This line of enquiry allows us new understandings of how these images functioned as both an inspiration to architectural imagination and practice, and the ways in which they have influenced how histories have been formulated. Instances of the relationship between the verbal and the visual are explored at the intersection of theory and archive. And these anachronistic juxtapositions work to disrupt established hegemonies about the description of the built past during the long eighteenth century. Perhaps most importantly, this study explores the gap between written and visual descriptions of architecture. More precisely, this book is about what the visual allows us to explore and convey that the verbal does not. In order to unpack this we need to take a few steps back and begin by thinking about how we might use words to describe a piece of text. We would instantly notice that the linguistic construction of our description runs parallel to the text we are describing.[1]

They are both progressive and follow syntactical formulae, which in the West we read left to right. My question here is how does this process inflect on our description of the visual world?

For those of us trained as art historians in the West, we are used to perceiving and reading pictures as we would a text – as a linear progression from left to right. Our analysis of composition is frequently biased by such readings. The flatness of the canvas helps underscore this mode of seeing and describing a painting as if it were a text.[2] But our experience of architecture is rather different. Architecture is both the flat articulated spaces of a building and the space that it encloses. It is at once an experiential and a visual phenomenon. As a consequence, our perception of architecture cannot be a process of reading or looking from left to right. Our eyes will move randomly across the surfaces of a building concentrating on chance details. Our bodily and visual experience of height, light, sound and texture cannot be described within/using the syntagmatic structures of discourse as, unlike the relationship between text and text, they do not run in parallel. As such, verbal descriptions can be at odds with the architecture or spaces they attempt to describe. What, then, does a visual description reveal, allow or release that a verbal one cannot? Does it, for example, tell us something about gender in relation to the representation and experience of the architecture of antiquity?

The linguistic qualities of images

With these caveats in mind, I want to begin with the concept of ekphrasis – the verbal description of a work of art or, indeed, its re-creation through language. The roots of this process in the literature of classical antiquity need not concern us here. Suffice to say that the rhetorical tradition of ekphrasis, first found in Homer and thence Philostratus, Lucian and other classical writers, is an established system of translating the visual into the verbal.[3] Importantly, here this is achieved through the action of choosing details and inevitably the choice of certain details means that the same object can be represented differently. Clearly, this process has had a substantial impact on the way in which we write about art and there are many erudite analyses of the influence of ekphrasis on the development of the history of art.[4] There is no doubt that description or narration is an essential process in the discipline of art history where the analysis of the visual is bound up in linguistic practices.[5] What I am arguing here is that the visual representation of architecture also operates as a kind of ekphrasis. It is at once a means of both describing an actual object and translating it into a different mode of representation. An image of architecture, like an ekphrasis, chooses details in order to narrate or describe its subject. The mode of graphic notation of these details operates in the same way as words (language) to present architecture in a certain way. The various graphic conventions of architecture conform to linguistic principles, and through their selective representation of details images work to interpret architecture. As a consequence, they make visible what may not have previously been apparent and engaging with the imagination, whilst making the building seem 'real'. This is important for my theme as I aim to argue that images of architecture – specifically here the architecture of antiquity – operate as a kind of language; they have descriptive qualities. The acts of verbal and visual description share a distance from that which is being described and it is this distance that makes ekphrasis possible.

The various types of images of the architecture of the past share common concerns. Perhaps most obviously are the issues of how to represent the three dimensions of the built environment in a coherent two-dimensional form and how to convey the idea of space and spatiality. Here, I want to privilege the images made of the past at a crucial moment when technology enabled new printing techniques. The printing press was an important and very obvious example of superiority over the ancient world and helped define the 'modern' period. Like its Renaissance predecessor – moveable type – the engraving in the long eighteenth century gave access to various forms of information about the past and in doing so appeared to overcome the barriers of time and space. The belief that it was possible to 'publish' the monuments of the past as engravings is not to be underestimated either for its novelty or by the differing motives for wishing to do so on the part of the antiquarian community. These diverse agendas ranged from preserving an artefact through its memorialisation in print to enhancing the perceived value and significance of a collection of antiquities. The act of representation presented fundamental choices about how monuments, including architecture, were described. Should they be textualised or should their materiality be translated into a readable two-dimensional form. Leading on from this, was textualisation a process that harked back to the descriptions of antiquity?

The relationship between text and image is important as a means of understanding how these histories of the classical past operated. And what we see here is the way in which visual illustration becomes an increasingly significant form of knowledge that is independent from the traditional antiquarian reliance on textual precedent. For instance, Bernard de Montfaucon published 15 volumes of *L'antiquité expliquée et représentée en figures* between 1719 and 1724. The wide-ranging work contained copperplate folio engravings of antiquities from ancient Egypt, Greece, Rome and elsewhere. Montfaucon uses illustrations to give clarity and order to what might otherwise appear the jumbled and divergent narratives of the past by acknowledging the significance of visual evidence when compared to textual sources. An English translation of this work was published in 1721–25 under the title *Antiquity Explained and Represented in Diagrams*. This prompted a number of antiquarians to reposition the role of images in the construction of histories. Rather than illustrations merely supporting an apparently known history, empirical observation of visual evidence could challenge the received wisdom of antiquity's textual sources.

That said, there remained a strong tradition of text-based antiquarian scholarship. Certainly this was the case with antiquarians such as Johann Joachim Winckelmann whose study of the past divorced artefacts from their contexts.[6] This was probably an attempt to raise the status of antiquarianism by rejecting the focus on physical remains. In his *Gedanken über die Nachahmung der griechischen Werke in der Malerei und Bildhauerkunst* (1755) Winckelmann introduced as systematic, chronological study of art history that provided a central plank in the evolving idea of chronology and progress in western culture.[7] But Winckelmann relied on textual descriptions of objects to write his verbal history which has remained the standard chronology for art history. Winckelmann's ideas also draw heavily on mid-eighteenth-century theories of language, which were seen as having developed its resources to allow a clear knowledge of things but excesses in style and rhetoric led to its degeneration. This locates Winckelmann's analysis, or system of history, as he preferred to call it, firmly in the verbal tradition. And this verbal system was translated into English only ten years after its original publication by the artist Henry Fuseli as *Reflections on the Painting and Sculpture of The Greeks*.[8] Winckelmann's major work, *Monumenti antichi inediti* is notorious for the poor quality of its engraved images and its lack of interest in the physicality of the monuments he records. Ostensibly a volume that records the great monuments under his care in the collection of the Pope, Clement XIII, Winckelmann chose instead to make physical monuments totally subservient to verbal texts. Indeed, his insistence on reading the iconography of monuments only in order to illuminate ancient texts saw the production of a volume in which engravings were not only inaccurate and aesthetically dull, but where bas-reliefs, statues and even paintings become almost indistinguishable. By removing ancient monuments from their historical and material contexts, Winckelmann insists that the material past is only of value in so far as its study aspires to the status of poetry.

The preoccupations of Winckelmann find a counterpoint in Gotthold Ephraim Lessing's *Laocoön* (1766). Lessing's choice of title is the well-known marble sculpture of the Trojan priest Laocoön and his two sons being attacked by snakes sent by the gods, which was in the papal collection of antiquities in the Vatican. The work was under the care of Winckelmann, who had been appointed Prefect of Antiquities to Pope Clement XIII in 1763. The Laocoön sculpture had been unearthed in 1506 and had remained one of the most popular pieces for visitors to Rome, not least the Grand Tourists in the eighteenth century. There is some irony here, however, as Lessing had not visited Rome before writing his *Laocoön*, so he relied on literary and pictorial representations of the work, indeed it may have been described by Pliny the Elder in his *Natural History* (XXXVI, 37). But this distance from the original did not diminish the impact of Lessing's ideas or his exploration of the relationship between verbal and visual descriptions of artworks. In *Laocoön* the relationship between painting and poetry as modes of representation is traced back to the authors of antiquity from Simonides' fifth-century BCE dictum 'painting is silent poetry, and poetry is talking painting' to Horace's perhaps better known adage some four centuries later '*ut pictura poesis*/as painting so is poetry' that has become almost synonymous with eighteenth-century preoccupations with landscape. Whilst acknowledging that pleasure is derived from both poetry and painting, Lessing sought to differentiate between the two.[9]

> If it is true that in its imitations painting uses completely different means or signs than does poetry, namely figures and colours in space rather than articulated sounds in time, and if these signs must indisputably bear a suitable relation to the thing signified, then signs existing in space can express only objects whose wholes or parts coexist, while signs that follow one another can express only objects whose wholes or parts are consecutive.
>
> Objects or parts of objects which exist in space are called bodies.
> Accordingly, bodies with their visible properties are the true subjects of painting.
> Objects or parts of objects which follow one another are called actions.
> Accordingly, actions are the true subjects of poetry.[10]

In this way, the visual world unfolds in space, whereas words follow one another in a sequence that connotes time.

Johann Wolfgang von Goethe recognised the importance of Lessing's *Laocoön*:

> One has to be a young man to visualize what an effect Lessing's *Laocoön* had on us, this work that swept us away from the regions of meagre contemplation and onto the open terrain of thought. The saying '*ut pictura poesis*', so long misunderstood, was now suddenly set aside, and the difference between the pictorial [*sic*] and verbal arts was now clear. The peaks of both now appeared separate, however closely they touched at the base … . The full consequence of this brilliant thought was illuminated for us as though by a flash of lightning. We cast off all previous critical instructions and judgments like a worn-out coat, we considered ourselves delivered from all evil, and we felt justified in looking down somewhat pityingly at the otherwise very magnificent sixteenth century.[11]

Indeed, Lessing's identification and exploration of the idea of the visual and linguistic sign continued to engage thinkers from Kant and Hegel to Foucault and Derrida, via Saussure.[12] For art historians, Lessing has largely remained as a part of the debates about representation in painting and its role in the historiography of art history, and about visual culture more broadly.[13] My concerns are different, as I focus on the distinction between the spatial and the temporal worlds as evident in graphic representations of ancient architecture as modes of ekphrasis. And it is here that we find the crossover between aesthetics and narratives of history, which was viewed as a branch of literature at this time. Whereas art-historical scholarship has focused on the relationship between word and image with particular reference to painting, my interest is in the role of the graphic arts as commissioned and circulated by eighteenth-century antiquarians. These images both acted as interlocutors between past and present, and explored the resonance between space and time.

I would like to concentrate here on the ways in which the improved techniques of production, together with the increasingly popular practice of cultural tourism, prompted innovative forms of visual representation that made three-dimensional objects widely available in a readable and coherent two-dimensional formula. In turn, these images engendered an ever-refining set of cultural values applied to and associated with antiquity. Prints equipped polite society with the critical faculties necessary to determine the associative values of modern and antique architecture and design. In this way we see how architecture and its images were seen as essential pieces of evidence about the past and their reproduction was an equally essential element of historical narrative as the reproduction of textual sources and histories. The separation of the visual image from written histories creates new visual histories, which in turn challenge the pre-eminence of the text. I want to ask what kind of rational debate might be operating around these representations and what purposes those debates serve. Moreover, were these images part of the increasing democratisation of aesthetics in the eighteenth century?[14]

History, time and space

The role of images in the construction of histories is germane to this book. One of the fundamental questions underpinning my line of enquiry is how we try to make the past visible. We are used to using words to narrate, describe or explain the past. The use of images in the formulation and telling of histories can be seen as a means of helping us to move away from the logocentricism I outline above. That said, we might also wish to question the belief in images as a form of immutable truth or evidence of the past. This also raises questions in my mind about the status of visual representations and how they operate as a mode of historical production.

The need to classify and codify in order to clarify for the modern world is a core concern in the production of images of classical antiquities. My focus here is on antiquarians, architects, and their patrons with a vested interest in establishing architecture based on classical antiquity as the modern style. Their favoured techniques of printing and engraving were commonly upheld as icons of modernity. As such, these techniques demonstrated one of the few ways in which modernity enjoyed superiority over the ancient world. Like moveable type, the engraving enabled and encouraged the production and consumption of information that transcended space and time. This transformation of the materialness of the past into a recognisable and readable two-dimensional form required a firm belief in the systems or modes of representation and, indeed, ekphrasis.

Textual historical narratives tend to favour the idea of 'progress' in western culture. Consequently, we might also argue that architectural images follow that model. Indeed, the measured, orthogonal drawings of Andrea Palladio or Nicholas Revett insist on a form of abstraction and reduction which aims to impose order on the 'inexact reality' of the remains of ancient architecture. That said, other kinds of printed representation allow us to trace a narrative of visual and experiential history that is independent of notions of progress. They articulate an emotive, psychological response to the architecture of the past which is outside of verbal expression and cannot be conveyed by other graphic means. In this way, images allow us not only to consider the role that prints played in the construction of visual histories but also the impact the printing press – the first means of mechanically reproducing an image – had on the idea of history itself. Moreover, the rediscovery of the past by antiquarians from the Renaissance onwards complemented known histories as well as revealing stories that had not been told in textual sources. Material objects can then act as an archive and tell a story. In this way, coins, medals, sculptures, prints and even architecture seem to have an immutable truth – but is this really the case?

The Enlightenment idea of history embraced at once the visual and the verbal subject so images played an important part in the construction of historical knowledge. Optical demonstration and visualisation were essential processes in the search to uncover the pure historical condition of humankind. This is seen, for instance, in the superlative position held by history painting in the academic hierarchy of subjects where painters of only the highest calibre depicted the past. In terms of an artist's academic training and the influence this had on public taste the past – history – was privileged over representations of the landscape or even portraiture. If, then, history was conceived as a visual subject how could it be related verbally and what were the consequences of this?

The discovery and ordering of the past played an important part in the life of modern Europe and even became a symbol of modernity. To this end, archaeology and the archaeological survey were used to excite the imagination and to proselytise ideas and to re-tell history. Here it is important to consider the intellectual climate in which these histories were constructed where reason played a pivotal role in the development of historical and linguistic thought and knowledge. And in this context the Aristotelian notion of the relationship between reason, memory and imagination was important in the construction of histories and was a keystone of aesthetic discourse in the eighteenth century.[15]

If we accept the Aristotelian notion that reason precedes verbalised ideas and imagination operates as a visual expression or sensation with memory sitting between reason and imagination, this sequence then begins to reveal something of the role of the status of the image in eighteenth-century architectural debate. In other words, we need a visual recollection of the object to provoke a response. This recollection can also be verbal, but in this case, following Aristotle's sequence, a reliance on the verbal implies the dilution of reason. Aristotle's ideas about imitation or 'mimesis' refer principally to literary aesthetics. But in the eighteenth century the interplay between the verbal and the visual and this questioning of the role of reason was current. For instance, Sir Joshua Reynolds asked to what extent the visual activity of painting could be taught through words.[16] But it is clear that the making of history, whether verbal or visual, required the imitation or representation of objects and events and the practice falls into two main categories: pictorial imitation or literary imitation. But both methods strive to provide an assemblage of 'facts'. We are familiar with textual 'facts' – descriptions of events or actions. But what constituted a visual 'fact' or fragment of knowledge? And were these facts ready for the manipulation of the historian in the same way as verbal ones and have they the same kind of originality?

The world in miniature

Visual histories usually comprised an assemblage of images, which may have been produced at different times by different artists or engravers, held together in a bound volume.[17] These kinds of publication were not uncommon in the eighteenth century nor were the different kinds of graphic notation used in the plates. These assemblages sometimes remained fluid so operating as an ever-changing discourse and this helps explain how these collections functioned as different collectors added to them or reconfigured their arrangement. Perhaps more importantly here is what happens to the past in these individual images and collections where it is miniaturised. Susan Stewart has argued that images (in her case photographs and postcards) preserve a moment in time and become souvenirs. The function of these souvenirs is to 'authenticate the past'.[18] And it is this represented past that is authentic, as it is a distance from present time and space. Indeed, Stewart contests that

> in antiquarianism we see a theory of history informed by the aesthetics of the souvenir. [...] the antiquarian seeks to both distance and appropriate the past. In order to entertain an antiquarian sensibility, a rupture in historical consciousness must have occurred, creating a sense that one can make one's own culture *other* – distant and discontinuous.[19]

In this way we can begin to see how these visual representations of the architecture of the past in miniature become souvenirs that speaks more to the time of their consumption than their production. The graphic image is crucial here, as it is part of the search for an imagined past which is created for consumption. And arguably, a collection of images orders and manipulates desire and so operates differently from a souvenir.[20]

Returning to our eighteenth-century Grand Tourists we can begin to think about how antiquarians seek to both distance and appropriate the past. An antiquarian sensibility makes one's own culture 'other' and time is seen as concomitant with a loss of understanding, so the distance of time is key here. This loss can be overcome through the awakening of objects and of narrative. The antiquarian looks for material evidence of the past and at the same time an intrinsic relationship between past and present. The search is, then, for an imagined past (devoid of narrative) which is created for consumption. Crucial here is the role of the imagination and the affect this has on notions of truth and authenticity. It has been argued that images of the antique attempt to replace the actual past with an imagined past. Prints made this vision readily available for consumption in the modern world.[21] This slippage between past and present is a moment of nostalgia which invites the individual to produce a narrative whereby an idealised lost past collides with the complexity of the present. In this sense nostalgia looks not only to the past but is defined by and acts to define the present. As a consequence, the original holds an ambiguous position as an object from the past and a representation in the present. The eighteenth and early nineteenth century witnessed numerous ways in which images of a reconstructed past were both used and produced. In this way the problematic relationship between the present and its pasts is disrupted.

The printed past

Architectural drawing or the visual language of architecture uses different kinds of graphic conventions which range from the pictorial which draws inspiration from stage sets and *veduta* painting to a discrete system of signs which represented three-dimensional architectural forms. The latter system of architectural drawings using perspective views, orthogonal elevation, details and working drawings was not merely imitative. Instead, buildings were disembodied and dissected, order was imposed on chaos – marks on paper evoked the built fabric. But this is only one kind of history than can be presented in visual terms. Indeed, Plato's attack on mimesis raised eighteenth-century awareness of how impressions of 'reality' could become corrupted and these ideas were just as current in contemporary aesthetic debate as the Aristotelian ideas about reason and imagination. The desire for exact knowledge from inexact things, that is the pure form reflected imperfectly in our world, was central to platonic thought. Yet the process of recording or copying – mimesis – creates something which is at twice remove from the perfect form. Orthogonal reconstruction, a form of parallel projection to represent three dimensions in two, became an established method of seeing and perceiving the architecture of the past. The rationalising system of representing architecture was part of a reductive process based on logos – the philosophical method for revealing the truth through linguistic means.

The hypothesis that thoughts and feelings could be expressed outside of verbal systems had currency in the eighteenth century as aesthetic philosophers moved away from the Albertian position that a picture is a window on the world and developed more speculative theories about the nature of vision. For instance, Bishop Berkeley's *An Essay Towards a New Theory of Vision* (1709) suggests that sight and the processes of mimesis or recording that follow on from it are part of a subjective gaze of an ethereal field. This signalled a profound shift in conceptions of vision and the act of viewing as the power and potency of non-verbal expression was recognised. But at the same time this recognition prompted the wish to neuter these images into an established Cartesian rationalist linguistic system of signs which separated the physiological from the psychological. The relationship between vision and cognition had currency in the eighteenth century. Can we, then, call this visual history a form of cognition? I have already stressed the links between the visual and human imagination. In addition, prints were used as a means of expressing knowledge which ran parallel to and intersected with other ways of communicating ideas. They were at once 'exterior aids but also interior transformations of consciousness'.[22]

Walter Benjamin argued that the authority or the aura of the original recedes in the act of mechanical reproduction.[23] But does the reproduced or printed image have special status? Associations are, after all, culturally determined and in the eighteenth century, if not before, a print would carry weight as it was a published document. The special status of prints and their concomitant authority was recognised at the very beginning of the eighteenth century by Roger de Piles in his 'De l'utilité des Estampes, et de leur usage' (1699) which was translated into English some fifty years later as 'Of the Usefulness and Use of Prints'. Piles expressed admiration for prints as displays of skill in their own right, but also as bearers of information mental aids and their receptiveness to diverse systems of classification. He also recognises the ability of prints to 'represent absent and distant things, as if they were before our eyes … we see countries, towns, and all the considerable places that we have read of in history, or have seen in our travels' and that these may replace travel for those 'who have no strength, leisure or convenience to travel'.[24] All of this was based on the democratic nature of prints. Their ability to prothelitise knowledge was doubtless important. And prints had the potential to represent 'all the visible productions of art and nature' to a wide range of publics who could afford them. But there is a paradox here. The democratising processes of the printing press also created a different kind of rarefied object in both material and intellectual terms. Prints came to represent what was not visible. As John Locke wrote in his *An Essay Concerning Human Understanding*:

> the materials of all our knowledge, are suggested and furnished to the mind only by sensation and reflection. When the understanding is once stored [the mind] has the power to repeat, compare, and unite them … and so can make … new and complex ideas.[25]

The fusion of artistic and 'archaeological' activity that is to say the different conventions of recording architecture come together in the realm of prints. Prints become 'facts' or fragments of knowledge – syntax and subject matter of a visual history which both shatter the tradition from which the image came as the image is dislocated from its original context and create the need for a new context. There is no such thing as an authentic print – reproducibility is part of the work and the lack of authenticity in prints is important as it constructs a new history, or archaeology of knowledge, as the act of reproduction emancipates art from its dependence on ritual. This process of democratisation removes the work of art from what Benjamin identifies as the cult value of the original to the exhibition value. This refers to the practice of displaying objects, here also representative of knowledge, which becomes part of a new cultural tradition. This had it roots in the sometimes-random assemblage of the cabinet of curiosities. Prints played an important part in such collections and were traded regularly so collections were fluid and the configuration of a group of prints continually changed. Perhaps this is partly to do with the social class of print collector who was looking to move up the social ladder using an increasingly impressive array of possessions? But it was not a process of amassing, as was the case with other objects. The practice of regrouping bodies of printed material also found expression in assemblages of prints which made up a publication on a certain theme. As such prints acquire a different status and meaning as the 'author', that is to say the collector or publisher, of their sequence or interrelationship could change and so present a diversity of histories.

Drawing the line

Drawing at once communicates a moment of inscription and exhibits a series of marks. But at the same time it provokes both mental images and ideas and feelings relating to more than just the actuality of their making. In this way, a drawing or the graphic line is a mark that functions as a sign. Clearly, here there is a relationship to language. And the logical extension of this would mean that most written scripts would qualify as drawings so prompting the question should all writing be considered drawing and vice versa – after all they are both products of the line and both are the products of flows of energy from brain to hand? It is helpful here to return to the importance of inscriptions and captions for Benjamin and to think about a review essay he published in French in 1938, 'Chinese Paintings at the Bibliothèque Nationale'.[26] Here he returns to a number of concerns articulated in his earlier work, especially the relationship between images and script, and modes of perception and cognition. Benjamin is especially interested in the significance of the calligraphic inscriptions included by Chinese artists in their paintings that cite the work of artists, styles or artworks from preceding periods. This artistic practice led Benjamin to see the act of copying or reproduction as central to Chinese painting. Importantly also for us is the juxtaposition of image and text on the same page. I am thinking here of the inscriptions and measurements that appear on images of architecture. We can see this, for instance, in the individual images produced by Thomas Major or Robert Adam, or in the substantial printed surveys by Piranesi or Stuart and Revett. The crucial thing here in relation to these kinds of descriptions is Benjamin's use of the term '*image-pensée*'. Benjamin refers to the art of Chinese painting as '*l'art de peindre est avant tout l'art de penser*' [first and foremost the art of thinking] and I wonder if this is helpful for our understanding of what these artworks actually do. Benjamin continues by observing 'the literary profession, which, in China, is inseparable from the profession of the painter'.[27] Indeed, the relationship between the thought and the image is crystallised by Benjamin in his summing up of the paintings in the Bibliothèque Nationale exhibition as exemplifying

> an antinomy which finds its 'resolution' in an intermediary element that, far from constituting a balance [*un juste milieu*] between literature and painting, embraces intimately the point at which they appear most irreducibly opposed namely, thought and image.[28]

Benjamin is also helpful as he addresses the idea of resemblance – do the images of the past bear any likeness to it? We have already noted that the past is miniaturised and commodified. Surely the question here is what leap of imagination is required to cross the spatial and temporal distance between the object and its description?

> And thinking, for the Chinese painter, means thinking by means of resemblance. Moreover, just as resemblance always appears to us like a flash of lightning (since nothing is more transient than the appearance of resemblance).[29]

Rationale

The spatial world of the image and the temporal world of the text share common ground as embodiments of human thought. My interest here is how these are brought to bear on the spatial and temporal aspects of the architecture of antiquity history as evident in prints and drawings made of it. And, leading on from this, how this pan-European currency in visual descriptions influenced architectural thought. My study begins with a consideration of the idea of the past in our period, especially how it was discovered and described. Here space and time inform the trope of ekphrasis, and this provides me with a thread or link between the verbal and the visual.[30] As we have seen in the reception of Lessing's *Laocoön*, the debates about verbal and visual representations have endured and continue to influence semiotics and critical theory. My approach uses the anachronistic juxtapositions of theory and archive to tease out potentially new ways of seeing the past through graphic descriptions of it, which hold within an alternative to the traditions of text-based scholarship. This also leads us to think about the varying methods of representing architecture – techniques of representation: orthogonal perspective, single point perspective, lack of picturesque or pictorial detail and so forth. All of which demonstrate choices about different modes of description or ekphrasis. I wonder here if, like the historian's sleight of hand in using the third person rather than 'I', does any of these modes of description at any point appear neutral? The theme of the embodied experience of the past runs through this study and is explored through the physical discovery and recording of antique architecture, the relationship between sight and touch and the ways in which gender can govern how the past is visually described. Above all, this book is a journey through the past as it is discovered, experienced, remembered and described.

Notes

1 On this point see Michael Baxandall, 'The Language of Art History', *New Literary History*, 10: 3 (1979), pp. 453–65.

2 There is, however, a vast literature on the way our eye moves across a picture surface that is very much at odds with the way art historians read a picture from left to right.

3 This was the subject of *Classical Philology*, 102:1 (2007) Special Issue on Ekphrasis, edited by Shadi Bartsch and Jaś Elsner; see also Murray Krieger, *Ekphrasis: The Illusion of the Natural Sign* (Baltimore: Johns Hopkins University Press, 1992) and W. J. T. Mitchell, 'Ekphrasis and the Other', *South Atlantic Quarterly*, 91 (1992), pp. 695–719, later published in his *Picture Theory: Essays on Verbal and Visual Representation* (Chicago: The University of Chicago Press, 1994), pp. 151–82.

4 See for instance Svetlana Leontief Alpers, 'Ekphrasis and Aesthetic Attitudes in Vasari's *Lives*', *Journal of the Warburg and Courtauld Institutes*, 23:3/4 (1960), pp. 190–215 and Patricia Rubin, *Giorgio Vasari: Art and History* (New Haven: Yale University Press, 1995); also Jaś Elsner, 'Art History as Ekphrasis', *Art History*, 33:1 (2010), pp. 10–27.

5 See for instance W. J. T. Mitchell, *Picture Theory* (Chicago: The University of Chicago Press, 1994) and *What Do Pictures Want?: The Lives and Loves of Images* (Chicago:

The University of Chicago Press, 2006); also Adrian Rifkin, 'Addressing Ekphrasis: A Prolegomenon to the Next', *Classical Philology*, 102:1 (2007), pp. 72–82.

6 A prime example of the concentration on text rather than the quality of the images can be found in Johann Joachim Winckelmann, *Monumenti antichi inediti, spiegati ed illustrati*, 2 vols (Rome, 1767). See also: Alex Potts, *Flesh and Ideal: Winckelmann and the Origins of Art History* (New Haven and London: Yale University Press, 1994); Maria Grazia Lolla, 'Monuments and Texts: Antiquarianism and the Beauty of Antiquity', in Dana Arnold and Stephen Bending (eds), *Tracing Architecture: The Aesthetics of Antiquarianism. Art History*, Special Issue, 25:4 (2002), pp. 431–49; and Katherine Harloe, *Winckelmann and the Invention of Antiquity: History and Aesthetics in the Age of Altertumswissenschaft* (Oxford: Oxford University Press, 2013).

7 A bilingual edition in German with a new English translation was published as *Reflections on the Imitation of Greek Works in Painting and Sculpture* (London: Open Court Classics, 1986).

8 Henry Fuseli, *Reflections on the Painting and Sculpture of The Greeks: with Instructions for the Connoisseur, and An Essay on Grace in Works of Art* (London: Printed for the Translator, and Sold by A. Millar in the Strand, 1765).

9 Whether he aimed to assert the primacy of one over the other remains open to debate. See for instance Ernst H. Gombrich, 'Lessing: Lecture on a Master Mind', *Proceedings of the British Academy*, 43 (1957), pp. 133–56 and his *Tributes: Interpreters of Our Cultural Tradition* (Oxford: Phaidon, 1984), p. 37, where he argued that Lessing wished to show the superiority of poetry. A selection of essays offering re-evaluations of Lessing from a range of disciplinary perspectives sheds light on this issue, see Avi Lifschitz and Michael Squire (eds), *Rethinking Lessing's* Laocoon*: Antiquity, Enlightenment, and the 'Limits' of Painting and Poetry* (Oxford: Oxford University Press, 2017).

10 Gotthold Ephraim Lessing, *Laocoön: An Essay on the Limits of Painting and Poetry*, trans. E. A. McCormick (Baltimore: Johns Hopkins University Press, 1984), p. 78.

11 Johann Wolfgang von Goethe, *Collected Works*, ed. V. Lange *et al.* (Princeton, New Jersey: Princeton University Press, 1995), vol. IV, p. 238.

12 Immanuel Kant, *Critique of Judgment* [1790], trans. W. S. Pluhar (Indianapolis: Hackett, 1987), p. 7; G. W. F. Hegel, *Aesthetics: Lectures on Fine Arts*, trans. T. M. Knox (Oxford: Oxford University Press, 1975); Ferdinand de Saussure, [*Cours de linguistique générale* (1916)], *Course in General Linguistics*, trans. Wade Baskin, ed. Perry Meisel and Haun Saussy (New York: Columbia University Press, 2011); Michel Foucault, *The Order of Things* (London: Tavistock Publications, 1970); Jacques Derrida, *Of Grammatology*, trans. Gayatri Chakravorty Spivak (Baltimore: Johns Hopkins University Press, 1997).

13 There is a vast literature, see for instance: Mieke Bal and Norman Bryson, 'Semiotics and Art History', *The Art Bulletin*, 73:2 (1991), pp. 174–208; Norman Bryson, Michael Ann Holly, and Keith Moxey (eds), *Visual Culture: Images and Interpretations* (Middletown, Connecticut: Wesleyan University Press, 1994); James Elkins, *The Object Stares Back: On the Nature of Seeing* (London: Routledge, 1996) and *On Pictures and the Words that Fail Them* (Cambridge: Cambridge University Press,

1998); W. J. T. Mitchell, 'The Politics of Genre: Space and Time in Lessing's *Laocoön*', *Representations*, 6:1 (1984), pp. 98–115; 'What Is an Image?' *New Literary History*, 15:3 (1984), pp. 503–37 and *Iconology: Image, Text, Ideology* (Chicago: The University of Chicago Press, 1986).

14 Jürgen Habermas, *The Structural Transformation of the Public Sphere: An Inquiry into a Category of Bourgeois Society*, trans. Thomas Burger and Frederick Lawrence (Cambridge: Polity Press, 1989). Habermas suggests that the eighteenth century saw the emergence of a 'public' in the modern sense. This body of rational individuals questioned the elite's dominance over the interpretation of images.

15 Aristotle introduces the concept of 'mimesis' in relation to Greek tragedy in his *Poetics*. This idea continued to inform thinking about representation and the rejection of Platonic systems of aesthetic representation. Aristotle's ideas about aesthetic thinking are further explored in *Metaphysics*. On this point see Aristotle, *Poetics*, trans. Malcolm Heath (Harmondsworth: Penguin Classics, 1996) and *Metaphysics*, trans. Hugh Lawson-Tancred, 2nd edn (Harmondsworth: Penguin Classics, 2004).

16 See Martin Postle, *Sir Joshua Reynolds: The Subject Pictures* (Cambridge: Cambridge University Press, 1995).

17 This is mapped, for instance, with specific reference to the Greek Doric temples at Paestum by Suzanne Lang, 'Early Publications of the Temples at Paestum', *Journal of the Warburg and Courtauld Institutes*, 13:1/2 (1950), pp. 48–64.

18 Susan Stewart, *On Longing: Narratives of the Miniature, the Gigantic, the Souvenir, the Collection* (Durham, North Carolina and London: Duke University Press, 1992), p. 139.

19 Ibid., pp. 140, 142 [emphasis in original].

20 Stewart, *On Longing*; see also Susan M. Pearce, *On Collecting: An Investigation into Collecting in the European Tradition* (London and New York, 1995).

21 Stewart, *On Longing*.

22 On this point see Walter J. Ong, *Orality and Literacy: The Technologizing of the World* (London and New York: Routledge, 1982).

23 Walter Benjamin, 'The Work of Art in the Age of Mechanical Reproduction', in *Illuminations*, ed. Hannah Arendt, trans. Harry Zohn (London: Fontana, 1973).

24 Roger de Piles, 'De l'utilité des Estampes, et de leur usage', in *Abrégé de la vie des peintres, avec des réflexions sur leurs ouvrages* (Paris: François Muguet, 1699), translated as 'Of the Usefulness and Use of Prints', in *The Art of Painting, with the Lives and Characters … of the Most Eminent Painters* (London: Printed for T. Payne, 1754), pp. 56, 58.

25 John Locke, *An Essay Concerning Human Understanding* [London, 1706], ed. and abridged by J. W. Yolton (London and Melbourne: Dent, 1976), p. 45. Locke's essay first appeared in December 1689 (although usually dated 1690). Four editions appeared during his lifetime, and a revised fifth edition appeared posthumously in 1706.

26 Walter Benjamin, 'Chinese Paintings at the Bibliothèque Nationale', in *The Work of Art in the Age of Its Technological Reproducibility, and Other Writings on Media*, ed. Michael W. Jennings, Brigid Doherty, and Thomas Y. Levin, trans. Edmund Jephcott, Rodney Livingstone, Howard Eiland, and others (Cambridge, Massachusetts: The Belknap Press of Harvard University Press, 2008), pp. 257–60.

27 Ibid., p. 258.
28 Ibid., p. 259.
29 Ibid.
30 On this point see, for instance, Brian Cosgrove, 'Murray Krieger: Ekphrasis as Spatial Form, Ekphrasis as Mimesis', in Jeff Morrison and Florian Krobb (eds), *Text into Image: Image into Text*; Proceedings of the Interdisciplinary Bicentenary Conference Held at St. Patrick's College, Maynooth (the National University of Ireland), September 1995 (Amsterdam: Rodopi, 1997), pp. 25–31.

The past 1

Part I: Travelling through the past

Before embarking on an exploration of the visual ekphrases of antique architecture, it is important to think about the ways in which it was encountered and recorded verbally. Crucial to this process is the growth in travel and with it knowledge of the ancient world. Indeed, travel and knowledge were intrinsically linked, as seen, for instance, in Baron d'Hancarville's assertion that 'Antiquity is a vast country separated from our own by a long period of time.' This statement is made in the Baron's ambitious, if ultimately flawed, study *Antiquités étrusques, grecques et romaines* (1767 but not published before 1776), which was based on the collection of William Hamilton, an antiquarian and the British envoy in Naples. Tourists from whatever era are travellers in search of experience. The connection between travel and knowledge is essential to an understanding of the importance of an actual and metaphorical journey into the past. The journey I want to trace is the one made by eighteenth-century antiquarians in the pursuit of experience and knowledge of the architecture of classical antiquity. In the opening years of the eighteenth century interest focused on Rome. Understanding of ancient Rome was enhanced through the study of textual descriptions of the writers of antiquity as well as direct knowledge of key sites included in the Grand Tour, which was just emerging as an essential part of the education of the elite.[1] This made an important link between the past as a foreign country and the actuality of foreign soil. Knowledge was amassed though the study and continued excavation of the archaeological remains of the classical past. In addition, textual sources, both from antiquity and later periods, and surveys of Rome made in the Renaissance provided important information. Horace Walpole's remark made in 1740 about the British tourist Joseph Addison applies equally to all European travellers at this time as shared interest in the discovery of antiquity dissolved national boundaries.

> Mr. Addison travelled through the poets, and not through Italy; for all his ideas are borrowed from the descriptions and not from reality. He saw places as they were, not as they are.[2]

My concern here is with the ways in which the architecture of antiquity was discovered and studied, and I question what kind of past was visited and remembered by Grand Tourists. The Grand Tour remains one of the best-known cultural activities of the long eighteenth century. A core number of European cities were visited, but the main purpose was to experience ancient Rome. Although later in our period the tour extended to include Naples, Sicily and Greece, the eternal city was never forgotten or avoided. Despite the political conflicts and perennial discomfort, the itineraries and experience were generally quite uniform.[3] Here the patrons of the future mixed with antiquarians and architects, and even academics. As Edward Gibbon remarked, 'according to the law of custom, and perhaps of reason, foreign travel completes the education of an English gentleman'.[4] That said, tourism was not solely the preserve of the English single male, as newly-weds, families and single women from across Europe also undertook these extended journeys. Notable here amongst British women travellers are Lady Mary Wortley Montagu and the Parminter sisters, Jane and Elizabeth, who travelled for almost 20 years with their cousin Mary and friend Miss Colville.[5] The many letters of Lady Mary Wortley Montagu give us an insight into the female touristic experience. Indeed, the title of Montagu's published letters refers to 'Sources that Have Been Inaccessible to Other Travellers'. Her initial focus was her travels in the Ottoman Empire but she spent the last 20 years of her life (1741–61) mostly in France and Italy. The letters themselves frequently draw attention to the fact that they present a different and, Montagu asserts, more accurate description than that provided by previous (male) travellers.

> You will perhaps be surpriz'd at an Account so different from what you have been entertaind with by the common Voyage-writers who are very fond of speaking of what they don't know.[6]

Montagu consistently derides the quality of European travel literature of the eighteenth century as nothing more than 'trite observations ... superficial ... [of] boys who only remember the best wine or the prettyest women'. There is no doubt that here Montagu identifies the common perception of male antiquarian activities. But my concern here is to look beyond the stereotypes and to think about the experience of antiquarians who travelled across Europe in search of the past during the eighteenth century.

At this point, I would like to focus on Rome as a prompt for the questions about memory, imagination, time and space that I explore throughout this book. Rome offered two different journeys through the city: the exploration of its past – that is to say, antiquity – and its present – that is to say, the modern city, including the more recent architecture of the Renaissance and Baroque periods. These simultaneous but distinctive interactions with Rome are indexical of the slippage between time and space. In turn they influence how antiquity was experienced and recorded. Nostalgia formed a common unifying bond amongst those who had undertaken the Grand Tour. And these memories of Rome fostered an imagined cultural connection with Roman antiquity. The growth of private collections of ancient artefacts and other memorabilia, including prints and drawings, was a key part of this cultural system. The amassing of objects and the copying or re-creation of architecture and sculpture from antiquity fuelled the nostalgia for Rome. This self-conscious construction of culture created an imagined classical past forged out of an invented memory that aligned with current beliefs and values. In this way, the documenting, recording and reinterpretation of antiquity created a dialogue, or indeed fluidity, between past and present.

The artefacts of antiquity became a kind of international currency that spoke the language of the elite, especially when displayed in private collections or re-invented through actual copies or re-working of buildings and architectural features. The Italian artist Pompeo Batoni was a renowned portraitist who recorded the cultural capital of many Grand Tourists. We can see this in his portrait of Francis Basset, 1st Baron de Dunstanville and Basset (1757–1835) (Figure 1). The picture shows the future baron in Rome on the Grand Tour, with the Castel Sant'Angelo and St. Peter's Basilica in the background. He is depicted holding a map of Rome and surrounded by the sort of collectibles that Grand Tourists brought back on their return. Some are real objects, others are fictitious – the ancient Roman altar on which he is leaning, for instance, is an invention that helps the composition of the portrait. The examples of the re-use of Roman architecture in the architectural design of the eighteenth century need only be noted here. However, I would like to signal how the nostalgia for these invented memories become a driving force in the English landscape garden movement. For instance, in the re-creation of the narrative of the *Aeneid* at Stourhead we see how Virgil's written description of a journey is transformed into a visual and spatial experience that evokes a fictitious recollection of Rome.[7]

But how was the Grand Tour itself remembered and described? Richard Lassels in his *The Voyage of Italy* (1670), which was part guidebook and part didactic treatise, was one of the first to identify the activity. And we have many accounts written by the guides who accompanied the tourists. For instance, Edward Wright looked back on his time as a Grand Tour tutor in his *Some Observations Made in Travelling Through France, Italy &c in the Years 1720, 1721 and 1722*, published in 1730. Such was the thirst for knowledge and the trans-European nature of this form of cultural exchange that in 1757 John and Joseph Noon arranged for a translation of the unpublished memoires of Monsieur de Blainville, formerly a secretary to the Embassy of the States General (i.e. France) in Spain. Published in three volumes as *Travels Through Holland, Germany, Switzerland, and other parts of Europe; but especially Italy.* The text is

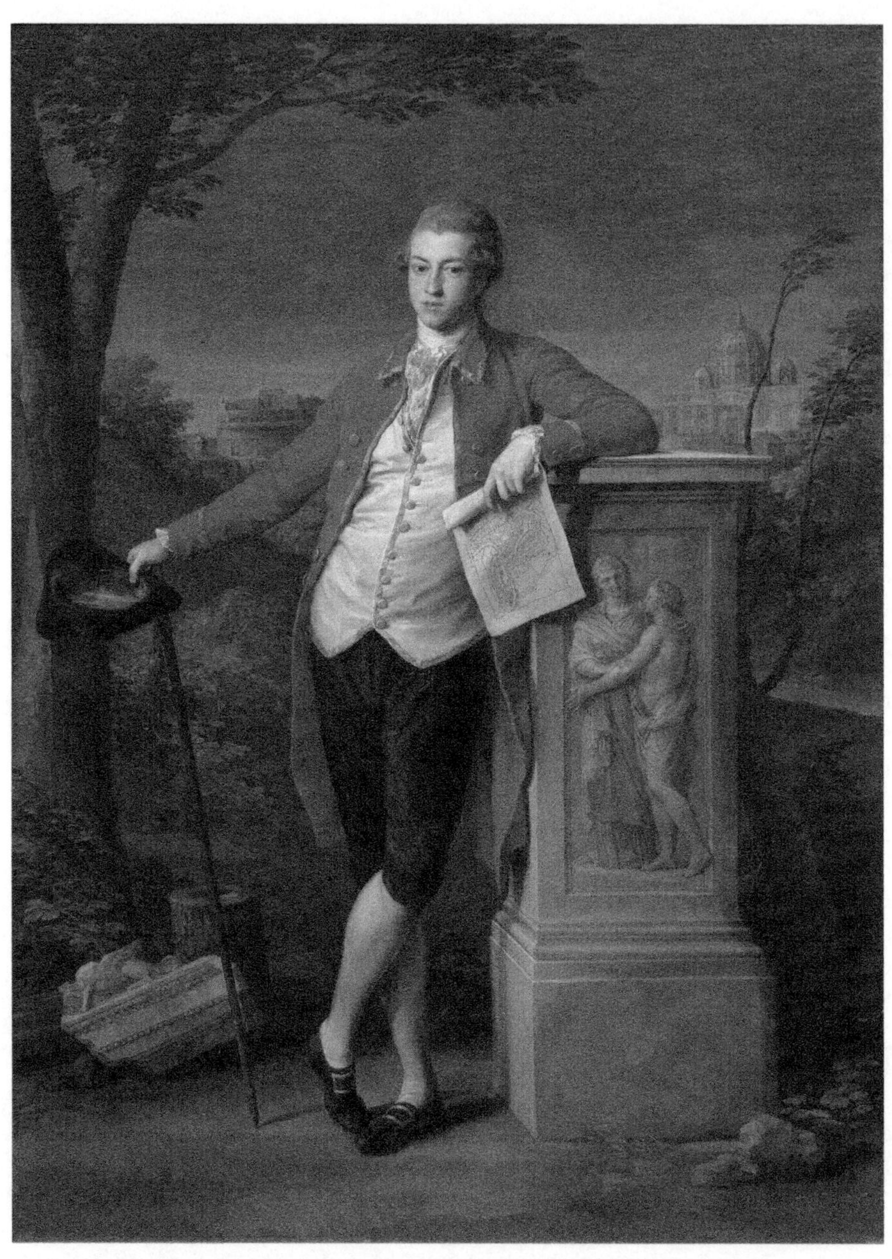

1 Pompeo Batoni, *Francis Basset, 1st Baron de Dunstanville and Basset*, oil on canvas, 1778

interspersed with remarks on well-known antiquarians including Montfaucon, Addison and others. We can also learn much about the touristic experience from the letters of the travellers themselves. As seen, for instance, in *Letters from Italy, in the Years 1754 and 1755*, published some twenty years later by the Earl of Cork and Orrery in 1773. Women's voices are part of this vast literature. For instance, although they covered a broader geography than the established Grand Tour, as we have seen, Lady Mary Wortley Montagu's letters also give us insights into the female experience of Italy.[8] The vast literature on travel is well documented and is not in itself my principal focus here. We can safely surmise that the number of publications and their availability to an increasingly literate public indicates an interest in the descriptions of the past as manifest in its physical remains.[9]

What fascinates me particularly about these descriptions of the Grand Tour is that they appear in epistolary format. This is important for our purposes, as the level of subjectivity this form of writing enabled provides fresh insights into the experience of Rome. We have personalised eyewitness accounts of the ruins of antiquity described in a manner that stands distinct from the descriptions or, indeed, ekphrases of the classical writers. The epistolary novel was an emergent form of writing at this time as seen in the work of authors such as Samuel Richardson whose *Pamela; or, Virtue Rewarded* appeared in 1740. Richardson, alongside other contemporary writers, believed that the epistolary format enabled the reader to gain access to a character's thoughts. We are very familiar with this kind of immediacy of writing where a character's thoughts and actions are described almost simultaneously. However, in the pre-Freudian world of the long eighteenth century this form of writing opened the door to what was to become known as the human subconscious. And it is helpful to use Freud anachronistically to understand the role of memory in the subjective experience of Rome. Importantly, too, Freud gives us some insight into the part prints played in the memorialisation of cities.

There is no doubt of the importance of the city – not least Rome – as a means of describing the workings of the mind. For instance in Freud's *Civilization and its Discontents* where Rome is a metaphor for the subconscious. Here I want to think about Freud's description of a series of dreams he had based on a yearning to visit Rome, as this helps us to understand how images operate in the realm of the imagination and how powerful they are as descriptive tools.

> I dream … that I am looking out of a carriage window at the [River] Tiber and the Ponte Sant'Angelo; the train starts to move, and I realize I have never set foot in the city. The view I saw in the dream was taken from a well-known engraving that I had fleetingly seen on a patient's drawing-room wall the day before. … Evidently, I am trying in vain to see, in a dream, a city that in a waking state I have not seen.[10]

The importance of invented memory is explored further by Freud in his discussion of memory itself. Freud uses Rome as a means of mapping the human subconscious which also helps us to understand responses to the architecture of the ancient world in the eighteenth and early nineteenth centuries. The relationship between the subconscious and memory is discussed in spatial terms and it is here that we find the convergence of the descriptive act, which is located in both space and time. The trans-historical/achronological description of Rome – both ancient and modern – is a spatial and temporal representation. By doing this Freud gives a flavour of what visitors to Rome actually saw and the importance of imagination to coax these monuments out of the past and into the present and so move them through time.

> Of the buildings which once occupied this ancient area he will find nothing, or only the scanty remains, for they exist no longer. [He or she would only be able] at the most to point out the sites where the temples and public buildings stood. Their place is now taken by ruins, but not by ruins themselves but of later restorations ... these remains of ancient Rome are found dovetailed into the jumble of the great metropolis ... . This is the manner in which the past is preserved in historical sites like Rome.[11]

Freud shows that Rome is a living entity where past and present resonate and inform each other. This was almost certainly the case in the mind of the eighteenth-century visitor and in the way the city was imagined. The co-existence of past and present is essential here. Can, then, images operate in the same way on the imagination? Perhaps in answer to this question, Freud continues:

> Rome and the palaces of the Caesars and the Septizonium of Septimus Severus would still be rising to their old height on the Palatine ... . In the place occupied by the Palazzo Cafferelli would once more stand – without the Palazzo having to be removed – the Temple of Jupiter Capitolinus; where the Coliseum now stands we could at the same time admire Nero's vanished Golden House ... . And the observer would perhaps only have to change the direction of his glance or his position in order to call up the one view or the other.[12]

The point that Freud is making here is important for our consideration of how architecture is imagined as he refers to the notion of time – buildings or at least their ruins endure. But we narrate buildings usually in an historical sequence, and this sequence cannot be expressed in spatial terms. Drawings or paintings do not have a narrative sequence or a temporal dimension; as such they can operate differently from a verbal ekphrasis, as they can respond/represent in ways that offer another kind of realism. Indeed, Freud's evocation of the imaginary image of Rome rests within certain linguistic constraints of verbal ekphrasis.

We might think that space or a city cannot have two different simultaneous contents and consequently that histories of the same geographical location must be juxtaposed. Yet this simultaneity is precisely the experience of visiting Rome – the compression of different temporalities – the ability to experience the past and the present at the same time. The sensation of knowing Rome, its relationship to the subconscious through dreams, or having a memory of it from prints before having visited it is not unique to Freud. Returning to the writings of our eighteenth-century travellers we can find similar responses to the experience of the city. James Russel's letters give an indication of the different kinds of touristic engagement with Rome. Russel's observation that visitors had 'great ideas … formulated to themselves, either from reading, or oral relations, having seen and heard the most ancient curiosities magnified too much' and, as a consequence, they did not anticipate the ruined state of Rome; the 'sackings, burnings, and ravages' perhaps chimes more with Walpole's observation about Addison. But Russel also signals the importance of the imagination, time and space when he remarks that he had encountered only a very few visitors who could

> stand upon the same spot of ground for a good while, as it were in deep contemplation. Where there was no appearance of any thing very remarkable or uncommon. Tho' such a one might be thought, by those who saw them, to be *non compos*, he might probably, from his knowledge in history, be calling to mind some brave action, performed upon that very spot; and enjoying a pleasure, not to be felt by any one, confined within the walls of the study or chamber.[13]

We also find echoes of Freud in the writings of Goethe who travelled in Italy in 1786–88. His *Italian Journey*, published considerably later (1816–17), draws on his letters and diaries and fuses the immediacy of these accounts with memories and reminiscences. Of particular note is his description of his arrival in Rome:

> Now I see all my childhood dreams come to life; I see now in reality the first engravings that I remember (my father hung the prospects of Rome in a corridor); and everything long familiar to me in paintings and drawings, copperplates and woodcuts, in plaster and cork, now stands together before me. Wherever I go I find something in this new world I am acquainted with; it is all as I imagined, and yet new.[14]

As noted, the growth of the novel, especially in an epistolary format, in our period gives us some insight into human thought. And this knowledge is embellished by the question of the different emotional and aesthetic responses to the visual world that preoccupied contemporary philosophers. John Locke's *An Essay Concerning Human Understanding* (1690) acknowledges the role of memory in the invention of fancy. Locke does not use the term imagination but his writing signals the beginning of two distinct linguistic traditions: the metaphorical language of poetry and the literal language of science. The former developed into the philosophy of association, which dominated aesthetic thinking and theory in the long eighteenth century. Arguably, and I explore this later, these two linguistic tropes are played out in the visual realm in the different ways of representing and describing the architecture of the ancient world.

The philosophy of association played an important part in the understanding and appreciation of antiquity in the long eighteenth century. For instance, Joseph Addison in his 'The Pleasures of the Imagination', written at the beginning of our period in 1712, identified two different kinds of pleasure that derived from buildings or artefacts – the pleasure of the object itself and that derived from remembered or fictitious objects. Edmund Burke's *Philosophical Enquiry into the Origin of the Sublime and the Beautiful* (1757) and Henry Home, Lord Kames's *Elements of Criticism* (1762) developed the Lockean idea and shed interesting light on the crucial issue of imitation. Sir Joshua Reynolds in his *Discourses on Art*, the lectures he gave at the Royal Academy, addressed the question of copying. In his 6th *Discourse*, Reynolds asserted that imitation was the best means to invention and that this should not be concealed. In his 13th *Discourse* Reynolds spoke specifically about architecture:

> architecture certainly possesses many principles in common with poetry and painting. Among those, which may be reckoned as the first, is that affecting the imagination by means of the association of ideas. Thus for instance, we have naturally a veneration for antiquity, whatever the building brings to our remembrance ancient custom and manners is sure to give this delight.[15]

David Hume in his *Enquiry concerning the Human Understanding* (1748) crystallised ideas about beauty, imitation and originality through their integration into an elitist definition of taste. Taste was the ability to contextualise an object or building whether it be an original or a copy. Socially formed taste should be an absolute preference that underscored pre-eminence and a right to rule. The experience of Rome and modes of describing and remembering the city were germane to the forging of this common experience.

The resonance between past and present is continued in the visual guides to Rome. Eighteenth-century tourists used sixteenth- and seventeenth-century images that were sometimes accompanied by text. In this way, they experienced ancient Rome through the eyes of the recent past and this helps to give us a flavour of the kind of engagement these travellers had with antiquity. Popular guides included Etienne Duperac's map of *Old Rome* (1577) (Figure 2) and Falda's *Li Giardini di Roma* (*c.*1683) (Figure 3). In these kinds of representations the ruined structures blended effortlessly with their overgrown surroundings giving visitors the impression that architecture and landscape had a symbiotic existence in antiquity. The nostalgia evoked by this kind of description of ancient Rome can be seen in the

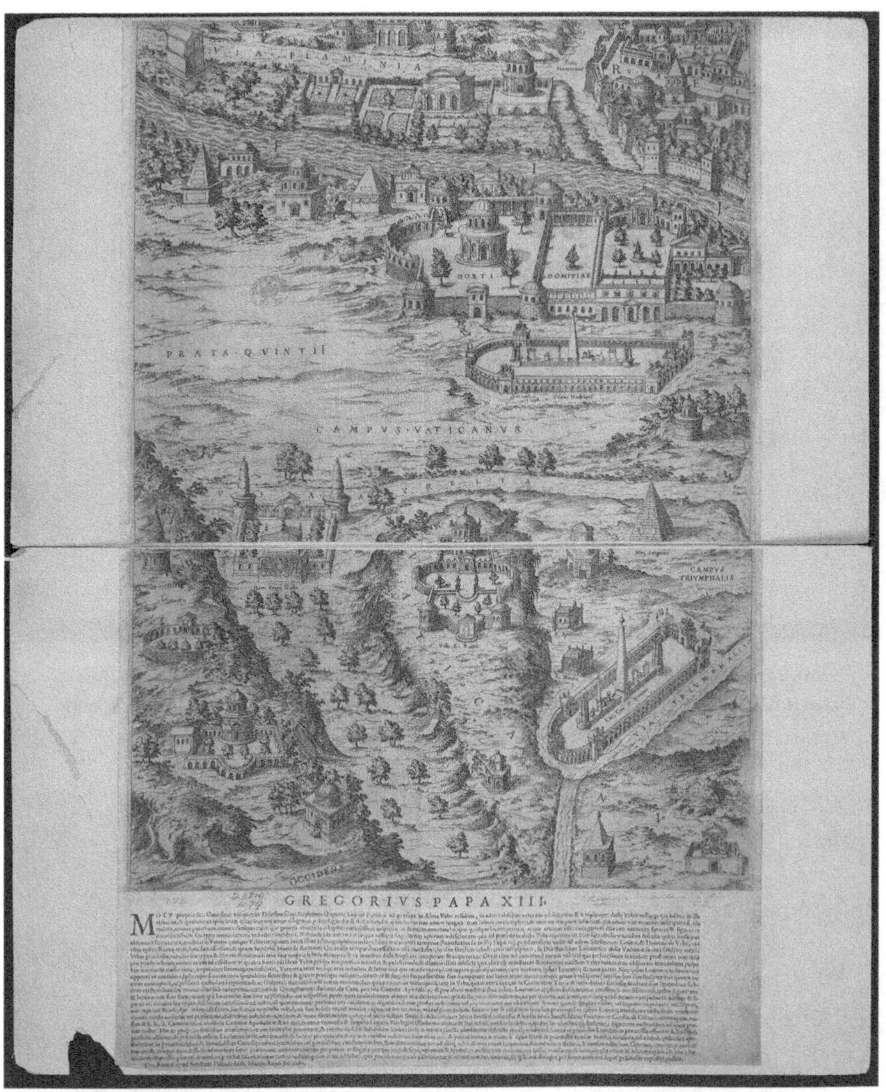

Etienne Duperac, 'A View, showing the position of several of the more important ancient Roman edifices' (*Urbis Romae Sciographia Ex Antiquis Monumentis Accuratiss Delineata* (1574–1691), engraving, 1604 **2**

garden designs of country houses – for instance the Temple of Venus at Stowe or the Pantheon at Stourhead (Figure 4). Here the visual descriptions of architecture used by visitors formulated historical narratives that had never existed. In addition, the nostalgia for these invented memories become a driving force in the English landscape garden movement that is

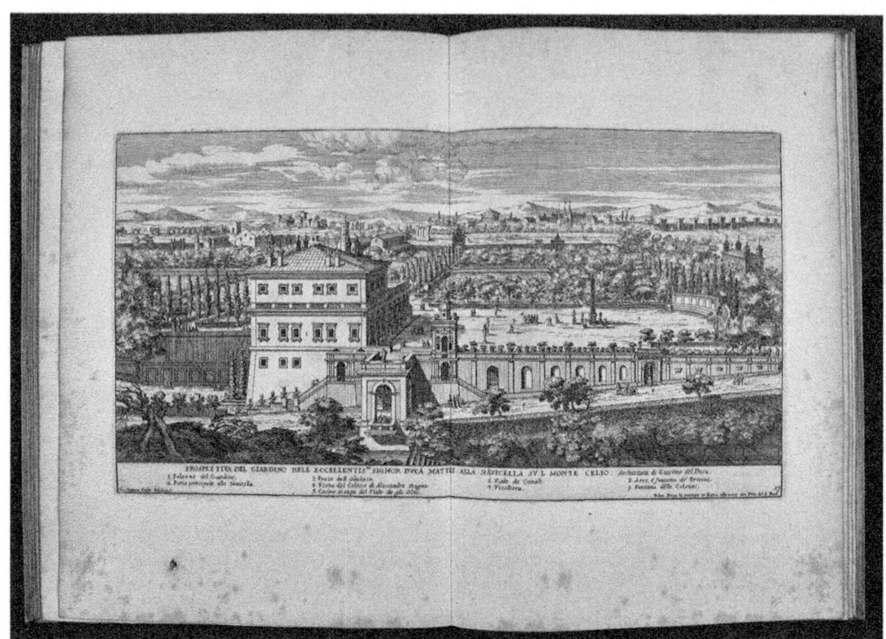

3 Giovanni Battista Falda, 'Prospettiva del Giardino dell eccellentis Signor Duca Mattei alla Navicella sul Monte Celio, Roma', from *Li Giardini di Roma*, engraving, 1690

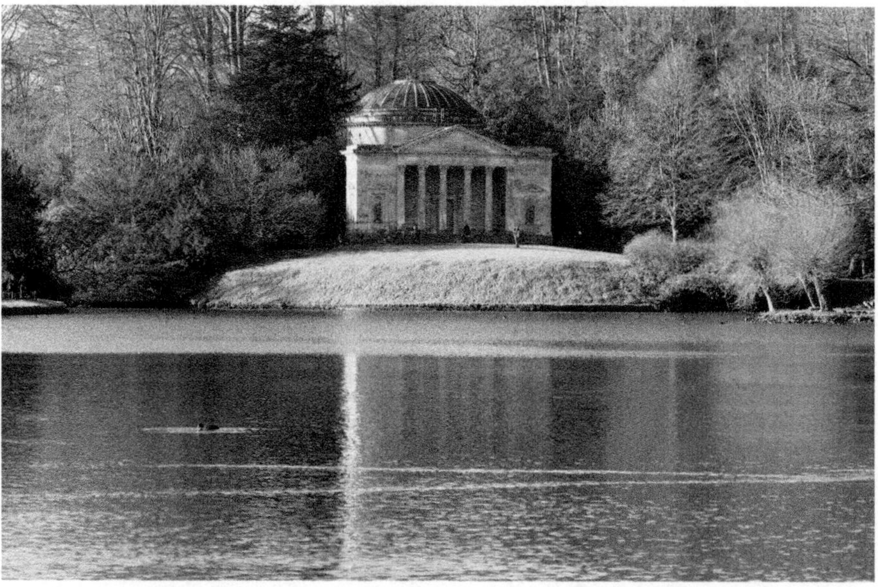

4 Henry Flitcroft, Pantheon in the garden at Stourhead, Wiltshire, UK, 1753–54

such a potent symbol of the cultural supremacy of the eighteenth-century elite.

The literary descriptions of the remains of the past, whether verbal or visual accounts, formed a pan-European currency of knowledge that transcended linguistic boundaries either through translation or the immediacy of their images. Improved printing techniques encouraged these sorts of publications, and their popularity, as manifest in the reprints and revised editions, tells us that the educated public had an appetite for this kind of material.[16] Many of these texts, especially prestige publications produced in quarto such as Campbell's *Vitruvius Britannicus*, or Stuart and Revett's *The Antiquities of Athens*, were supported by subscribers whose names appear in the front matter, and this gives us some idea of the intended audience. Although, ownership of a book does not necessarily ensure it is read, we can safely assume that these publications were objects of desire that met a certain cultural need and connoted a certain status through their ownership.[17]

Notes

1 There is a vast literature on the Grand Tour. See for instance Jeremy Black, *The British Abroad: The Grand Tour in the Eighteenth Century* (Stroud: Alan Sutton, 1992) and Rosemary Sweet, *Antiquaries: The Discovery of the Past in Eighteenth Century Britain* (London and New York: Hambledon and London, 2004).

2 Horace Walpole and George Montagu, *Correspondence of Horace Walpole, with George Montagu, Esq, [and others]* (London: Henry Colburn, 1837), vol. xiii, p. 231.

3 For a detailed analysis of the itineraries, see for instance Andrew Wilton and Ilaria Bignamini, *The Grand Tour, The Lure of Italy in the Eighteenth Century*, Tate Gallery exhibition catalogue (1996) and John Ingamells (ed.), *A Dictionary of British and Irish Travellers to Italy 1701–1800* (London and New Haven: Yale University Press, 1997).

4 Edward Gibbon, *Memoirs of My Life*, ed. Georges A. Bonnard (London: Nelson, 1966).

5 Brian Dolan, *Ladies of the Grand Tour* (London: Harper Collins, 2001), especially chapter 6, pp. 194 ff.

6 *The Complete Letters of Lady Mary Wortley Montagu*, ed. Robert Halsband, 3 vols (Oxford: Clarendon Press, 1965–67).

7 For a full discussion of the gardens at Stourhead see Kenneth Woodbridge, *Landscape and Antiquity Aspects of English Culture at Stourhead: 1718–1838* (Oxford: Clarendon Press, 1970).

8 On this point see Halsband, *Complete Letters of Lady Mary Wortley Montagu*.

9 The practice of travel writing is discussed in, for instance, Chloe Chard, *Pleasure and Guilt on the Grand Tour:Travel Writing and Imaginative Geography 1600–1830* (Manchester: Manchester University Press, 1999).

10 Sigmund Freud, *Interpreting Dreams*, new trans. J. A. Underwood (Harmondsworth: Penguin, 2006), pp. 209–10.

11 Sigmund Freud, 'Civilization and its Discontents', in A. Dickson (ed.), *Civilization, Society and Religion*, The Penguin Freud Library, vol. 12 (Harmondsworth: Penguin, 1991), pp. 257–8.

12 Ibid.

13 James Russel, *Letters from a Young Painter Abroad to his Friends in England* (London: W. Russel, 1750), vol. 2, pp. 178–9.

14 Johann Wolfgang von Goethe, *The Italian Journey*, ed. Thomas P. Saine and Jeffrey L. Sammons, trans. R. Heitner (New York: Suhrkamp, 1989; reprint, *Princeton*, New Jersey: *Princeton University Press, 1994*), p. 104.

15 Sir Joshua Reynolds fifteen discourses on art were delivered at the Royal Academy and published individually from 1769–91. They are reprinted as Sir Joshua Reynolds, *Discourses on Art*, ed. Robert R. Wark (San Marino, California: Huntington Library, 1959).

16 On this point see John Brewer, *The Pleasures of the Imagination: English Culture in the Eighteenth Century* (London: Harper Collins, 1997).

17 The dispersal of many country house libraries in the later nineteenth century has resulted in the loss of many of these collections but does sometimes give us the benefit of sales inventories. On this point see Peter H. Reid, 'The Decline and Fall of the British Country House Library', *Libraries & Culture*, 36:2 (2001), pp. 345–66.

Part II: Writing the past

In order to explore the grammar and syntax of a visual ekphrasis I need first to step back and think about textual descriptions of ancient architecture. Ancient texts such as Pliny's *Natural History* were used as a guide to the remains of the classical world, but my particular interest here is the predicates for the verbalisation of the architecture of antiquity. One of the most influential texts in this regard is Vitruvius's treatise *De architectura* (*The Ten Books on Architecture*); written in the first century BCE, it is a survey of classical (principally Greek) architecture by a Roman author. The book provided a comprehensive survey of the classical style of building and supplied a ready-made taxonomic apparatus with which to discuss architectural design.[1] Vitruvius codified the classical orders of architecture and instilled into them a language and grammar which made them intelligible, and this technique of representation was well in advance of methods of recording and representing architecture visually.

It may at first appear that the male human subject does not take centre stage in these contexts, but the actuality is otherwise; for instance, the predisposition to accept whatever *is* as natural, whether in regard to academic enquiry or our social systems. This is aided by our linguistic acknowledgement of woman as 'different': that we use 'she' instead of the presumably neutral 'one' – in reality the white-male-position accepted-as-natural, or the hidden 'he' as the subject of all scholarly predicates – is a decided advantage, rather than merely a hindrance or subjective distortion.[2] This impacts on all modes of cultural production where the white western male viewpoint is unconsciously and unquestioningly accepted as *the* viewpoint of the historian.

We can see the ways in which the normative masculine predicates for architecture are germane to Vitruvius's theories of proportion and design when he maps out the anthropocentric proportions and associations of the different orders. This strengthens the relationship of classical architecture to a human-based appreciation of style, as does the idea of the Vitruvian – the perfect forms of the circle and the square which are shown as directly related to masculine proportions, a point to which I shall return. For instance, the Doric order being based on the proportions of the masculine body connotes strength and severity. By contrast, the Ionic order, with its proportions drawn from the feminine body, is presented as a kind of compromise between the virility of the Doric and the delicacy of the (un-gendered) Corinthian (Figure 5). The narratives around the orders found in Vitruvius's text embellished them further as transmitters of particular modes of discourse, based in part on Greek history or mythology. As Vitruvius remarks:

> Propriety is that perfection of style which comes when a work is authoritatively constructed on approved principles. … The temples of Minerva, Mars, and Hercules, will be Doric, since the virile strength of these gods makes daintiness

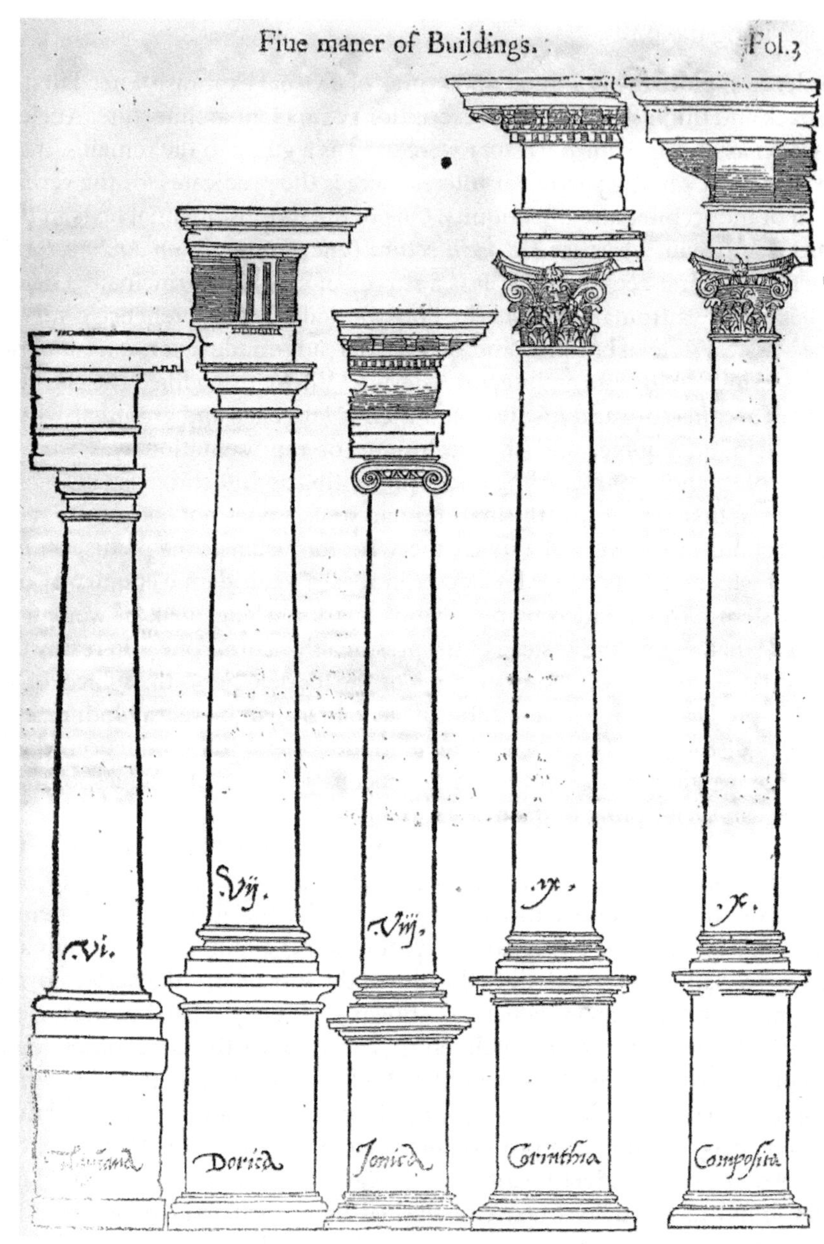

5 Sebastian Serlio, the classical orders, from *Five Books of Architecture*, book IV, fol. 3, 1611 (English edition)

> entirely inappropriate to their houses. In temples to Venus [and] Flora … the Corinthian order will be found to have peculiar significance, because these are delicate divinities… . The construction of temples of the Ionic order to Juno, Diana, [and] Father Bacchus … will be in keeping with the middle position which they hold; for the building as such will be an appropriate combination of the severity of the Doric and the delicacy of the Corinthian.[3]

Here the ideas of appropriateness and system are outlined by Vitruvius. And it is clear that in his view the orders could signify qualities that transcended the binary gender divide – at least as far as mythological divinities are concerned. But the historical narratives encapsulated in the orders perhaps reveal a different attitude towards the gender of mortals (Figure 6).

Vitruvius explains the caryatid, a draped female form which takes the place of columns, in this enchanting history:

> among the ornamental parts of an architect's design for a work, there are many the underlying idea of whose employment he [the architect] should be able to explain … . the marble statues of women in long robes, called Caryatides … [can be explained thus]. Caryae, a state in Peloponnesus, sided with the Persian enemies against Greece; later the Greeks, having gloriously won their freedom by victory in the war, made common cause and declared against the people of Caryae. They took the town, killed the men, abandoned the State to desolation, and carried off their wives to slavery, without permitting them, however, to lay aside the long robes and other marks of their rank as married women, so that they might be obliged not only to march in the triumph but to appear forever after as a type of slavery, burdened with the weight of their shame and so making atonement for their State. Hence, the architects of the time designed for public buildings statues of these women, placed so as to carry a load, in order that the sin and punishment of the people of Caryae might be known and handed down even to posterity.[4]

Vitruvius's reinforcing of classical architecture with these associated values enabled the construction of an enduring canonical style imbued with a set of social and cultural beliefs expressed through a human-based system of proportions. In this system, nature and femininity are *mastered* and subdued in the process of verbalising the architecture of the past.

The Ten Books were an important source of Leon Battista Alberti's *De re aedificatoria* circulated in manuscript from 1452 and published in 1485 (later translated into Italian by the author).[5] Alberti had a resounding influence on many other Renaissance architects and theorists and was still widely read in the eighteenth century. But Vitruvius's classical canon had a broader appeal and was a fundamental part of the formulation of the principles of taste. For instance, Giorgio Vasari's *The Lives of the Artists*, which appeared in the

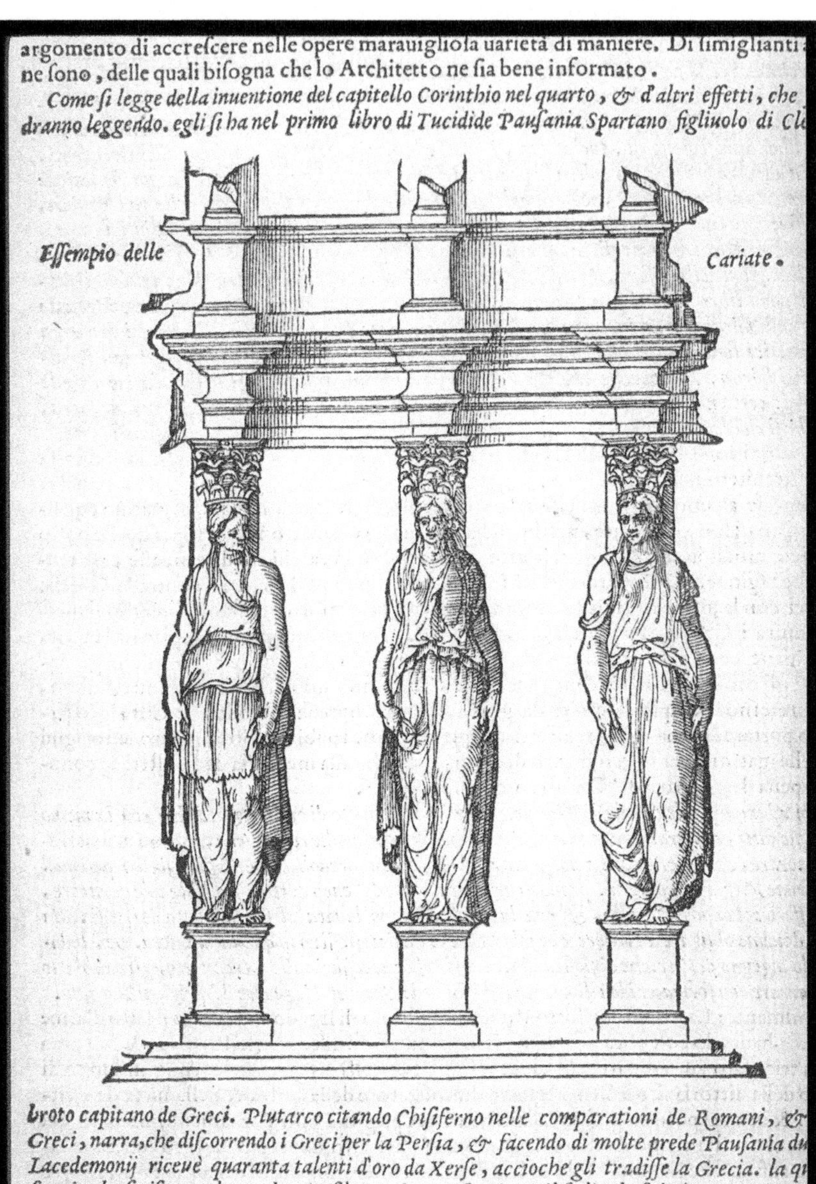

argomento di accrescere nelle opere marauigliosa uarietà di maniere. Di simiglianti ne sono , delle quali bisogna che lo Architetto ne sia bene informato .

Come si legge della inuentione del capitello Corinthio nel quarto , & d'altri effetti , che dranno leggendo. egli si ha nel primo libro di Tucidide Pausania Spartano figliuolo di Cle

broto capitano de Greci. Plutarco citando Chisiferno nelle comparationi de Romani, & Greci , narra, che discorrendo i Greci per la Persia , & facendo di molte prede Pausania du Lacedemonij riceuè quaranta talenti d'oro da Xerse , acciochè gli tradisse la Grecia. la qu sa poi , che si riseppe , hauendo Agesilao padre perseguitato il figliuolo fin' al tempio di Pa & edicalcha otturò con mattoni le porte del tempio , & iui per fame lo fece consumare ;

6 Vitruvius, 'Essempio delle Cariate' [Caryatids] from *De architectura* [*On architecture*], *c.*1567 (annotated and illustrated Italian edition)

latter half of the sixteenth century in Italy, drew on the Vitruvian ideal. In his Preface to part three of the *Lives* Vasari remarks:

> By rule in architecture we mean the method used of measuring antiques and basing modern works on the plans of ancient buildings. Order is the distinction made between one kind of architectural style and another … Doric, Ionic, Corinthian, Tuscan. Proportion is a universal law of architecture.[6]

Indeed, the Vasarian concepts of *regola*, *ordine*, *misura*, *disegno* and *maniera* (rule, order, measure, drawing, style) remain touchstones of academic formal criticism and the benchmark of perceived perfection against which other traditions were always to be found wanting.

The judgements of Vitruvius and Vasari were handed down through subsequent generations of writers and influenced, for instance, Winckelmann's *Remarks on the Architecture of the Ancients* (1762), which privileged the classical ideal. The veneration of classical architecture was also promoted through the Academies of Art and Design, which flourished throughout Europe, where design was taught through rules and formulae.[7] Academic architecture relied heavily on these textual sources for the formulation of its classical style; moreover, many architects and cognoscenti also used them as guides to the buildings of antiquity and Renaissance Italy.

The confluence of the verbal and the visual produced potent manifestos for classical architecture as seen in Andrea Palladio's *I quattro libri dell' architettura* or *The Four Books of Architecture* (1570), which was used across Europe as a guide to the architecture of antiquity as well as Palladio's own buildings. *The Four Books* first became available in English in 1715 when Giacomo Leoni published an edition translated from an inadequate French version. Neither the quality of the text nor the images – which were woodcuts – proved satisfactory, but an improved English edition, published by Isaac Ware, did not appear until 1738. Nevertheless, *The Four Books* were a crucial interlocutor between the architecture of antiquity and those with an antiquarian interest in the seventeenth and eighteenth centuries.[8] The work comprises reconstructions of the architecture of the ancient Roman world with textual commentaries as well as similar-style representations of Palladio's own buildings. The techniques of architectural drawing developed and employed by Palladio established the visual epistemological system that re-affirmed and promoted the continuance of the 'normative' classical (male) building.

Palladio's debt to Vitruvius is manifest throughout this text and underpinned both the way is which he theorised about ancient architecture and the way in which he reconstructed it. Indeed, Palladio had illustrated a translation of *The Ten Books* from Latin into Italian published by one of his Veneto patrons, Daniele Barbaro, in 1556. The process of visualising Vitruvius's verbal discourse on antique architecture must have been an important formative process in Palladio's education as an architect and antiquarian. In 'The Author's Preface to the Reader' Palladio remarks:

> It was always my opinion, that the ancient Romans [in building] vastly excelled all those who have been since their time, I proposed myself Vitruvius for my mentor and guide … . I began very minutely with the utmost diligence to measure every one of their [antique buildings] parts… that might entirely from them, comprehend what the whole had been, and reduce it into design … . I therefore, hope that the manner of building may with universal utility be reduced, and soon brought to that pitch of perfection … . [and] to treat of architecture, as orderly and distinctly was possible for me.[9]

It is through his novel and evocative conjunction of text and image that Palladio became an essential interlocutor between the architecture of the ancients and the Renaissance and eighteenth-century antiquarian. The enduring popularity of *The Four Books*, even amongst those who did not understand the Italian text (or were baffled by the poor translations of it), is testament both to the power of the graphic representations of architecture and his reconstructions and analyses of the ruins of ancient Rome.

The Four Books rely on innovative techniques in architectural drawing to present plans, elevations, sections and details of their subjects, both ancient and modern, which are complemented by textual descriptions of the buildings (Figure 7). Book IV on antique architecture, where Palladio attempts to reconstruct the buildings of ancient Rome, demonstrates at once the potency of the technique of representing the architecture of the ancient world and the way in which it is made to conform to a set of predetermined conventions governed by abstract notions of geometry which were seen to pertain to the patrician ideology of classical architecture. The order or perfect form of the circle or square based on male proportions as seen in the *Vitruvian Man* was used to impose order on images of buildings to promote a rational, linear, geometric, and ultimately male, world based on pre-existing verbal laws – the rationalising, 'masculine' forces of analysis based on verbal histories.

Orthogonal perspective was one of the principal techniques of drawing the architecture of the past employed by Palladio. This kind of representation provided accurate measurements of buildings as they were 'flattened' against the picture surface – the only illusion of depth being shading to imply some kind of spatial recession. Orthogonal perspective preserved the proportional systems of architecture which would have been sacrificed if other techniques of representation had been used. In this way orthogonal representation stood in distinct contrast to the preoccupation in sixteenth-century Italy with the creation of the illusion of pictorial space through aerial and linear perspective. Instead of a realistic image of a building, this technique placed emphasis on

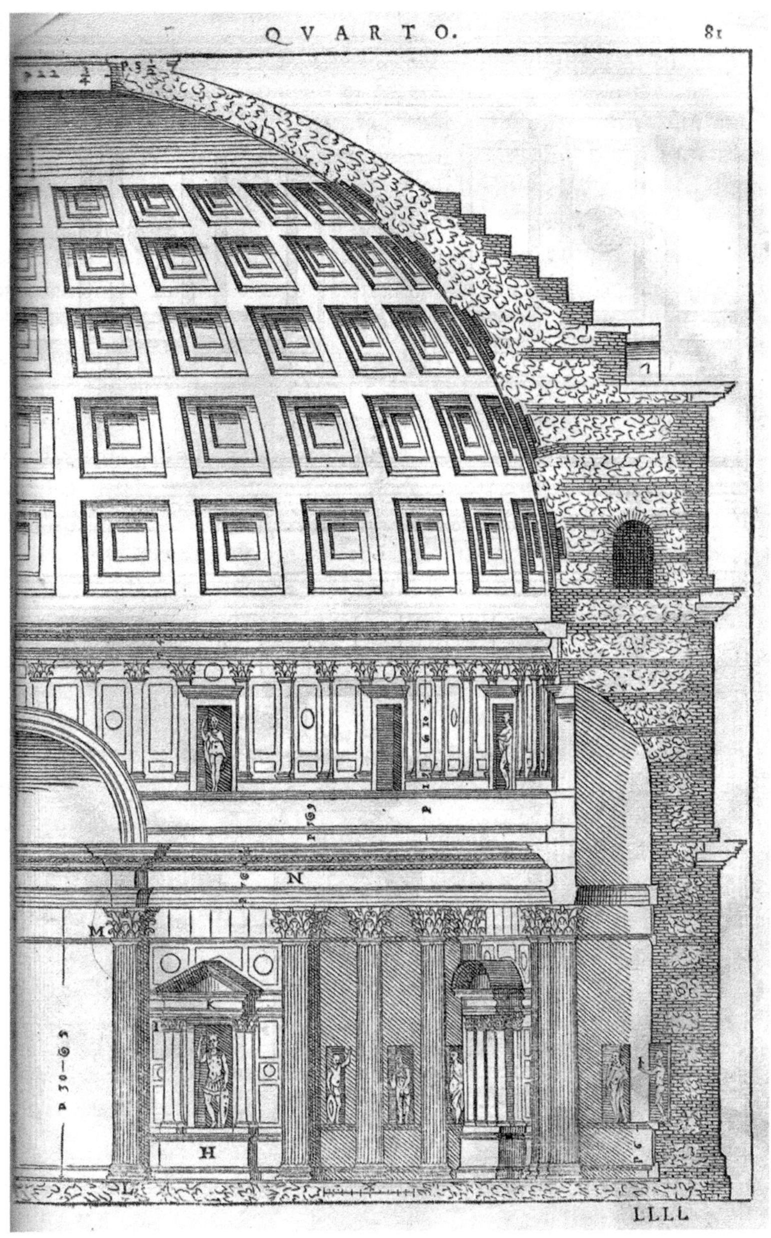

Andrea Palladio, 'Interior of the Pantheon, Rome', from *I quattro libri dell'architettura*, book IV, chapter XX, p. 81, 1570

proportions and measurements, which were accurately represented. This returns us to the Lockean juxtaposition of the metaphorical language of poetry and the literal language of science, and as we have already seen, the verbal preoccupation with rationality, measurement and the reduction of these principles into good (*all'antica*) design. Here we find the graphic, visual equivalent of this system of understanding classical architecture. Clearly, orthogonal perspective is an effective tool in the scientific reconstruction of ancient architecture and it provided those who wished to emulate this mode of building with an easily readable blueprint to do so – complete with measurements. These extractable signs, linguistic procedures for pictorial clarification, created a universal science of recording and expression of a common ideal. This logocentric system fitted into the Cartesian rationalist philosophy which found its best expression in the formulaic use of antique architecture in styles often called Palladian and neo-classical but which in fact bore little relation to the actuality of antiquity. This tradition of architectural design and its histories establish theoretical hegemonies and aesthetic practices that promote the ideology of a patrician élite, which is based on 'tangible reality', that was ultimately a male discourse. But it is important to remember that Palladio did not represent what was actually there. The plates in Book IV are Palladio's reconstructions of Roman ruins based on his linguistic principles of architecture, albeit these relate to a long-established tradition. Moreover, the measurements Palladio provides of both antique and his own architecture are not always accurate and were sometimes optimistic interpretations of proportional formulae.[10] In other words, Palladio is no more truthful than other descriptions of Rome. He provided only a way of seeing or reading the architecture of the past using a particular set of linguistic principles and not a universal truth. We can see, then, how Palladio's epistemological systems and modes of graphic notation that were grounded in antiquity were part of the process of distancing architecture from its physical context. The rationalising system of representing architecture was part of a reductive process based on logos – the philosophical method for revealing the truth through linguistic means.

Notes

1 On the point of language and criticism see the full discussion in Michael Baxandall, *Giotto and the Orators* (Oxford: Oxford University Press, 1986).

2 On this point see Kathleen Canning, 'Feminist History after the Linguistic Turn: Historicising Discourse and Experience', *Signs*, 19:2 (1994), pp. 368–404.

3 Vitruvius, *The Ten Books on Architecture*, trans. Morris Hickey Morgan (Cambridge, Massachusetts: Harvard, 1914), book I, chapter 2, paragraph 5, pp. 14–15.

4 Ibid., book I, chapter 1, paragraph 5, pp. 6–7.

5 The most recently available translation is Leon Battista Alberti, *On the Art of Building in Ten Books*, trans. Joseph Rykwert, Neil Leach, and Robert Tavernor (Cambridge Massachusetts: MIT Press, 1988).

6 Giorgio Vasari, *The Lives of the Artists,* trans. George Bull (Harmondsworth: Penguin, 1971), p. 249.

7 This is evident in the establishment of the Académie française, founded in Paris in 1634 and the Royal Academy in London, founded almost a century later in 1768. See Anton W. A. Boschloo, *et al.* (eds), *Academies of Art between Renaissance and Romanticism, Leids Kunsthistorisch Jaarboek V–VI* (1986–87) ('s Gravenhage: SDU Uitgeverij, 1989).

8 For instance, Inigo Jones used his copy of *I quattro libri dell'architettura,* which is held in the Library at Worcester College, Oxford, as a guide to his tour of architecture in Italy. Jones checked Palladio's measurements and found them wanting, and his remarks are noted in the margins. This has been published in facsimile as *Inigo Jones on Palladio, being the notes of Inigo Jones in the copy of I quattro libri dell'architettura di Andrea Palladio, 1601 in the library of Worcester College, Oxford* (Newcastle-upon-Tyne: Oriel Press, 1970).

9 Andrea Palladio, *I quattro libri dell'architettura* [1570] facsimile of translation by Isaac Ware, ed. Adolf K. Placzek (New York: Dover Publications, 1965). This passage appears in the unpaginated prelims to the text.

10 Jones, *On Palladio.*

Part III: Gendering the past

The interaction between these textual and visual sources for the architecture of classical antiquity based on a male predicate coheres around the notion of the Vitruvian Man. And this gets right to the heart of one of my concerns in this book – the impact of these verbal discourses on our perception of visual descriptions of architecture. Part of what I want to explore here is that this viewpoint inherent in the discourses of the architecture of antiquity is also only a construct and that there are other ways of *seeing* and *writing* about the architecture of the past based on different predicates. Particularly here I focus on the notion of gender and how this inflects on our experience of architectural space and the way architecture can be described.

Man is the measure of all things?

The *Vitruvian Man*, also known as *Le proporzioni del corpo umano secondo Vitruvio* [The proportions of the human body according to Vitruvius], is a pen and ink drawing by Leonardo da Vinci from around 1490 (Figure 8). Leonardo depicts a man in two superimposed positions with his arms and legs apart and inscribed in a circle and square. The image is complemented by notes Leonardo made on Vitruvius and the drawing and text are sometimes called the Canon of Proportions – a point to which I shall return. Leonardo is illustrating this passage from Vitruvius's *De architectura*:

> For the human body is so designed by nature that the face, from the chin to the top of the forehead and the lowest roots of the hair, is a tenth part of the whole height; the open hand from the wrist to the tip of the middle finger is just the same; the head from the chin to the crown is an eighth, and with the neck and shoulder from the top of the breast to the lowest roots of the hair is a sixth; from the middle of the breast to the summit of the crown is a fourth. If we take the height of the face itself, the distance from the bottom of the chin to the under side of the nostrils is one third of it; the nose from the under side of the nostrils to a line between the eyebrows is the same; from there to the lowest roots of the hair is also a third, comprising the forehead. The length of the foot is one sixth of the height of the body; of the forearm, one fourth; and the breadth of the breast is also one fourth. The other members, too, have their own symmetrical proportions, and it was by employing them that the famous painters and sculptors of antiquity attained to great and endless renown.
>
> Similarly, in the members of a temple there ought to be the greatest harmony in the symmetrical relations of the different parts to the general magnitude of the whole. Then again, in the human body the central point is naturally the navel. For if a man be placed flat on his back, with his hands and feet extended, and a pair of compasses centred at his navel, the fingers and toes of

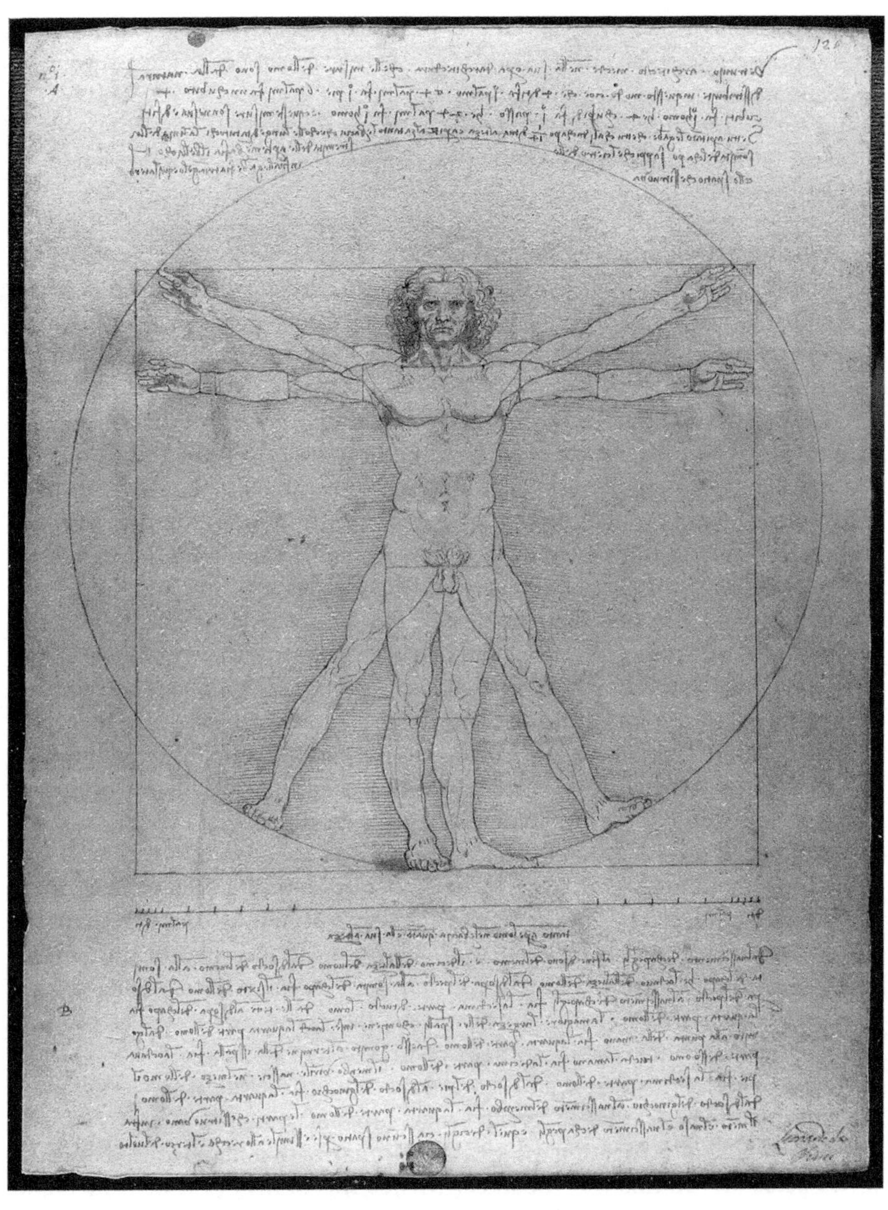

Leonardo da Vinci, *Vitruvian Man*, pen and ink on paper *c*.1490

8

> his two hands and feet will touch the circumference of a circle described therefrom. And just as the human body yields a circular outline, so too a square figure may be found from it. For if we measure the distance from the soles of the feet to the top of the head, and then apply that measure to the outstretched arms, the breadth will be found to be the same as the height, as in the case of plane surfaces which are perfectly square.[1]

The *Vitruvian Man* provides a template for seeing, recording and reconstructing architecture. We have seen this, for instance, in Palladio's *The Four Books of Architecture* where antiquity is reconfigured according to a proportional system based on the male body. My question here is does this make space a masculine construct?

This makes me think of Jacques Lacan's famous analysis of the toilet signs 'Ladies' and 'Gentlemen', where he argues that the signs on the toilet door do not stand for the content of the signifier, which is the toilet, but for the chain of associated signifiers assigned by history, culture and social mores separately and reciprocally to the sexual differentiation implied in them. Lacan asserts that the relationship between signifier and signified is arbitrary and there is no one correspondence between them, still less between the signifier and the thing referred to 'no signification can be sustained other than by reference to another signification'.[2] In other words, the content of the signified is determined only by its relationship to other signifiers in the signifying chain. Is it, then, our culturally determined views that make space represent masculinity or femininity? But it is more than this. If we return to Lacan through his reworking of Freud in terms of the theory of language, woman is ascribed the status of not only the 'other' sex, but also the 'other' of language as he asserts 'there is always something about her and in her which escapes discourse'.[3] Lacan is here bringing 'woman' to the spaces of the text or the scene of writing. But this maps on to the problematic of how we write women into space as something other than a represented object. If 'woman', or the 'feminine' represents those spaces that have escaped structured symbolic discourse, then how are women as subjects of space transforming the discourses of it? Women both assume a space in history and refuse historical and temporal boundaries. These acts necessitate the making of new textual and visual spaces that account for women's experiences, as well as interrogating the spatial boundaries that have worked towards their exclusion.[4] In this way the linear (dis)course of history is disrupted and transformed.

I want to push this point a little further with a provocation. We have already seen how Vitruvius ascribed gendered associations to the different kinds of classical columns. But what happens if we replace the *Vitruvian Man* with the *Vitruvian Woman* (Figure 9)? Most obviously, the canon of proportions that we have seen dominates the theories and practices, representations and

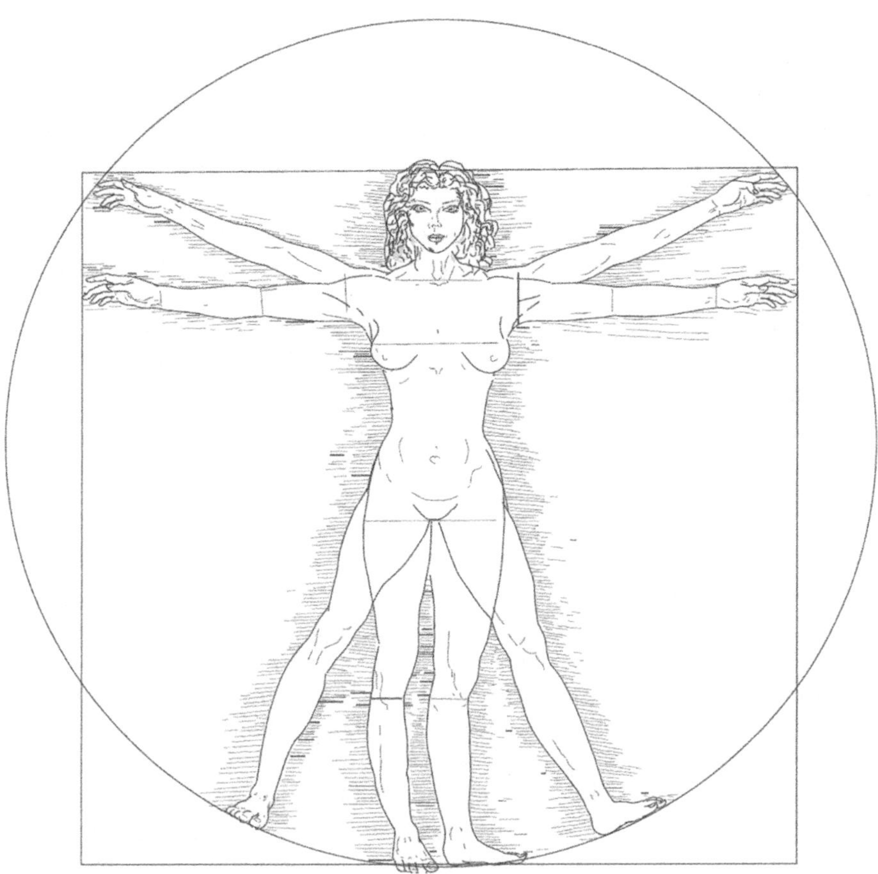

Vitruvian Woman, digital image 9

reconstructions of antique architecture, would be rather different if based on the female body. But the visual representation of a woman with her arms and legs apart and inscribed in a circle and square would not perhaps in the first instance imply that woman is the measure of all things. Instead, our polite sensibilities might initially be challenged. Indeed, this can be explained further if we think about women's space and spatial experience – or spatial bodily existence – as both an object constituted by space as well as being a spatially constituted subject. Central to this is the feminine body, which is positioned in space by a set of patriarchal co-ordinates that impose modes of performativity that constitute our notion of woman. Simply put: the *Vitruvian Woman* connotes subjugation and sexual readiness. And we will see later how drawing in perspective can also create a space predicated on masculine proportions that subjects the feminine body to the male gaze.[5]

Let me unpack this in a little more detail – the visual modes of performativity as evident in the *Vitruvian Woman* operate in a similar way to the phallogocentric linguistic predicates of the text. Iris Marion Young identifies space as an agent of confinement that restricts women's bodily movements and pushes them to absent themselves from space to become invisible occupying no space whatsoever, 'a space surrounds us in our imagination that we are not free to move beyond; the space available to our movement is a constricted one'.[6] At one level the female body is an object for which the gaze imposes and confirms certain patterns of comportment. Restricted movements in a real or imagined space that are 'lady-like' assert woman as subject by avoiding the objectification of the gaze. Female bodily movements cannot, then, fill the spaces inhabited by woman, in our case the circle and the square.[7]

This makes me think more generally about our phenomenological, bodily sense of space. Imagine, for instance, the lights failing in a room and we have to negotiate the space through touch, crawling along feeling the floor, walls and doorframe in order to move our bodies in space. Cognitive scientists accept that the body shapes the embodied mind and that this is shaped by the experiences of the body. But the experiential world is more than just a physical place. We experience the world within a certain social and cultural milieu that conditions our view of it and imposes a kind of performativity on us as regards our occupation of that space.[8] And this is relevant for the description of ancient architecture. The bodily experience of architectural space is a core ingredient for a verbal or a visual ekphrasis, and this is a point I will return to later in this book.

This analysis of the gendered construction of the languages of architecture might at first appear to jar against the comfortable image of genteel, gentlemanly travel and the polite activity of rediscovering the antique in the eighteenth century. But it is precisely this cosy image of eighteenth-century antiquarianism that needs to be disrupted and unsettled. The rational Enlightenment project was not objective, and its subjectivity continues to impinge on our understanding and qualitative evaluation of antique architecture. And this takes us right to the heart of the Cartesian rationalist system of imposing pre-formulated ideas of order on the known world. This issue relates more generally to the way culture is constructed and evaluated – culture is masculine and nature, that which is unruly and irrational or not subject to rational laws, is feminine. In this way gender becomes a signifier of power through its discourses of the white western male subject and his binary opposite – the white western female.[9] If gender is, then, a social construction through its production by discourse there must be a moment before the sovereign white male subject began to dominate our linguistic and knowledge systems. Part of my aim in this book is to attempt to 'unlearn' the discourses of classically inspired architecture and using the trope of visual ekphrasis I attempt to retrace their evolution back to a moment before the linguistic constraints of the rational male subject were imposed.[10]

Notes

1 Vitruvius, *The Ten Books*, book III, chapter 1, paragraphs 2–3, pp. 72–3.
2 Jacques Lacan, *Ecrits, A Selection*, trans. Alan Sheridan (New York: W.W. Norton, 1977), pp. 150–2.
3 Ibid.
4 Feminist writers such as Teresa de Lauretis argue women have never occupied a place in discourse other than as the object of representation. By creating new spaces of discourse women can occupy a position in the discourse as well as maintaining their marginal status so they can be re-visioned rather then being viewed in the dominant discourse. See Teresa de Lauretis, *Technologies of Gender: Essays on Theory, Film and Fiction* (London: Macmillan, 1987), p. 25.
5 See Chapter 3 of this book.
6 Iris Marion Young, *'Throwing Like a Girl' and Other Essays in Feminist Philosophy and Social Theory* (Bloomington: University of Indiana Press, 1990), p. 146.
7 See Young, 'Throwing Like a Girl'. For Young this represents the tension between woman's immanence and transcendence, her role as subject and object.
8 This kind of phenomenological notion of space is not solely the preoccupation of cognitive scientists. Kant had posed similar questions over two centuries earlier believing that space was a form imposed by our minds on the world.
9 On this point see Judith M. Bennett, 'Feminism and History', *Gender and History*, 1:3 (1989), pp. 251–72.
10 This idea is discussed by Jacques Derrida in his essay 'To Unsense the Subjectile', in Jacques Derrida and Paule Thévenin (eds), *The Secret Art of Antonin Artaud*, trans. Mary Ann Caws (Cambridge, Massachusetts: MIT Press, 1998), p. 105 esp.

Part IV: Imaging and imagining the past

I would like now to focus on three case studies in the form of brief provocations, if you will, to explore these ideas and to set up some of the key concerns of this book. I am particularly interested in the relationship between image and imagination. Additionally, if we accept that these images are a form of history, I explore how space and time are narrated, especially within the masculinist constructs I have outlined. We have seen how Rome was a constant presence in the engagement with the past and how its both authors and subsequent studies of its monuments had influenced architectural theory and practice in the Renaissance. By contrast, politics and geography had contrived to make the architecture of ancient Greece more remote. The country had mostly been inaccessible for European travellers since the mid fifteenth century when it became part of the Ottoman Empire. By the middle years of the eighteenth century diplomatic relations between Turkey and Europe had improved and, as a consequence, the more daring of our Grand Tourists could experience at first hand the many examples of ancient Greek architecture and other artefacts.

My first provocation is a consideration of James Stuart and Nicolas Revett's volumes entitled *The Antiquities of Athens*.[1] Plans for this survey were made in Rome when Stuart and Revett in discussion with various antiquarians, including the antiquarian and artist Gavin Hamilton, decided to visit and record the ancient monuments of Athens with a view to publishing the results in three volumes. These were intended to contain 191 plates and the whole enterprise was to be brought to its published conclusion over a period of four years. Only one year was to be spent in Greece for the purposes of excavating, measuring and recording the buildings themselves. The project was wildly optimistic both it its scope and the timescale within which it was to be realised. We must remember that Athens, alongside the rest of the antique architecture in Greece, had remained largely untouched for centuries. Like its cultural counterpart, Rome, many of the ancient monuments in Athens were in ruins or formed a part of later buildings. But Rome had been subjected to over three centuries of archaeological and historical investigation where the combination of the trowel and the text had succeeded in revealing much of its built past. In this way, in contradistinction to the on-going excavations and exploration of ancient Rome, the eighteenth-century re-discovery of ancient Athens could not benefit from the work that had been carried out by previous generations of antiquarians. The ancient monuments were largely undisturbed and the fabrication of knowledge about their past and their reconstruction for the present was new territory that remained to be charted. As a consequence, a brief outline of the historical circumstances surrounding the enterprise is helpful context.

Stuart and Revett's aims for their ambitious project were expressed in the Proposal published in 1748, which was intended to attract subscribers to finance the venture. Stuart and Revett had 'resolved to make a journey to Athens; and to publish at our return, such Remains of that famous City as we may be permitted to copy, and that appear to merit our attention'. Their stated reasons for doing so foregrounded the historical need for such a survey, rather than the 'neat profit' that was also envisaged.

> But Athens the Mother of elegance and politeness, whose magnificence scarce yielded to that of Rome, and who for the beauties of a correct style must be allowed to surpass her; has been almost entirely neglected. So that unless exact copies of them be speedily made, all her beauteous Fabricks, her Temples, her Palaces, now in ruins, will drop into Oblivion; and Posterity will have to reproach us, that we have not left them a tolerable Idea of what was so excellent, and so much deserved our attention; but that we have suffered the perfection of an Art to perish, when it was perhaps in our power to have retrieved it.[2]

By 1751 Stuart and Revett had secured more than 500 subscribers and thus the appropriate funds plus the essential 'recommendatory letters to all the principal persons of the places' they intended to visit and record.[3] The work on site had taken two years during which time Stuart made notes and made sketches for his gouache paintings of the actual state of the principal monuments, whilst Revett produced meticulous reconstructions and measured drawings. On the pair's return to London, Stuart supervised the engraving of the plates, prepared the text and designed the binding. The first volume, only, appeared in 1762 and, owing to unforeseen circumstances, including an outbreak of plague, focused on only five buildings in the northern part of Athens. The survey work had been time consuming but the resulting publication set the tone for the remaining volumes. Stuart and Revett noted in the Preface that they intended to record the remaining ancient monuments of Greece in the same way that

> Rome, who borrowed her Arts, and frequently her Artificers, from Greece, has by means of Serlio, Palladio, Santo Bartoli, and other Ingenious men, preserved the memory of the most Excellent Sculptures, and Magnificent Edifices, which once adorned her.[4]

At first glance this statement can be interpreted as part of the rhetoric of the Greco-Roman controversy that dominated European cultural and aesthetic debate in the middle years of the eighteenth century. More importantly for us is the way in which Italian Renaissance architects and theorists are identified as the interlocutors between ancient Rome and the present. And this had led to the privileging of Roman over Greek. Here this new history would in the eyes of Stuart and Revett

> meet with the Approbation of all those Gentlemen, who are Lovers of Antiquity, or have a taste for what is Excellent in these Arts, as we are assured that

> those Artists, who aim at Perfection must be infinitely more pleased, and better instructed, the nearer they can draw their Examples, from the Fountain-head.[5]

The remaining volumes of *The Antiquities* suffered further delay. Revett resigned from the project before the appearance of Volume I and ceded his interest to Stuart. Stuart's heavy drinking and premature death in 1788 meant Volume II appeared *c.*1789/90 under the editorship of William Newton, with Volume III edited by Willey Reveley following a couple of years later. A fourth volume edited by Joseph Woods, based partly on surviving papers, followed much later in 1816.[6] There is no doubt that *The Antiquities* helped shape the European understanding of ancient Greece and introduced a new vocabulary to architectural design. The primacy of Greek over Roman classicism as the model for contemporary architecture as asserted by Stuart is indeed analogous to the views of Winckelmann in his highly influential *History of the Art of Antiquity*[7] that appeared at around the same time as the first volume of *The Antiquities*.[8]

Volume I of *The Antiquities* provides an introduction to the authors and the rationale behind the project as a whole. Common to all the volumes is the system for presenting each monument comprising a detailed explanation followed by a contemporary view of it in its surroundings.[9] The images were based on views sketched and possibly also partly painted in gouache on site by Stuart and conform to traditions of landscape painting.[10] These 'pictorial' views were followed by Revett's accurately drawn elevations, cross sections, ground plans, underneath views and details of its architectural elements.[11] The measurements supplied were given to a thousandth of an inch – a technical impossibility given the use of brass rulers and the distortions that resulted from the ambient temperature of the site itself. Indeed, Stuart most likely calculated these near infinitesimal measurements whilst he worked on producing the volumes in London. The success and failure of *The Antiquities of Athens* both as an antiquarian endeavour and as an advocate for Grecian-styled architecture have been ably argued elsewhere, and it is not my purpose here to reiterate or challenge these analyses.[12] Rather, my questions focus on how the desire for knowledge encouraged travel across both geographies and time. The images in *The Antiquities* help us to retrace the journey of discovery undertaken by Grand Tourists and the ways in which the fragments of the past were transformed into factual information. Most importantly, I am curious to know what the images in *The Antiquities* actually do. Let me begin by thinking about how Stuart and Revett saw the monuments themselves. It is important to remember that Greek art and architecture was not well known in Europe and it presented a distinctive, if not slightly exotic, aesthetic when compared to the more familiar remnants of ancient Rome. But rather like the Grand Tourists who travelled 'through the poets', Stuart and Revett's guide to the architecture

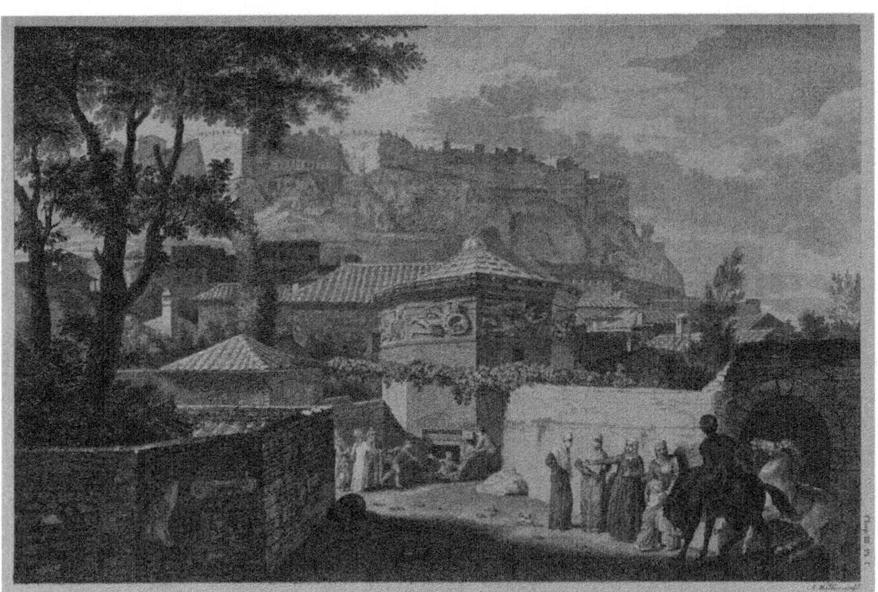

James Stuart and Nicholas Revett, 'A View of the Tower of the Winds', from *The Antiquities of Athens*, Volume I, chapter III, plate I, 1762 **10**

of Athens was textual. They believed that Greek architecture should be studied according to its 'conformity to the doctrine of Vitruvius, and the descriptions of Strabo, Pausanias etc'.[13]

Volume I of *The Antiquities* included the Horologion (clock tower) of Andronicus of Cyrrhus, also known as The Tower of the Winds and the plates are excellent examples both of Stuart's skill as a painter, and Revett's dexterity and diligence in producing measured reconstructions. We can use the various images of it to trace the antiquarian journey of discovery as the building is encountered, reconstructed and dissected (Figure 10). The series of plates devoted to The Tower begin with a contemporary, topographical view showing us how it was encountered by Grand Tourists. The Tower was partly included in another building and we have the anecdotal details of figures in contemporary Turkish dress that add an almost ethnographic dimension to the narrative. As a consequence we can get a good sense of how the past was encountered in these newly accessible sites. Stuart's view of The Tower shows us the east, northeast, and north sides of the building and that the remainder of the building was 'concealed in the Wall of a neighbouring house; which the Owner was prevailed on to pull down' in order that the pair could study all the sides of octagonal building.[14] The ground level had risen around The Tower and the pair had excavated the site by digging trenches fifteen feet down to the original level of the pavement. As such, the Tower and its history were exhumed from the earth and it was reconstructed by Revett using the additional information that was uncovered. Further excavations several feet down inside the building exposed a marble floor and internal arrangements that revealed the original function of the building, which was a water clock.

In contrast to Stuart's topographical view, Revett's images of The Tower offer no narration of context or indeed history: the passage of time is not evident. We are left then with the question of what kind of ekphrasis, if any, do the images offer? Here I want to think about the graphic conventions used by Revett – a discrete system of signs which represented three-dimensional architectural forms. The latter system of architectural drawings using perspective views, orthogonal elevation, details and working drawings was not merely imitative. Instead, buildings were disembodied and dissected, order was imposed on chaos – marks on paper evoked the built fabric. But the act of drawing is blind – The Tower was not in the sightline of the draughtsman when it was being recorded; an image is held in his imagination and it is the rhetorical devices of this imagined image that determine the mode of ekphrasis. Revett's studies of *The Tower and its interior order* demonstrate this technique (Figures 11 and 12). Here the ruined edifice is reconstructed in orthogonal elevation and is presented out of its physical context. There is no surrounding landscape and there is no texture to the stone or patina of age. This method of representation relies on the viewer's imagination, as the construction of this artificial composition is the creation of something other than the object under scrutiny. Revett's reconstructions of the architectural details of The Tower of the Winds on subsequent pages of the publication re-present the temple – or parts of it – on a completely different scale so privileging different kinds of information about it and prompting a different kind of cognition, response or understanding of it. The abstraction of detail that became a hallmark of 'scientific' or archaeological survey drawing also became a system of standardisation akin to the dictionaries and encyclopaedias which proliferated in the eighteenth century. This produced a legible language of signs, which could be subjugated to verbal argument and could, if desired, follow linguistic systems. By this I mean that there appears to be no authorial voice; it is apparently objective rather than subjective observation. But Revett's descriptions of The Tower manifest many authorial choices. Indeed, his mode of ekphrasis allows me to pursue further the linguistic analogies. The reconstructed image of the temple is decontextualised, floating in space offering no sense of scale or texture. This mode of ekphrasis also offers the deconstruction of The Tower as seen in the study of the detail of its internal mouldings including the cornice, soffit and column capitals. The Tower is broken up into its constituent parts which are reconfigured in an authorial sleight of hand that seems anonymous and objective. But the quasi 'science of seeing' is very much the product of the

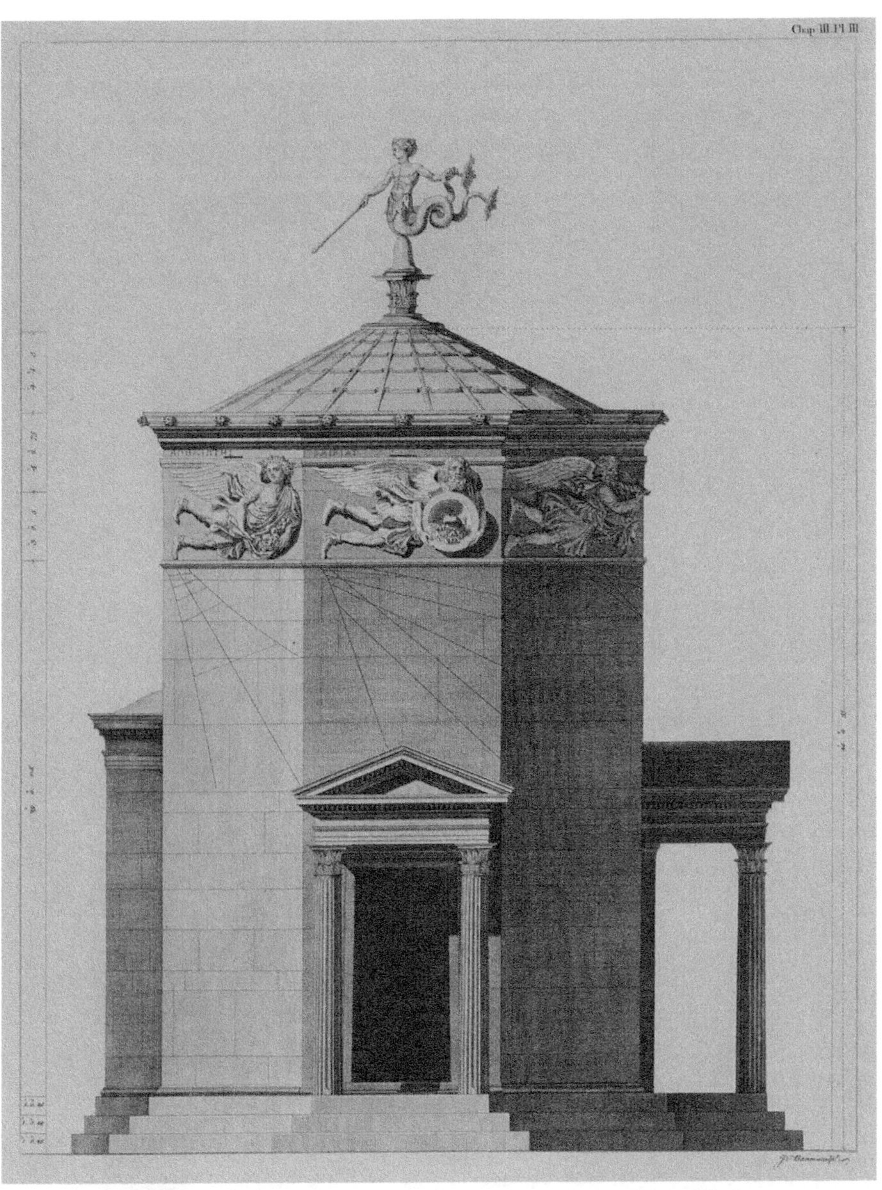

James Stuart and Nicholas Revett, 'Elevation of the Tower of the Winds', from *The Antiquities of Athens*, Volume I, chapter III, plate III, 1762 **11**

imagination as tempered by the masculinist notions of the *Vitruvian Man*. The perfect form of the circle or square was used to impose order on images of ruins to promote a rational, linear, geometric world based on pre-existing

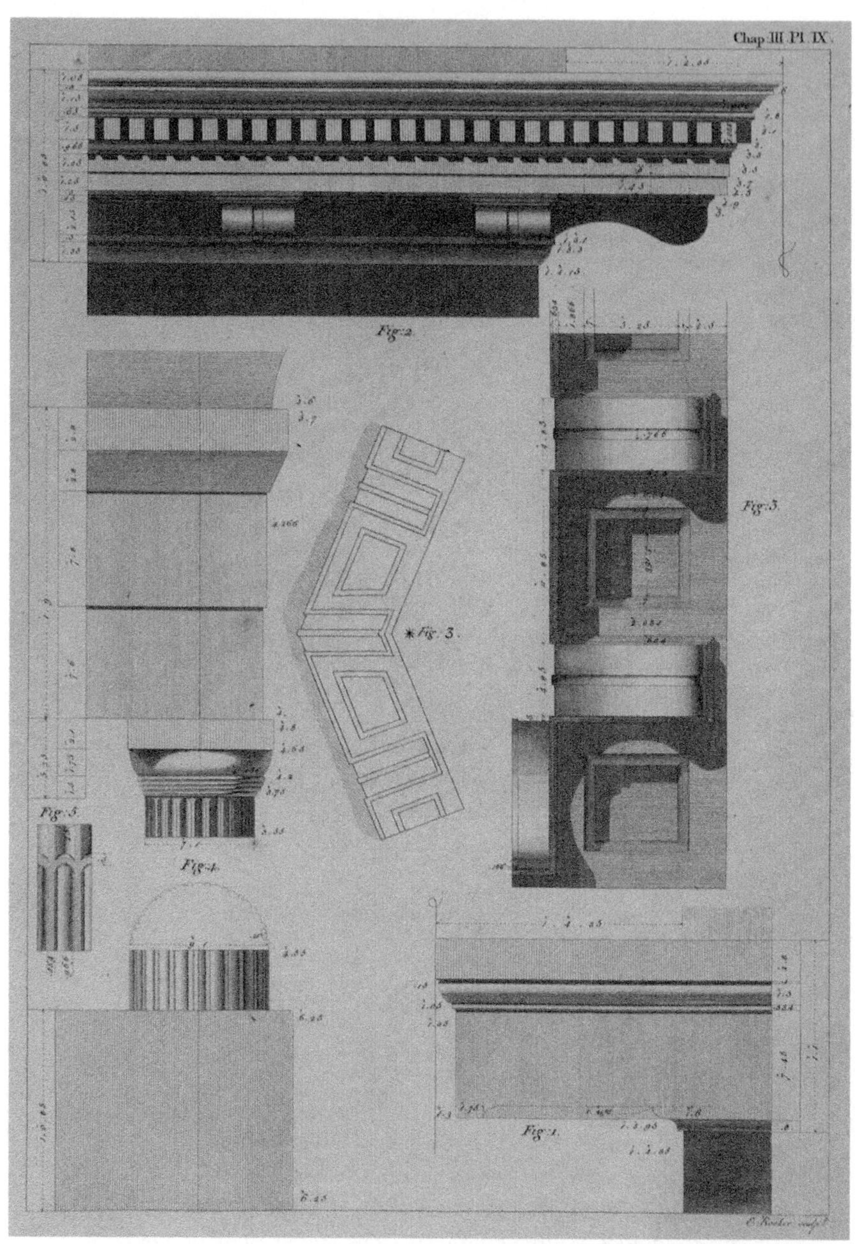

12 James Stuart and Nicholas Revett, 'Study of details of the interior, Tower of the Winds', from *The Antiquities of Athens*, Volume I, chapter III, plate IX, 1762

verbal laws that evoked a Lockean view of the world based on empirical observation.[15] These extractable signs, linguistic procedures for pictorial clarification, created a universal science of recording and expression of a common ideal. This visual tradition of representing architecture established theoretical hegemonies based on 'tangible reality' which required the imagination to make the image 'real'. But what of the operation of the imagination in other images that have a more narrative character?

The images of The Tower show us how modes of visual ekphrasis can operate. The artificial constructions and imitations of the temple recall the methods and approaches set out by Palladio in his *Four Books* use 'mimesis' and other rhetorical devices to create a set of pictorial conventions, based on Vitruvius, which re-perform the past. Like the camera with its zoom lens the studies in *The Antiquities* focus in and re-present the original in such a way as to make it conform to cognitive thought processes that enable its memorialisation. And this mode of description facilitates the re-use of the various elements of this aesthetic by eighteenth-century architects as the printed reconstruction enables its physical reconstruction, or re-performance to make it real again. In this way, the printed images of The Tower, like the reconstructions of ancient Roman architecture, encouraged an invented cultural memory that reconfigured the relationship between past and present as the past. Indeed, in 1760, before the publication of *The Antiquities*, Stuart recreated The Tower in the grounds of Shugborough for Thomas Anson.

There were of course other ways of seeing and describing ancient architecture. *The Antiquities* were part of a crowded field of publications offering systemic studies of the monuments of Greece and elsewhere that appeared in the mid eighteenth century.[16] Frequent comparison is made between Stuart and Revett's volumes and Le Roy's *Les ruines des plus beaux monuments de la Grèce*, which appeared just before *The Antiquities* in 1758.[17] To this day, Le Roy is often favoured as the voyageur-philosophe who presented the monuments in their cultural contexts, rejecting the accuracy of empirical recording for a more evocative technique of visual ekphrasis. And there were some sharp published exchanges between Stuart and Le Roy about the importance of accurate measurement. These debates do not need to be rehearsed here.[18] But I do want to think about the contrasting ways in which architecture can be described.

Perhaps in response to Le Roy's publication, Stuart used his topographical view to document the extent of their archaeological endeavours and to show that they did not simply measure and draw. In his view of The Tower of the Winds, we see how it was set against the fortified walls of the Acropolis. And we see the labourers they employed excavating the doorway and the removal of some fourteen feet of earth to reveal the original exterior and interior levels of the building. The images of The Tower in *The Antiquities* record certain 'facts' in some detail, as their subject is an actual building. The graphic techniques of recording used in the images operate like language – the changing effect of metre and rhythm; detail and impression create different moods and modes of description. The vision of The Tower is bifurcated: Stuart's narrative image functions like a touristic snapshot capturing the contemporary scene, whilst Revett's reconstructions and dissections are almost arid in their attention to measurement.[19] What both these modes of seeing and describing have in common is that they exist in the present. But where is the past in these images?

My second provocation considers how ancient monuments made the past visible and the ways in which certain modes of visual description acknowledged the passage of time. The rediscovery of the three Greek Doric temples at Paestum in southern Italy meant the area became an important diversion for the Grand Tourists with a special interest in the architecture of the ancients. The temples were known in the eighteenth century as the Basilica, the Temple of Ceres and the Temple of Neptune and alongside the temples on the Acropolis in Athens and at Agrigentum in Sicily they represent the most outstanding extant examples of Greek Doric architecture. Many images circulated of the temples and this helped promote knowledge about them and placed them within established histories of architecture.[20] In broad, the images were akin to the types produced by Stuart and Revett. For instance, the studies by Thomas Major (1768) conformed to the mode of description employed by Revett.[21] By contrast, many of the more pictorial images rather like those by Stuart of Athens, offered some sort of narrative of the site but were not necessarily original views. They were instead based on a single set of prints that were circulated across Europe.[22] Here I want to focus on a series of plates of the Temples at Paestum that stand outside of these traditions through their focus on temporality. Giovanni Battista Piranesi's *Differentes vues de quelques restes de trois grands edifices qui subsistent encore dans le milieu de l'ancienne ville de Pesto autrement Posidonia*, was published two months after his death, in 1778, by his son Francesco (Figure 13).[23] The plates show the temples as ruins and here I concentrate on the image of the Temple of Neptune, which was the best known of the three. The representation of the visual fragments – in other words the actual physical state of the temple – is at once an image of the actuality of the ruins themselves and a carefully constructed re-performance of the temple. The scale and size of the temple in relation to the size of the print is important here as they fill the frame, and the inclusion of human figures that are dwarfed by the massive bulk of the buildings underscores the awesome appearance of the temples as they were encountered by eighteenth-century visitors.

Time is encapsulated in these images through the description of the slippage between past and present. As Marguerite Yourcenar remarks, Piranesi's images of the monuments of the past are 'a meditation on the duration or the slow erosion of things, on the opaque identity of the block continuing, within the monument, its long existence of stone as stone'.[24] Moreover, she notes his human

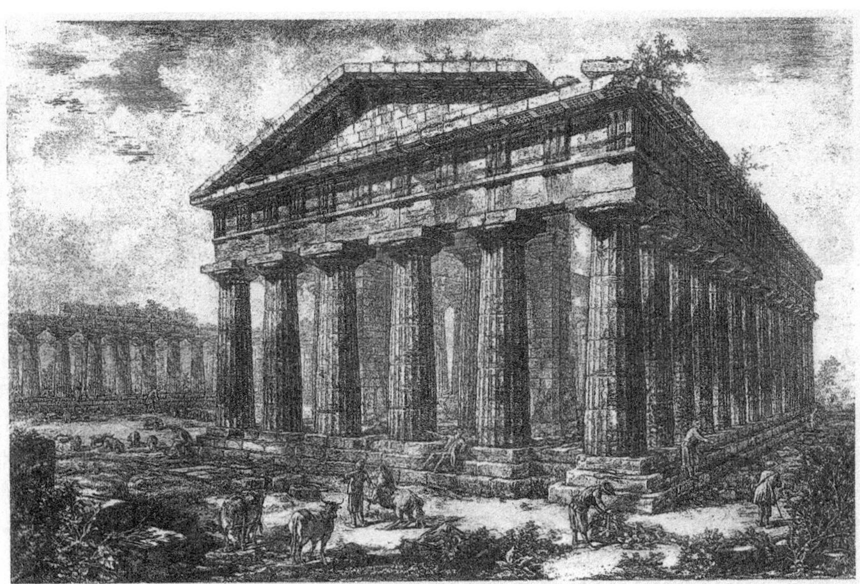

Giovanni Battista Piranesi, 'Temple of Neptune at Paestum', from *Differentes vues de quelques restes de trois grandes edifices qui subsistent encore dans le milieu de l'ancienne ville de Pesto autrement Posidonia qui est située dans la Luganie*, plate X, 1778 **13**

figures serve only to accentuate the height and perspectival depth of his architectural subjects. Time is also embedded in the technique of representation as Piranesi's use of the medium of etching is akin to the process of physical deterioration we witness in his representations of ancient ruins.[25] Etching involved a process of erosion to achieve the lines that create the printed image. This is achieved by immersing a varnished copperplate inscribed with the image in a bath of acid, which then bites into the copper surface the artist has exposed.[26] In this way the technique echoes the way in which Piranesi revealed the past; both are corrosive processes that re-enact the loss inherent in the decay of ruins over time and the antidote to this loss is the re-enactment of survival of the ruins and the past in their representation. Indeed, compared to plates prepared for engravings, those for etchings are far more vulnerable to the depredations of time when it is used for multiple prints. The copperplate becomes degraded and requires reworking in order to maintain the quality of the line.

Compared to Stuart's topographical views or Revett's reconstructions, which are the inheritors of the traditions of landscape painting and the Vitruvian/Palladian view of architecture respectively, Piranesi's images are a very different way of seeing which guides the mind to a different form of cognition. Piranesi re-presents a different kind of past which draws attention to the surface texture of the temples, their ruined state and emphasises their imposing aesthetic. The image is about the past being encountered in the present. There is the patina of age and the notion of the passage of time alongside the narrative context of the contemporary eighteenth-century figures and the landscape itself. But this mode of visual description makes me think about the 'gap' between the subject and the way in which it is represented. It is here in the gap – the moment of blindness – between looking and recording images, and seeing images and interpreting, where imagination comes into play. Piranesi's views almost do the work of the viewer for him or her, as little is apparently left to the imagination.

For my third provocation, I would like to return to Rome to explore how leaps of the imagination facilitate the slippage between past and present. So far I have considered different modes of ekphrasis in relation to buildings. But what of the potency of images as a mode of ekphrasis of a city and, indeed, what better example than Rome. Once again the work of Piranesi comes to the fore as we see how a visual description of a city works to re-create an apparent reality, which is in fact an interpretation. But how can the notion of 'Rome' be encapsulated in one image and what effect/affect does this have? Topographical conventions produce tropes of narrative fiction or invented memory that perform linguistically as a means of describing and evoking a city. And these are not based on the actuality or reality of a city. 'Truth' has to be sacrificed in order that a comprehensive representation of something as complex as a city can be produced. And we need to be able to 'read' this. This is evident in maps such as Duperac's (Figure 2) and Falda's survey of the gardens of Rome (Figure 3). In both examples the features of the city have been presented from a single viewpoint, albeit this may be a fictitious one. This results in the compression of the spatial dimensions of Rome – most obviously its three-dimensionality is reduced to two, but we also have no notion of shifting viewpoints or indeed parallax. The momentariness of the maps of Duperac and Falda also reduce the temporal vision of Rome as we see the city's past in the present. But the notion of a history predicated on images brings with it the assumption that the ancient world can be mapped and known by its visual representations. And this prompts us to think about what kinds of information can be represented in any particular image.

During the 1750s and 1760s, Piranesi took to illustrating architectural remains by combining on a single sheet different types and scales of representation. Many of Piranesi's images of Rome were published in the volumes of his *Le antichità romane* (1756). Indeed, Piranesi was one of the first antiquarians to convey the layering of time or a 'vertical history' within a single image.[27] Often he inserted the letters of the alphabet against parts of a building and these referred to extended captions either within or outside the frame of the image. There was some precedent for this in cartography and indeed in antiquarian publications, but what marks out these images is not only the range of different kinds of information they made available but also the recognition of gaps in historical knowledge and the need to imagine connections which were not otherwise visible. By juxtaposing a mass of competing and sometimes apparently contradictory verbal and visual information, Piranesi offered a lost past which might be brought back into existence by seeing the connections that others had not yet made. Piranesi's method relies on the image as the prime means of ordering current knowledge: the text here serves largely in a supporting role as a description of those images. Thus, what is at stake here is how we perceive, amass, and structure knowledge and the means of its visual representation. Piranesi's multi-informational images offered the past as a specific time and place and made the artist the discoverer of a lost world.

There remains a radical disjunction between a belief in the empirical observation embodied in accurate measurement and the fundamental unknowableness of the past. Multi-informational images jostle with deeply-shaded elevations and peopled perspectives in their attempts to describe the architecture of the past. Whilst those attempts rely at times on the documentary evidence of historical sources, what we also see, however, is the increasing ability of the antique print to tell its own story, a story often quite independent from those textual accounts which had so long dominated the past.

Piranesi's views of Rome were so evocative that, in an almost pre-echo of Freud, Grand Tourists who had seen his work before visiting the city could be disappointed with the real thing. For instance, Goethe who owned the first of the four volumes of Piranesi's *Le antichità romane*, remarked in his *Italian Journey*, that 'his first sight of the ruins of Rome had failed to measure up to Piranesi's views of them'.[28] Indeed, Horace Walpole was lavish in his praise urging his contemporaries to

> study the sublime dreams of Piranesi, who seems to have conceived visions of Rome beyond what it boasted even in the meridian of its splendour. Savage as Salvator Rosa, fierce as Michael Angelo, and exuberant as Rubens, he has imagined scenes that would startle geometry, and exhaust the Indies to realize. He piles palaces on bridges, and temples on palaces, and scales heaven with mountains of edifices. Yet what taste in his boldness! What grandeur in his wildness! What labour and thought both in his rashness and details![29]

Piranesi originally intended the *Ichnographia* or *Campus Martius* (Figure 14) to be part of the *Le antichità romane* (1756). Instead, his grand and intricate sixteen-page foldout etching measuring three square metres became an independent map or plan of this ancient Roman district that nestles in the curves of the River Tiber. The *Campus Martius* (1762) was dedicated to Scottish architect Robert Adam, as an acknowledgement of their friendship. In the dedication Piranesi notes that Adam had encouraged him 'to engrave the remains of the buildings ... and to produce a bird's eye view of the whole area'.[30] The dedicatory tablet,

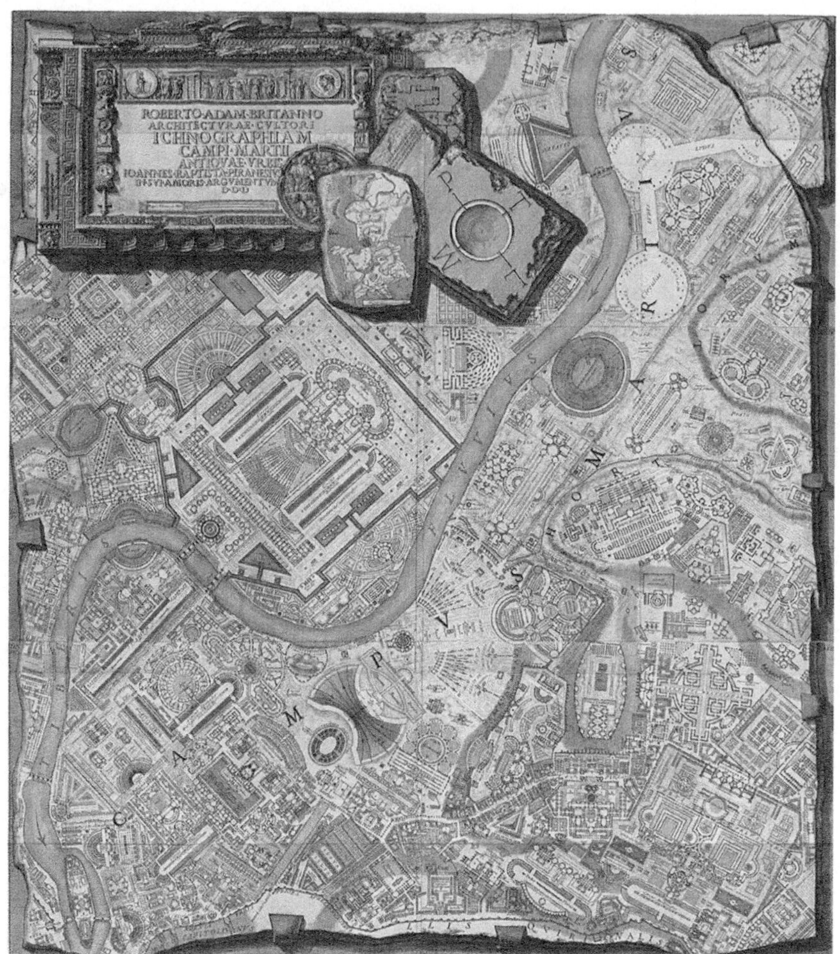

14 Giovanni Battista Piranesi, *Iconographiam Campi Martii antiquae urbis* (Map of the Campus Martius of ancient Rome), etching in six plates, 1757

dated 1757 when the work on the giant plan began, appears on the *Ichnographia* and is in itself an archaeological fiction. It takes the form of a fragment bearing the portrait heads of both Adam and Piranesi and it appears to rest on top of the pattern of Rome that lies beneath it, obscuring some of the detailed information. This layering of the history of the friendship of Adam and Piranesi with the history of Rome points to the importance of the imagination in the production of this innovative plan, its multi-informational properties, and the slippage between past and present. The *Ichnographia* stands distinct from other maps of Rome; we have already considered Duperac's and Falda's representations of the city. A more recent example was Giambattista Nolli's large plan of Rome (1748), which provides a foil to Piranesi's view through its sober, documentary focus on the contemporary built environment of eighteenth-century Rome.

Street plans and contemporary layouts are not Piranesi's primary focus. Instead the ground plans of ancient Roman buildings from various periods of the city's past together with fictitious structures form an intricate pattern. And Piranesi acknowledges his use of speculative evidence and the importance of his imagination in his dedication to Robert Adam:

> I am rather afraid that some parts of the Campus which I describe should seem figments of my imagination and not based on any evidence: certainly if anyone compares them with the architectural theory of the ancients he will see that they differ greatly from it and are actually closer to the usage of our own times. But before anyone accuses me of falsehood, he should, I beg, examine the ancient [marble] plan of the city…, he should examine the villas of Latium and that of Hadrian at Tivoli, the baths, the tombs and other ruins, especially those beyond the Porta Capena, and he will find that the ancients transgressed the strict rules of architecture just as much as the moderns. Perhaps it is inevitable and a general rule that the arts on reaching a peak should then decline, or perhaps it is part of man's nature to demand some licence in creative expression as in other things, but we should not be surprised to see that the ancient architects have done the very things which we sometimes criticise in buildings of our own times. Here then, my dear Adam, is the Campus Martius, not as perfect perhaps as you wanted but as complete as I could manage, given the complexities of the subject and the lapse of time… . Whatever your judgement may be about this little work, I am happy to have done as you asked and to have provided for posterity a monument to our friendship.[31]

In his *Campus Martius*, Piranesi saw the creative potential of archaeology as a stimulus to design as well as its practical application to solving technical problems. The extensive publication was based on a great deal of archaeological exploration and was intended to demonstrate the Roman genius for design. Piranesi set out to indicate the potential of the evidence illustrated on a vast urban scale to stimulate the imagination of contemporary architects. The plates were preceded by 15 pages of dense text in three columns, followed by a catalogue and index of the plates, including a list of ruins represented in the plates. Sequences of plates were one of Piranesi's favourite forms of visual argument, and he introduced the collection of topographical views, and illustrations of fragments and inscriptions with a series of plans that traced Rome from its beginnings on the banks of the Tiber. These sources culminate in the six-plate *Ichnographia* as an apotheosis of the potential of Roman urban design to be an essential source of inspiration for subsequent generations. The architecture and urban planning of Rome is represented in ground plan configured as a series of shapes and patterns and we accept it as real. The intricate arrangement of the plans of complex structures from different points in time continues in every direction and appears to go beyond the broken edges of the fictive marble fragment on which it appears to be displayed. It is not Rome as seen by the visitor, but it can be used as a guide of sorts where the spatio/temporal narrative of Rome is compressed into a visual pattern. We have already noted that our Grand Tourists' disappointment at the real Rome compared to Piranesi's visual descriptions of it pre-echoed Freud. We can, then, surely see the *Ichnographia* as an illustration of the temporal layering of Rome that Freud used to describe the workings of the mind.

And there is no doubt that the selective representation of details, whether by Freud or Piranesi, has an effect on how the city is seen, read and remembered. It is important here to think historically, as our present-day knowledge and familiarity with cities we have never visited is greatly enhanced by new technologies. Before photography, videos and the internet, prints were the main means of visual description or memorialisation of cities. How do we begin to understand this process? Returning, then, to the Rome in Piranesi's *Campus Martius* it is at once Rome and not Rome; a superposition of space and time of the eternal city and an abstract pattern.

My three provocations prompt me to think about visual images as a form of writing. And the question I want to raise here is the idea of a single authoritative authorial voice – or at least the illusion visual images can give of the existence of such a phenomenon. The seductive power of a visual ekphrasis is the illusion of total knowledge of what is being represented or described. We have confidence that visual images have the power to describe their subject completely – that is to say, what is seen. But we do not accept this in language after the linguistic turn. So if we challenge this view of the visual we are left with a plurality of voices in the visual ekphrasis of architecture and there are gaps between this speech or mode of description and the image (architecture) itself. Ekphrasis, whether verbal or visual, surrounds the object of description with projected meanings. So the definition of deconstruction as there being 'always more than one language' suggests that description is most truthful when the illusion of the single authorial voice is abandoned. This also reasserts the importance of the viewer, as the act of 'reading' images implies a dialogic relationship between viewer and viewed – a relationship where image and imagination are at play.

Notes

1 James Stuart and Nicholas Revett, *The Antiquities of Athens: Measured and Delineated by James Stuart, FRS and FSA, and Nicholas Revett, Painters and Architects* (London: Printed by John Haberkorn, 1762). For a detailed outline of the volumes see Eileen Harris assisted by Nicholas Savage, *British Architectural Books and Writers, 1556–1785* (Cambridge: Cambridge University Press, 1990), pp. 439–49.

2 James Stuart and Nicholas Revett, *Proposals for publishing an accurate description of the Antiquities of Athens* (1748).

3 Thomas Hollis to John Ward, letter dated 26 February 1751, as quoted in Dora Wiebenson, *Sources of Greek Revival Architecture* (London: A. Zwemmer, 1969), pp. 75–7.

4 Stuart and Revett, *The Antiquities of Athens*, vol. I, note to Preface.

5 Ibid.

6 For the debates around the chronology of the volumes of *The Antiquities of Athens* see Harris and Savage, *British Architectural Books and Writers*, and Nicholas Savage, Alison Shell, Paul W. Nash and others, *Early Printed Books 1478–1840*: Catalogue of the British Architectural Library, Early Imprints Collection (London: Bowker-Saur, 1995).

7 Johann Joachim Winckelmann, *Geschichte der Kunst des Alterthums* (Dresden: Walther, 1764). Published in English as Johann Joachim Winckelmann, *History of the Art of Antiquity*, trans. Harry Frances Malgrave (Los Angeles: Getty Research Institute Texts and Documents, 2006).

8 Winckelmann was, however, disappointed with Volume I of *The Antiquities of Athens* as he questioned the lavish scale used to represent what in his view were 'minor monuments'. On this point see Wiebenson, *Greek Revival Architecture*, p. 113.

9 The images are listed in Susan Weber Soros (ed.), *James 'Athenian' Stuart 1713–1788: The Rediscovery of Antiquity* (New Haven and London: Yale University Press, 2006), pp. 591–5.

10 These are discussed in Julius Bryant, 'James "Athenian" Stuart: The Architect as Landscape Painter', V&A online journal, Issue 1, Autumn 2008. www.vam.ac.uk/content/journals/research-journal/issue-01/james-athenian-stuart-the-architect-as-landscape-painter/.

11 On this point see Bruce Redford, *Dilettanti: The Antic and the Antique in Eighteenth-Century England* (Los Angeles: Getty Research Institute, 2008), chapter 2, esp. pp. 52 ff.

12 See for instance: Lesley Lawrence, 'Stuart and Revett: Their Literary and Architectural Careers', *Journal of the Warburg Institute*, 2:2 (1938), pp. 128–46; Jacob Landy, 'Stuart and Revett: Pioneer Archaeologists', *Archaeology*, 9:4 (1956), pp. 252–9; Frank Salmon, 'Stuart as Antiquary and Archaeologist in Italy and Greece', in Susan Weber Soros, *James 'Athenian' Stuart*, pp. 107–17; and Frank Salmon's introduction to a reduced format facsimile edition of *The Antiquities of Athens: Measured and Delineated by James Stuart, FRS and FSA, and Nicholas Revett, Painters and Architects, London 1762* (Princeton, New Jersey: Princeton Architectural Press, 2008).

13 As quoted in Eileen Harris assisted by Nicholas Savage, *British Architectural Books and Writers*, p. 442.

14 Stuart and Revett, *The Antiquities of Athens*, p. 17.

15 On this point see Bruce Redford, 'The Measure of Ruins: Dilettanti in the Levant, 1750–1770', *Harvard Library Bulletin*, 13:1 (2002), pp. 5–36.

16 For instance Robert Wood, *The Ruins of Palmyra* (London, 1753) and *The Ruins of Balbec* (London, 1757). Many expeditions were also financed by The Society of Dilettanti, and Revett was subsequently employed as a draughtsman on some of these missions.

17 See Robin Middleton's introduction to Julien-David Le Roy, *The Ruins of the Most Beautiful Monuments of Greece*, trans. David Britt (Los Angeles: Getty Research Institute, 2004) and more generally Christopher Drew Armstrong, *Julien-David LeRoy and the Making of Architectural History* (London: Routledge, 2011). See also Redford, *Dilettanti*.

18 These are discussed for instance in Redford, *Dilettanti*, pp. 60 ff.

19 Stuart also inserted images of both he and Revett in situ and often in Turkish dress. For instance, in the view of the Monument of Philopappus above Athens, Stuart and Revett wear Turkish kaftans and are shown chatting with James Dawkins while his fellow antiquarian Robert Wood notes down inscriptions from the monuments. Both Dawkins and Wood visited Athens in May 1751 and, as noted, published volumes on the antiquities of Palmyra and Baalbec.

20 On this point see Dana Arnold, 'Facts or Fragments? Visual Histories in the Age of Mechanical Reproduction', *Art History*, 25:4 (2002), pp. 450–68.

21 Thomas Major, *The Ruins of Paestum, Otherwise Posidonia, in Magna Grecia* (London: Published by T. Major, in St. Martin's Lane. Printed by James Dixwell, 1768).

22 The interrelationship between the images of the temples at Paestum is discussed in Suzanne Lang, 'The Early Publications of the Temples at Paestum', *Journal of the Warburg and Courtauld Institutes*, 13:1/2 (1950), pp. 48–64.

23 There is a vast literature on Piranesi and his influence on the study and understanding of antiquity. See for instance: John Wilton-Ely, *The Mind and Art of Giovanni Battista Piranesi* (London: Thames & Hudson, 1978) and *Piranesi as Architect and Designer* (New Haven, London and New York: Yale University Press and The Pierpont Morgan Library, 1993); Nicholas Penny, *Piranesi* [1978] repr. (London: Bloomsbury, 1988). The following offer insights into how Piranesi's etchings worked as representations of time and space: Richard Wendorf, 'Piranesi's Double Ruin', *Eighteenth-Century Studies*, 34:2 (2001), pp. 161–80; Robert Etheridge Moore, 'The Art of Piranesi: Looking Backward into the Future', in Robert E. Moore and Jean H. Hagstrum (eds), *Changing Taste in Eighteenth-Century Art and Literature* (Los Angeles: William Andrews Clark Memorial Library, 1972); Jennifer Bloomer, *Architecture and the Text: The (S)crypts of Joyce and Piranesi* (New Haven and London: Yale University Press, 1993).

24 Marguerite Yourcenar, *'The Dark Brain of Piranesi' and Other Essays*, trans. Richard Howard (New York: Farrar, Straus and Giroux, 1984), p. 100.

25 I discuss the techniques of printmaking and their relationship to time together with other themes addressed in this book in more depth in Chapter 2, Part I of this book.

26 On this point see Antony Griffiths, *Prints and Printmaking* (London: British Museum Press, 1980) republished (Berkeley and Los Angeles: University of California Press, 1996).

27 For a fuller discussion of the notion of 'vertical history', see Leonard Barkan, *Unearthing the Past: Archaeology and Aesthetics in the Making of Renaissance Culture* (New Haven and London: Yale University Press, 1999), p. 20 where Barkan asserts 'Rome is almost purely a symbol. With the exception of a very brief period, the history of Rome is a history of the idea of a city that used to be'.

28 Goethe, *The Italian Journey*, p. 363.
29 Horace Walpole, *Anecdotes of painting in England*, 4th edn, 4 vols (London: Printed for J. Dodsley, 1786), vol. IV, p. 398.
30 Translation from Jonathan Scott, *Piranesi* (London: Academy Editions, 1975), pp. 166–7.
31 Ibid.

2 Time

Part I: The wanton chase of history

I would like to think about the relationship between drawings and prints both in terms of their materiality and the role graphic representation played in the discovery of the ancient world and as a means of developing and disseminating architectural ideas in the eighteenth century. At the outset, I would like to flag two things. First is that the term [architectural] drawing encompasses both the action and the artefact. Implicit in this is the idea of the embodiment of movement in drawing. Second, although prints are the principal focus of this study, we must remember that prints usually begin as drawings. I will discuss the differences in effect and affect between these two media later. Here, I want to collapse both techniques into the single category of graphic representation. In this way we can see the graphic line, whether in a print or a drawing, as a form of writing that prompts a critical awareness of the various visual, technical and semiotic modes of description. If we accept that the field of relations both historical and actual in which the graphic line operates is in constant flux then we see how it changes its identity over time and consequently has fluid potential, capacities, and indeed uses within its field of cultural production at any given moment.

Time lines

I would like to begin by thinking about the significance of the line, which both of these graphic art forms, together with writing, have in common.[1] Certainly, the eighteenth-century understanding of the line stresses its protean nature. For instance, we might think about Dr Samuel Johnson's (1709–84) *Dictionary of the English Language* first published in 1755, which sought to provide some fixity of meaning for the English vocabulary. Of particular note from the 17 meanings supplied for the noun 'line' are the definitions 'Longitudinal extension'; 'Delineation, sketch'; 'Contour, outline'; 'Method, disposition'; and 'Extension, limit'.[2] All of these descriptions of the word 'line' accord in some way with the interests in this chapter and, indeed, more broadly of this book.

At this point it is helpful to step back a little and think about the surface that the graphic line inhabits, what these lines do and how we read them. Here we find a perhaps surprising but nevertheless fruitful coalescence between Renaissance and Enlightenment thought and contemporary cultural theory. My starting point is the fifteenth-century Italian theorist and practitioner Leon Battista Alberti (1404–72), specifically here his *De pictura* published in Latin in 1435 and translated into Italian as *Della pittura* a year later.[3] Despite being a product of the humanistic, academic approach to the visual, Alberti's *De pictura* confronts, albeit perhaps unintentionally, the tensions of the language of the image and the language of the text.[4] And this Saussurian dialectic between different sign-systems has remained part of the discourse of semiotics and art, and art practice to the present day.[5]

As the title suggests, *De pictura* is primarily a book about painting, but there is a substantial amount of discussion about drawing as the basis for pictorial representation and with this the problems of denoting space and surface. And here, the visual properties of the line are an essential part of Alberti's theory. We should also remember that Alberti was an architect with a keen interest in perspective, a point I shall return to later.[6] Indeed, the richness of the text and the references to writings of Horace and Cicero emphasise the connection between Alberti's treatise for the visual depiction of the world and the classical linguistic trope of ekphrasis.[7] Moreover, the palpable struggle Alberti has in finding suitable vocabulary to express his ideas about the visual in both the Latin and Italian versions makes this work germane to our study. As Creighton Gilbert remarks: 'he [Alberti] was breaking new ground and seeking language for it'.[8] We might begin with Alberti's discussion of the notion of a line becoming a surface:

> a point is a figure which cannot be divided into parts … . These points, if they are joined one to the other in a row, will form a line. With us a line is a figure whose length can be divided but whose width is so fine that it cannot be split. Some lines are called straight, others curved. A straight line is drawn directly from one point to another as an extended point. The curved line is not straight from one point to another but rather looks like a drawn bow. More lines, like threads woven together in a cloth, make a plane.[9]

Alberti sees the line as operating thus:

> I say the function of a painter is this: to describe with lines and to tint with colour … observed planes of any body so that at a certain distance and in a certain position from the centre they appear in relief, seem to have mass and to be lifelike.[10]

Staying with the line, rather than the tint, Alberti's knowledge both as a geometrician and as a painter presents a kind of creative friction. We see this, for instance, when he addresses the concept of the outline: 'Permanent qualities are of two kinds. One is known by the outermost boundary which encloses the plane.'[11] As a geometrician, Alberti knows that although a line can separate one area from another, its only dimension is that of length. But he also acknowledges that a line is formed of matter (the ingredients of ink, for instance) and as such must have three dimensions. These questions of point, line, plane and outline are key to Alberti's concept of drawing that underpins his theory of artistic practice. Importantly here for our study, Alberti's work was made available in English by Giacomo Leoni, who had also recently translated another key Renaissance resource for architectural theory and imagery: Palladio's *I quattro libri dell'architettura or The Four Books of Architecture* (1570).[12] Leoni published Alberti's writings on *Painting, Architecture and Sculpture* in three volumes. The first edition appeared around 1726 followed by three subsequent editions. The text is printed in English and Italian in parallel, making Alberti's ideas available for eighteenth-century British artists such as Hogarth and Reynolds.[13]

Of particular relevance for our concerns is Alberti's emphasis on the interrelatedness of liveliness and line. Using as his example the movements of properly depicted hair, Alberti advises:

> The seven movements are especially pleasing in hair where part of it turns in spirals as if wishing to know itself, waves in the air like flames, twines around itself like a serpent, while part rises here, part there.[14]

William Hogarth expands these ideas in his treatise *The Analysis of Beauty* (1753).[15] 'The most amiable in itself is the flowing curl; and the many waving and contrasted turns of naturally intermingling locks.'[16] In *The Analysis of Beauty* Hogarth addresses the eighteenth-century art world.[17] Indeed, the *Analysis* has been described as 'the first sustained anti-academic treatise in the history of aesthetics'.[18]

But perhaps more importantly, here, Hogarth talks about the line. He was, after all, essentially a graphic artist whose prints and print cycles narrated contemporary life.[19] Their success in communicating Hogarth's social commentary was due to the effectiveness of the line. He also discusses the link he perceives between the line and memory 'to make my studies and my Pleasures go hand in hand by retaining in my mind lineally such objects as fitted my purpose best'.[20] Indeed, Hogarth's method of lineal memory-study connects with his system of lineal beauty: 'I was extremely glad to find the line which I had conceived to be part of what might be formed into a system.'[21]

In chapter five of the *Analysis* entitled 'Of Intricacy', Hogarth posits that in contrast to straight and curved lines there also exists a 'waving line and a 'serpentine line' that he names the 'line of beauty' and 'the line of grace' respectively. The distinctive quality of these lines is 'intricacy' and this 'leads the eye [on] a wanton kind of chase'.[22] For Hogarth 'Intricacy' is to an extent a new aesthetic criterion; it relates to the way in which the object or work engages the viewer and satisfies the 'love of pursuit'.[23]

Hogarth goes on to discuss the constant use made of lines by mathematicians, as well as painters, in describing things upon paper. He remarks that these linear descriptions 'hath established a conception of them [the lines], as if actually existing on the real forms themselves'.[24] 'Intricacy' is, then, a strange principle based on the notion of the pleasure of pursuit. Every difficulty in understanding or grasping the object enhances the pleasure of overcoming it, to continue the pursuit. By extension, understanding or overcoming the object is connected to knowledge and this knowledge is based on the way in which the object is described. There is a direct connection here to the line of beauty along which every image is built up. We read or understand these images through the movement of our eye. This is discrete from the movement of our 'Mind's eye' that follows a duplicate course of the line, a principal ray of light moving along with the line of sight. For Hogarth, the continuous movement of our 'Mind's eye' triggers the notion of intricacy. In this way Hogarth links the line with the imagination and the way in which the eye moves across a picture surface. And this movement might not be left to right as in the act of reading. Here we see how in the eighteenth century the line is attributed with having agency. Just as the printed word leads the eye across the page so does the line by employing various strategies, for example a straight, curved or wavy shape, in order to engage the viewer.[25]

Alberti and Hogarth have shown us the visual properties of the line. In addition, Hogarth has attributed it with agency, if not also with an embodied sense of movement resulting both from the eye's 'pursuit' of the line and the artist's action in drawing it.

> That the waving line, or line of beauty, varying still more, being composed of two curves contrasted, becomes still more ornamental and pleasing, insomuch that the hand takes a lively movement in making it with pen or pencil.[26]

But I also want to consider how a different conceptualisation of the line can work to disrupt established historical narratives. Hogarth hints at this when he discusses the way the line 'leads the eye [on] a wanton kind of chase'.[27] This agency when combined with the mnemonic and descriptive qualities of the line identified by Hogarth, challenges, or at least presents an alternative truth to, linear verbal histories.[28]

Lines of flight

If we return to Hogarth's 'wanton chase' we can see how the line connects with our notions of Modernity where history and its chronology are disrupted and the visual is no longer contained by these norms. This has been discussed elsewhere, not least by Ronald Paulson.[29] Here I would like to think about the connection between Hogarth and Gilles Deleuze – unlikely bedfellows but (and please forgive me) the line draws them together.

The idea of motion makes me think about Deleuze and the way in which he privileges the geographies of movement over history. In this way we can begin to unpick the linear and chronological viewpoints that are a hallmark of western historical thinking. As a consequence it is possible to see how visual descriptions of the architecture of the past can be independent of the progressive chronologies that dominate textual histories. But first I want to untie the line. Deleuze and Guattari speak of the concept of the rhizome that enables new connections to be made:

> Every rhizome contains lines of segmentarity according to which it is stratified, territorialised, organised, signified, attributed, etc., as well as lines of deterritorialisation down which it constantly flees. There is a rupture in the rhizome whenever segmentary lines explode into a line of flight, but the line of flight is part of the rhizome. These lines always tie back to one another.[30]

The line of flight, like the line, has no beginning or end, but always a middle. And it is in this middle or 'in between' that everything takes place.[31] If we think about the Deleuzian notion that it is not what the line is but what it can do or be, then a line can be a mark, a trace, a contour or an outline, which is both seen and unseen.[32] In this way, a line can form visible and invisible pathways and these fluid processes work to locate memory and recollection and ultimately time through their shifting, crossing and repeating. For Deleuze, the line both frees us from linear histories whilst operating as a process of historicisation. As we have seen, the line forms the basis of textual and visual histories. But the eye engages with history in a different way when looking at it rather than reading it – it is not sequential left to right movement, instead it is a more random 'wanton kind of chase' of history.

There is a further connection here between Hogarth and Deleuze. As noted earlier, for Hogarth the waving line is the 'line of beauty' and the serpentine line is the 'line of grace'.[33] Their varied form means they contribute most to producing beauty. The serpentine line 'gives play to the imagination, and delights the eye'. In addition, Hogarth admires 'the effects of quantity' as a source of beauty. Here we reach the sublime as an aesthetic category of expression and pleasure: 'vastness', 'horror', 'awe', 'immense', 'colossal', 'grandeur'. '[I]t is quantity which adds greatness to grace.'[34] Deleuze's 'line of flight' produces a transport or lift which can be interpreted as a kind of sublime. Indeed, Deleuze describes this as 'a sort of delirium … . There is something demoniacal or demonic in a line of flight. … What demons do is jump across intervals, and from one interval to another'.[35]

Where, then, is the demon in Hogarth's theory if his line allows us to jump across established textual (linguistically masculine) narratives? The *Analysis* begins with a quotation from Milton's *Paradise Lost*:

> So vary'd he, and of his tortuous train
> Curled many a wanton wreath, in sight of Eve,
> To lure her eye. — Milton.

But the complete verse reads:

> With tract oblique
> At first, as one who sought access, but feared
> To interrupt, sidelong he works his way.
> As when a ship by skilful steersman wrought
> Nigh river's mouth or foreland, where the wind
> Veers oft, as oft so steers, and shifts her sail;
> So vary'd he, and of his tortuous train
> Curled many a wanton wreath, in sight of Eve,
> To lure her eye. *Paradise Lost* (9.510–18)

'He' is Satan, and he is at once feminised through the allusion to the ship and its movement as well as masculinised by the allusion to the 'skilful steersman'. I am drawn here to the use of the word 'wanton'.[36] Hogarth makes a further reference to Milton's Eve in his discussion of hair (see also above). 'The poet knows it, as well as the painter, and has described the wanton ringlets waving in the wind.'[37] Here Hogarth alludes to 'her unadorned golden tresses wore / Dishevell'd, but in wanton ringlets' in *Paradise Lost* (4.305–6).

Eve's hair attracts Satan, but more importantly the waviness of her ringlets is echoed in Satan's serpentine movements as he approaches her. Indeed, Ronald Paulson has remarked that 'Milton could reasonably be interpreted as implying that Satan's wiles are derived from the female line'.[38] But as W. J. T. Mitchell notes, Hogarth never mentions this in the text itself, despite numerous references to serpents and the promotion of a serpentine line as the epitome of visual allure.[39] However, there is a strong visual clue in the image of the line of beauty that appears on the title page of the *Analysis*. The serpentine line that floats in a pyramid atop a plinth entitled 'Variety' is in the form of serpent, with a serpent's head and a pointed tail. It is also vertical, so its shape forms the letter S. Satan is, then, present in the feminised, demoniacal serpentine line. Is this then a way to disrupt masculinist (verbal) histories/descriptions through Deleuze's lines of flight?

Producing the line

It is the 'gap' between the physical line and what it can do that is significant here. And at this point it is important to think about the physical properties of the line as it appears in graphic representations of architecture in the eighteenth century. As we have seen, Hogarth spoke of the movement of the artist in producing the image and by implication (to a present-day reader at least) the embodiment of action in the line of beauty.

> That the waving line, or line of beauty, varying still more, being composed of two curves contrasted, becomes still more ornamental and pleasing, insomuch that the hand takes a lively movement in making it with pen or pencil.[40]

Leading on from this, I want to think about the processes, materials and techniques of drawing and its relationship to the finished product in terms of its affect and effect. I also want to think about prints in the same way, particularly here in the light of the notion of mechanical reproduction. What happens to the descriptive process in both and when it is transferred from drawing to print? And what happens to history?

Paper was the usual support for both prints and drawings. If we remember that Alberti instructed the artist 'to describe with lines'[41] and 'more lines, like threads woven together in a cloth, make a plane'[42] then a line or outline separates space and defines a plane. In this way, the surface – namely the colour and texture of the paper – forms part of the image or description of the object. Towards the latter half of the eighteenth century this surface changed, as the lined, slightly ridged effect of 'laid' paper was replaced by the more even, smoother texture of 'wove' paper.[43] Lines were drawn on this surface with reed or quill pens and, from the early nineteenth century, with metal nibs. Ink was also applied with fine brushes, but when it was diluted and applied with fuller brushes, it was called 'wash'.[44] Most architectural line drawings used high quality brown or black inks of varying intensities.[45] For our purposes it is helpful to think of them as a form of watercolour. If applied in thin enough layers and allowed plenty of drying time it is possible to add washes on top, which can be coloured with a variety of pigments. In other words, these kinds of inks allowed a layering and gradation of line and tone and consequently a working and reworking of the image. Instruments such as compasses, trammels and set squares were used to achieve the shapes of various forms and to create the illusion of perspective.[46] These techniques afforded drawing more painterly effects that were not easily transferable to prints.

If you will forgive the expression, when compared to drawings prints have generally had a rather bad press. We need only think of Vasari, who included engraving amongst the arts of *disegno*, but considered it as merely reproductive, not to be confused with true *disegno*.[47] For Vasari, *disegno* was principally the art of drawing or draughtsmanship that distinguished the supremacy of Florentine painting over other regions of Italy in the representation of form. Engraving was remote from this process, as it involved reproduction rather than (in Vasari's view) the production of an original work of art. Even Diderot, who was the son of a cutler, argued for the 'pulling [of] the mechanical arts up from the debasement where prejudice has held them for so long'.[48] Despite Diderot's entreaties, this view persisted into our period as the Royal Academy in England did not see engraving as equal to drawing.[49] That said, very few final drawings for prints have survived, as the process of turning it into an engraving resulted in their near destruction.[50] Often a mirror, or a second drawing made with a mirror, was used to transfer the drawing so that the print corresponded with the original.[51] All of these processes indicate both the complexities of the practice of printmaking, but more importantly for us they demonstrate the distance between the printmaker, the image, and the surface.

There are the three principal kinds of printing processes in our period: relief, intaglio and planographic. The most common kinds of prints, including engravings, etchings, and mezzotints were produced using the intaglio method.[52] The intaglio printing process is the reverse of relief printing, as the image is cut, or 'bitten' (using acid), into the surface of a metal plate. When the plate is inked, the ink is pushed into the incised lines. The plate is then passed through a press with a sheet of dampened paper which pulls the ink out of the lines and transfers them to the paper producing a reversed image of that incised on the plate.[53] The force of pressure applied by the press, which was powered by the exertion of the printmaker, results in an outline of the metal plate itself being impressed into the paper. This is known as the plate mark. Prints in the age before machine-powered presses were, then, produced by the efforts of the body.[54] And the physical act of pressing plate to page, as part of the mechanics of reproduction, cannot be underestimated and I will come back to this point.[55] Here, I want to concentrate on the ways in which the image was transferred on to the plate, as there are significant differences between the techniques of engraving and etching. In the case of the former, a burin, a small, V-shaped chisel set into a wooden bulb-like handle, was the most common tool used in engraving to cut the lines into the plate. The relationship between the burin, plate and the movement of the engraver is key, as the act of engraving is fundamentally that of two linear movements, one straight and the other circular. The engraver produces straight lines by moving the burin diagonally across the plate, usually from right to left placing the plate in front of him or herself.[56] In this way the movement of the engraver is embodied in the creation of the line. By contrast, curved lines are more complex requiring the combined movement of the burin and the plate. The latter is placed on a cushion filled with sand and rotated against the burin. Instead of the draughtsman's hand moving across the surface, here the surface moves across the draughtsman's hand, so reversing the relationship between draughtsman and surface we have just seen in the creation of straight lines. In this way the production of the serpentine, feminised line disembodies the efforts of the engraver and gives agency to the line itself.

Etching was a more spontaneous 'painterly' process and required much less bodily effort than carving into metal. But the embodied presence of the draughtsman remained. The surface of the plate was covered with an acid-resistant ground and the image was scratched into this using a needle. The plate was then dipped in acid which bit channels or lines into the metal plate. Although this permitted a more direct relationship between engraver and surface, the end result was dependent on way the acid bit into the metal plate. Nevertheless, this became the favoured intaglio printing method in our period.[57]

What happens to the line in prints?

It might appear obvious, but unlike a drawing or painting, the line *is* the intaglio print. The ink used for this process was a very viscous oil-based substance. The thick texture of the ink resulted in a line that stands in slight relief to the paper surface. In addition, the printed line was a strong black colour. As such, prints lacked the variation of colour, texture and tone often found in drawings, as cross-hatching was the principal means of depicting shade. Whereas a drawing can use washes to represent shade, a print can only use lines – they might appear as parallel sequences or as cross-hatchings. Here the length and width and relative intensity of the lines are crucial to the gradations from light to dark. In this system of lines, form is built up of lines that relate to each other, rather like flat washes of different tints in a drawing. In order to increase this effect, lines could be both etched and engraved on the same plate, and washes could be added by hand later. But unlike drawing, however, the draughtsman is at a distance from the printed line; it is produced by a mechanical process, a point to which I shall return.

There are, then, significant differences in effect between drawing and print. In the former, we find greater gradation of colour and the embodied movement of the draughtsman in the pressure applied to the nib as it glides across the surface. Like writing, drawing is produced at the speed of the body – the time it takes for the hand to move across paper. Prints and the printed word are ultimately produced through mechanical means. Accordingly, they lack the spontaneity of the embodied movement of the draughtsman's line. Moreover, the surface also acts differently – the plate mark defines the area of vision. Also, we must not forget that each print or impression is subtly different. The movement of the plate as it is pressed by the printmaker against the surface subtly alters the line making it increasingly less crisp. As a consequence prints can be graded according to the sequence in which they are produced – the clarity of second, third or fourth impressions gradually diminishes along with the perceived 'value' of the print. This also means that each impression is an image made at a different point in time and has subtle distinctions from its predecessor and successor. Mass reproduction also alters this state and the time the viewer may spend reading or looking, and this can in turn manipulate the speed of thought. The processes involved in the production of a print become an interlocutor between draughtsman and page, and viewer and image.

Techniques of looking and reading

The resonance between the graphic practices of the long eighteenth century and contemporary cultural theory fruitfully continues in the work of Walter Benjamin. Benjamin attempted to conceptualise the significance of painting, drawing and graphic illustration within the shifting historical contexts. These contexts both included that in which his own work was produced and the situations of the production and initial reception of these images. Importantly, his writings also reveal the degree to which any discussion of an 'image' is for Benjamin inextricably linked to his reflections on writing as a medium for the presentation of figural images and the communication of meaning. In other words, these concerns go straight to the heart of our enquiry into the relationship between verbal and visual histories.

Here I begin with the untitled fragment known as 'Painting and the Graphic Arts' and the related essay 'Painting, or Sign and Mark', both of which were composed in the latter part of 1917. On one level, these writings are a response to the artistic climate of the time, not least the work of Picasso, Kandinsky and Klee. But they also address broader concerns that are helpful in our consideration of the significance of drawing and graphic illustration (i.e. prints, for our purposes) within shifting historical contexts. Although brief and unfinished, these texts also try to categorise drawings and prints in terms of the essential features of each medium.

> A picture wants to be held vertically before the viewer. A floor mosaic lies horizontally at his feet. Despite this distinction, it is customary simply to view a work of graphic art as a painting. There is, however, a very important and far-reaching distinction to be made within the graphic arts: it is possible to look at the study of a head, or a Rembrandt landscape, in the same way as a painting, or in the best case to leave the sheets in a neutral horizontal position.[58]

Importantly, here, we learn from Benjamin that painting, and drawing and prints can be conceived of as pictures and signs respectively. If we then follow the principle that pictures are set vertically and signs horizontally, our habits of viewing and reading are, then, historically determined.

> We might say that there are two sections through the substance of the world: the longitudinal section of painting and the transverse section of certain graphic works. The longitudinal section seems representational – it somehow contains things; the transverse section seems symbolic – it contains signs. Or is it only in our reading that we place the pages horizontally before us? And is there such a thing as an originally vertical position for writing, [for example,] engraving in stone?[59]

In other words, the level of drawing is horizontal and that of painting is vertical. As such there are two 'sections' or 'cuts' through the 'substance of the world': the 'longitudinal section of painting and the transverse section of certain graphic works'. The longitudinal section of painting 'seems representational' as it looks as if it contains things, whilst the transverse section (or cross section) of prints and drawings gives the idea of being symbolic as it contains 'signs'. In this way prints and drawings may appear to have no meaning unless arranged for viewing in a horizontal position in the same way as we would set out a text to be read. This emphasis on 'reading' leads Benjamin to question if, conversely, there might ever have existed a vertical position of writing or script. At this point it is helpful to remember how collections of prints or drawings were collated and consulted by antiquarians. Individual sheets were frequently bound together in albums; sometimes this was done by a collector or dealer at a later date.[60] As we have seen, albums could contain work by different artists and the groupings of images could cohere around a theme or particular site.[61] Moreover, Piranesi's images of Herculaneum and the temples at Paestum produced at the very end of his life were collated, transferred to print and published by his son (Figure 15). Here, the squares that were overlaid enabled the image to be copied to the plate. Consequently, Piranesi's drawing did not appear in reverse once printed.

The second of Benjamin's early writings of interest here is the text 'Painting, or Sign and Mark', also from 1917.[62] As before, it was a response to remarks on contemporary art practice, especially Cubism, but also has broader implications for our concerns here. Benjamin construes the mark as the 'medium of painting'; by contrast he considers drawing and other forms composed by means of 'graphic line' (in our case prints) as belonging to the 'sphere of the sign'. Benjamin argues that rather than focusing upon any particular material surface, a drawing's identity has to do with a certain transitive relationship to its ground (whatever material form it takes).

> The graphic line marks out the area and so defines it by attaching itself to it as its background. Conversely, the graphic line can exist only against this background, so that a drawing that completely covered its background would cease to be a drawing.[63]

This notion of a line becoming a surface finds a perhaps unexpected echo in the writings of the fifteenth-century theorist Alberti who, as we will remember, remarked in his *De pictura* that

> a point is a figure which cannot be divided into parts ... . These points, if they are joined one to the other in a row, will form a line.[...] More lines, like threads woven together in a cloth, make a plane.[64]

If we accept this view that the mark is the medium and consequently the visual language of a painting, drawing or print, in order for it to relate to the world and for it to be understood an image needs a name. Indeed, the power of the act of naming – a linguistic process – finds a reprise in Benjamin's assertion from the mid 1920s of the crucial relationship between images, captions and inscriptions. What is remarkable here is the decisive role given to writing, inscription and naming, along with the spatial marks on monuments and

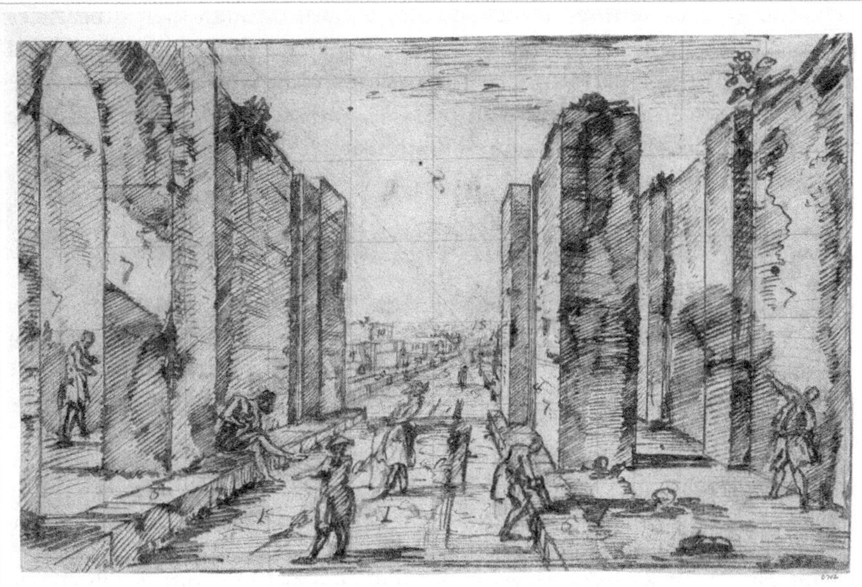

Giovanni Battista Piranesi, 'View through the Herculaneum Gate, Pompeii', 15
pen and brown ink over black chalk, 1778

gravestones. '[T]he linguistic word,' he writes, 'lodges in the medium of the language of painting.'[65] And this is particularly relevant to us as many images of the architecture of the past often include (lengthy) captions and measurements as seen, for instance in the Duperac map of Rome (Figure 2), as well as representations of inscriptions on the buildings themselves.

But what is important here is the distance between the printed word and the image of the printed word. Inscriptions could be transcribed into the moveable type of a letterpress, but this removed the words from their original context. In addition, this process of transcription rather than description made the recording of antiquity less authentic. In direct contrast to Winckelmann's privileging of the word, here we find an insistence on the importance of the original and its accurate reproduction. Surely this points the way to the belief that in the future there will be new ways of seeing the past and that a visual description – even if it is of an antique text – holds within it an alternative to the traditions of text-based scholarship.

Drawing on memory

At the beginning of this chapter I signalled that I would initially collapse drawing and prints into a single category of graphic representation. Here I would like to distinguish between these two media and their methods of production to explore their affects and effects both through their differences and similarities. This allows me to explore the ways in which these visual descriptions of the architecture of the past intersect with and re-articulate established historical narratives. In the following sections I want to explore how the practices of graphic representation inflect on processes of history, especially memory and time.

Notes

1 For a general discussion of the concept of the line see Tim Ingold, *Lines: A Brief History* (London: Routledge, 2007). In addition, for a more nuanced discussion of linearity in architectural theory and practice see Catherine Ingraham, *Architecture and the Burdens of Linearity* (New Haven and London: Yale University Press, 1998).

2 Samuel Johnson, *A Dictionary of the English Language: in which the words are deduced from their originals, explained in their different meanings and authorized by the means of the writers in whose works they are found*, 6th edn, 2 vols (London: Printed for A. Millar, 1766).

3 I am using John R. Spencer's excellent translation of Leon Battista Alberti, *On Painting*, 2nd edn (New Haven and London: Yale University Press, 1966). For a discussion of the nature and structure of the treatise see D. R. Edward Wright, 'Alberti's *De pictura*: Its literary structure and purpose', *Journal of the Warburg and Courtauld Institutes*, 47 (1984), pp. 52–71 and Mark Jarzombek, 'The Structural Problematic of Leon Battista Alberti's *De pictura*', *Renaissance Studies*, 4:3 (1990), pp. 273–86.

4 For a fuller discussion see Eric Cameron, 'The Depictional Semiotic of Alberti's *On Painting*', *Art Journal*, 35:1 (1975), pp. 25–8.

5 On this point see Ferdinand de Saussure, *Course in General Linguistics*, ed. Charles Bally and Albert Sechehaye in collaboration with Albert Riedlinger, trans. Wade Baskin (New York: McGraw-Hill, 1966), p. 66.

6 See Leon Battista Alberti's treatise on architecture, *De re aedificatoria*, written between 1443 and 1452.

7 Creighton E. Gilbert suggests that the framework of Alberti's treatise relies on Horace, see 'Antique Frameworks for Renaissance Art Theory', *Marsyas*, 3 (1943–45), pp. 87–106. In addition, John R. Spencer, identifies specific details in Alberti that point to Cicero, see '*Ut rhetorica pictura*: A Study in Quattrocento Theory of Painting', *Journal of the Warburg and Courtauld Institutes*, 20:1/2 (1966), pp. 26–44.

8 Creighton E. Gilbert, *Italian Art 1400–1500: Sources and Documents* (Englewood Cliffs, New Jersey: Prentice Hall, 1980), p. 51.

9 Leon Battista Alberti, *On Painting*, trans. John R. Spencer, 2nd edn (New Haven and London: Yale University Press, 1966), Book I, pp. 43–4.

10 Ibid., Book III, p. 89.

11 Ibid., Book I, p. 44.

12 Andrea Palladio (1508–80), *I quattro libri dell'architettura* (*The Four Books of Architecture*) first published in four volumes in 1570 in Venice. It comprised text

accompanied by woodcuts after the author's own drawings. Book I was first published in English in 1663 in a London edition by Godfrey Richards. The first complete English language edition was published in London by architect Giacomo Leoni in 1715–20. I discuss this important work in greater depth later in the previous chapter.

13 Alberti's work was made available in English by Giacomo Leoni, who had also translated Palladio's *The Four Books*. See note above. Four editions of *De pictura* appeared between 1726 and 1755. See Eileen Harris and Nicholas Savage, *British Architectural Books and Writers*, pp. 107–9. The English title page of Volume I reads, 'The Architecture Of Leon Battista Alberti In Ten Books. Of Painting In Three Books And Of Statuary In One Book. Translated Into Italian By Cosimo Bartoli. And Now First Into English, And Divided Into Three Volumes By James Leoni, Venetian, Architect; To Which Are Added Several Designs Of His Own, For Buildings Both Public And Private. Vol. I.' The title pages of Volume II read, 'Della Architettura Di Leon Battista Alberti Della Edizione Di Giacomo Leoni Tomo II' and 'The Architecture Of Leon Battista Alberti Published By James Leoni, Vol. II.' Although the title pages are dated 1726, plates [52–4] of Volume II are dated 1727, and the licence (copyright privilege) bound into Volume I is dated 1730.

14 Alberti, *On Painting*, Part II, p. 8.1.

15 William Hogarth, *The Analysis of Beauty* (London: Printed by John Reeves for the Author, 1753). For a survey of the many editions of the *Analysis* see Stanley E. Read, 'Some Observations on William Hogarth's *The Analysis of Beauty*: A Bibliographical Study', *Huntington Library Quarterly*, 5:3 (1941–42), pp. 360–73 and William Hogarth, *The Analysis of Beauty: With the Rejected Passages from the Manuscript Drafts and Autobiographical Notes*, ed. Joseph Burke (Oxford: Clarendon Press, 1955).

16 Hogarth (1753), *The Analysis of Beauty*, chapter V, p. 28.

17 There are many studies of Hogarth. See for instance Ronald Paulson, *Hogarth's Graphic Works*, 3rd edn (London: The Print Room, 1989) and his expanded three-volume biography of *Hogarth* (New Brunswick, New Jersey: Rutgers University Press, 1991–93).

18 Michael Kitson, 'Hogarth's "Apology for Painters"', *Walpole Society*, 41 (1966–68), p. 65.

19 On the last page of *The Analysis* Hogarth includes a list of prints published by him that are 'to be had at his House in Leicester Fields'. Hogarth (1753), *The Analysis of Beauty*, verso of p. 153 and recto of p. 154.

20 Hogarth (Burke ed. 1955), *The Analysis of Beauty*, p. 206.

21 Ibid., p. 231.

22 Hogarth (1753), *The Analysis of Beauty*, chapter V, 'Of Intricacy', p. 25.

23 For an alternative reading of the line see Frédéric Ogée, 'The Flesh of Theory: The Erotics of Hogarth's Lines', in Bernadette Fort and Angela Rosenthal (eds), *The Other Hogarth: Aesthetics of Difference* (Princeton, New Jersey: Princeton University Press, 2001).

24 Hogarth (1753), *The Analysis of Beauty*, chapter VII, 'Of Lines', p. 37.

25 On this point see, for instance, Michel Baridon, 'Hogarth's "Living Machines of Nature" and the Theorisation of Aesthetics', in David Bindman, Frédéric Ogée, and

Peter Wagner (eds), *Hogarth: Representing Nature's Machines* (Manchester: Manchester University Press, 2001), pp. 85–101.

26 Hogarth (1753), *The Analysis of Beauty*, chapter VII, 'Of Lines', p. 38.

27 Ibid., chapter V, 'Of Intricacy', p. 25.

28 Ibid., chapter VII, 'Of Lines', p. 37; William Hogarth (Burke ed. 1955), *The Analysis of Beauty*, pp. 206, 231.

29 See for instance Ronald Paulson, 'The Aesthetics of Modernity: Hogarth', in *Breaking and Remaking: Aesthetic Practice in England, 1700–1820* (New Brunswick, New Jersey: Rutgers University Press, 1989), pp. 149–202.

30 Gilles Deleuze and Félix Guattari, *A Thousand Plateaus: Capitalism and Schizophrenia*, trans. Brian Massumi (London: Athlone Press, 1988), p. 10.

31 Ibid., pp. 6–15.

32 Gilles Deleuze and Félix Guattari, *On the Line*, trans. John Johnston (New York: Semiotext(e), 1983), p. 19 esp.

33 Hogarth (1753), *The Analysis of Beauty*, chapter VII, 'Of Lines', p. 38.

34 Ibid., chapter VI, 'Of Quantity', p. 30.

35 Gilles Deleuze and Claire Parnet, *Dialogues* (Paris: Flammarion, 1977) and trans. Hugh Tomlinson and Barbara Habberjam (London: Athlone Press, 1987), p. 40.

36 For a fuller discussion of this see Abigail Zitin, 'Wantonness: Milton, Hogarth, and *The Analysis of Beauty*', *Differences*, 27:1 (2016), pp. 25–47.

37 Hogarth (1753), *The Analysis of Beauty*, chapter V, 'Of Intricacy', p. 28.

38 Ronald Paulson, *Hogarth's Harlot: Sacred Parody in Enlightenment England* (Baltimore and London: Johns Hopkins University Press, 2003), p. 194.

39 W. J. T. Mitchell, 'Metamorphoses of the Vortex: Hogarth, Turner and Blake', in Richard Wendorf (ed.), *Articulate Images: Sister Arts from Hogarth to Tennyson* (Minneapolis: University of Minnesota Press, 1983), pp. 125–68 and p. 132 esp.

40 Hogarth (1753), *The Analysis of Beauty*, chapter VII, 'Of Lines', p. 38.

41 Alberti, *On Painting*, Part III, p. 89.

42 Ibid., Part I, pp. 43–4.

43 'Laid' paper made from linen or cotton rag was used. This has distinctive qualities, as the fibrous pulp made from the soaked and beaten fabric was spread on a wire grid. The liquid drained the wires leaving a lined effect on the surface of the paper. For 'wove' paper a fine mesh replaced the wire grid resulting in a more even surface.

44 My thanks to Dr Frances Sands for the information on drawing materials.

45 The pigments used for brown inks were usually umber or sienna and those for black inks were usually soot, burnt ivory or burnt grape vines. Sepia ink is surrounded with confusion. True sepia is obtained from the inky secretion of the cuttlefish bound with gum arabic. It gives a smooth transparent effect. It is often, incorrectly, used to describe various tones of brownish wash, especially in connection with Old Master drawings. In fact it was only widely used in the 19th century. Ex info Dr Frances Sands.

46 See Maya Hambly, *Drawing Instruments 1580–1980*, London, Sotheby's Publications, 1988.

47 See the life of Marcantonio Raimondi especially in Giorgio Vasari, *Le Vite de' Piu Eccellenti Pittori, Scultori, e Architettori Scritte da M. Giorgio Vasari Pittore et*

Architetto Aretino, Di nuovo dal medesimo riviste et ampliate con i ritratti loro et con l'aggiunta delle vite de' vivi, & de' mort,i Dall'anno 1550 infino al 1567. Prima, e Seconda Parte. Con le tavole in ciascun volume, delle cose piu notabili, de' ritratti, delle vite degli artefici, et de i luoghi dove sono l'opere loro. Con Licenza E Privilegio Di N.S. Pio V. Et Del Duca Di Fiorenza E Siena (Florence: Giunti, 1568). A broader historical and geographical purview of the practice of drawing can be found in Deanna Petherbridge, *The Primacy of Drawing: Histories and Theories of Practice* (New Haven and London: Yale University Press, 2010).

48 Denis Diderot and Jean le Rond d'Alembert (eds), *Encyclopédie, ou dictionnaire raisonné des sciences, des arts, et des métiers* (Paris: Briason, 1751–65).

49 Gordon Fyfe, *Art, Power, and Modernity: English Art Institutions, 1750–1950* (London and New York: Leicester University Press, 2000), p. 111.

50 This was done by coating the reverse of the paper with carbonate of lead and then tracing it by pressing along the contours of the figures to transfer the image onto the plate.

51 Antony Griffiths, *Prints and Printmaking: An Introduction to the History and Techniques* (Berkeley and Los Angeles: University of California Press, 1996).

52 On this point see Griffiths, *Prints and Printmaking* and Tim Clayton, *The English Print, 1688–1802* (New Haven and London: Yale University Press, 1997).

53 Engravers could use a mirror to transfer the image to the plate. On this point see Griffiths, *Prints and Printmaking*.

54 The physical processes of printing are described in detail in Carl Goldstein, *Print Culture in Early Modern France: Abraham Bosse and the purposes of print* (Cambridge: Cambridge University Press, 2012), p. 22 esp.

55 Griffiths, *Prints and Printmaking*. See also William M. Ivins, Jr., *Prints and Visual Communication* (Cambridge, Massachusetts: MIT Press, 1969).

56 Lia Markey, 'The Female Printmaker and the Culture of the Reproductive Print Workshop', in Rebecca Zorach and Elizabeth Rodini (eds), *Paper Museums: The Reproductive Print in Europe, 1500–1800* (Chicago: David and Alfred Smart Museum of Art, University of Chicago, 2005).

57 The invention of a tool known as an echoppe by Jacques Callot enabled better control of the line. This together with the technical information that was widely available in Abraham Bosse, *Traité des manières de graver en taille-douce sur l'airain, par le moyen des eaux-fortes & des vernis durs & mols: Ensemble de la façon d'en imprimer les planches, & de construire la presse*, first published 1645 but reprinted many times. The book became a standard work, was translated into English, Italian, Dutch, German, and Portuguese, with multiple editions in those languages and two further editions published in eighteenth-century France, and became the basis for virtually all subsequent discussions of the practice. See Goldstein, *Print Culture*, chapter 1 esp.

58 Walter Benjamin, 'Painting and the Graphic Arts', in *The Work of Art in the Age of Its Technological Reproducibility, and Other Writings on Media*, ed. Michael W. Jennings, Brigid Doherty, and Thomas Y. Levin, trans. Edmund Jephcott, Rodney Livingstone, Howard Eiland, and others (Cambridge, Massachusetts: The Belknap Press of Harvard University Press, 2008), p. 219.

59 Ibid.

60 On this point see Antony Griffiths, 'Print Collecting in Rome, Paris, and London in the Early Eighteenth Century', *Harvard University Art Museums Bulletin*, 2:3, *Print Collecting* (1994), pp. 37–58 and Clayton, *The English Print*.

61 See Prolegomenon, p. 8.

62 'Painting, or Sign and Mark', in *Walter Benjamin: Selected Writings, Volume 1, 1913–1926*, ed. Marcus Bullock and Michael W. Jennings (Cambridge, Massachusetts: Harvard University Press, 1996), pp. 83–6. Benjamin's essay, unpublished in his lifetime, was written in response to Gershom Scholem's remarks on Cubism.

63 Ibid., p. 83.

64 Alberti, *On Painting*, Part I, pp. 43–4.

65 Walter Benjamin, 'Painting and the Graphic Arts', in *The Work of Art in the Age of Its Technological Reproducibility, and Other Writings on Media*, ed. Michael W. Jennings, Brigid Doherty, and Thomas Y. Levin, trans. Edmund Jephcott, Rodney Livingstone, Howard Eiland, and others (Cambridge, Massachusetts: The Belknap Press of Harvard University Press, 2008), p. 86.

Part II: Drawing the line

The serpentine line has demonstrated the ways in which graphic representations can work to subvert (or feminise) established narratives. Here I would like to think about what happens to the description of architecture when it is a drawing rather than a print, and in turn what this might tell us about how histories are formulated. This returns us to my opening questions about the imagination, memory and subjectivity.

Let's reflect, first of all, on the relation between line and drawing. We might begin with the Deleuzian paradigm of drawing as a process of 'becoming', where time and memory are in constant flux.[1] Indeed, if we think about drawing as being suspended between gesture and thought, it becomes a process of visualising thought in an attempt to remember. In this way, we rely on our past experience, imagined or real, that can be disturbed and recollected through the process of drawing. Moreover, our thoughts or memories are derived from the senses and from experiences other than visual perception. And I question the primacy of seeing as a means of experiencing and recording architecture. This points towards the importance of other senses in drawing, including the haptic, which together with the absence of sight, is a core concern of this book. This makes us re-think the pre-eminence given to visual experience by phenomenologists. In this way, the graphic line allows us to explore the binaries of sight and touch and of the visible and the invisible.

Questions about sight and recognition are not unique to present-day philosophers and theorists. Indeed, these issues were debated in our period. For instance, the philosopher John Locke, in *An Essay Concerning Human Understanding* (1690), considered the question of whether a person born blind who became sighted would be able to recognize objects previously known only by touch.[2] The question remains a favourite amongst philosophers as the rhetorical scenario allowed speculation as to the nature of learning and understanding.[3] Bishop Berkeley addressed this question in *An Essay Towards a New Theory of Vision* (1709), which I discuss in depth later in this book. But importantly here, in the final part of his *Essay*, Berkeley considers the difference between perception by sight and by touch and of whether we ever perceive the same thing by both faculties.

> Hence it follows that a man born blind and afterwards, when grown up, made to see, would not in the first act of vision parcel out the ideas of sight into the same distinct collections that others do, who have experienced which do regularly coexist and are proper to be bundled up together under one name. … all these ideas offered at once to his view, he would not distribute into sundry distinct combinations till such time as … he comes to know which are to be separated and which to be collected together.[4]

Leaping across the centuries we find similar concerns in the work of Jacques Derrida. In his dialogic work *Memoirs of the Blind*, Derrida recounts his own attempt to write without seeing.

> A hand of the blind ventures forth alone or disconnected, in a poorly delimited space; it feels its way, it gropes, it caresses as much as it inscribes, trusting in the memory of signs supplementing sight.[5]

Indeed, Derrida presents us with paradox – at the moment when the pen touches the surface it conceals the point at which the actual mark is being made. 'The inscription of the inscribable is not seen.'[6] Whoever is drawing is then blind to the actuality of the line's making or becoming. It is only visible once the pen moves on and the line becomes part of the past. Is the line (or in Derrida's words *le trait*), then, the act of making history? For Derrida drawing is certainly a work of memory. 'Memory or not, and forgetting as memory, in memory and without memory'.[7]

Michael Newman discusses Derrida's use of the word 'trait' and posits the notion of drawing as contact: 'Whatever else it might be, drawing, in its moment of genesis, is contact. Thus its origin lies not in vision and light, but in blindness and obscurity'.[8] Importantly for us, Newman extends this idea to include the notion of the body:

> What is at stake in this is an ethos, an 'ethic' not in the sense of a moral law, but as a way of being-in-the-world, that would include habits and bodily comportment towards things and others. It is an ethos of adherence, of touching and being touched, in the world and at the limit.[9]

There are innumerable examples of architectural prints and drawings in our period and I do not intend to present a one size fits all interpretation of them. What I would like to get at here is how through memory and imagination our preconceived ideas about architecture inflect on its description. We have already seen how the male human body has steered the methods of visual representation of the architecture of the past. And we have explored how the draughtsman is embodied in the process of drawing. Here, I would like to extend this to see how the male body works to re-negotiate architecture through memory and imagination.

These questions cohere around a building we know exists but we have never seen: the Villa of the Papyri, which disappeared underground with the eruption of Mount Vesuvius in 79 CE. The volcano buried the history of its surrounding area, including the Roman cities of Pompeii and Herculaneum.[10] During the eighteenth century the remains of Pompeii were unearthed so the image and history of the site became intelligible and imaginable. In contrast to its neighbour Herculaneum, the type of volcanic ash that covered Pompeii made excavation possible. Ironically, the mud that had engulfed Herculaneum preserved the city but its removal would have meant the destruction of the buildings, so the city remained underground. I have chosen the Villa of the Papyri as my case study as it goes straight to the core of the debates around the representation of the materiality of the past that we have seen on the writings of Winckelmann. What, then, of the architecture of the past that could not be seen? And how could it be drawn and how was the draughtsman embodied in this process of linear description?

Drawing blind

It is first of all important to remind ourselves of the way in which the Villa of the Papyri was discovered and explored in the eighteenth century. The Villa was known only through a series of subterranean excavations, and contemporary accounts speak of the discovery of the architectural form and contents of the Villa through the process of mining. Whilst the contents of the Villa were brought to the earth's surface, its spaces remained underground. Despite the intense activity surrounding the rediscovery of the Villa at this time, by antiquarians such as Goethe and Winckelmann, and not least the more intrepid Grand Tourists, the building remained unseen.

Its spaces were explored through a series of vertical access shafts and horizontal tunnels that serviced temporary chambers.[11] These chambers were excavated sequentially, as the rubble was cleared from one room it was placed in the previously hollowed out space. The way in which the excavators twisted their way through the space under the earth's surface – literally digging in the dark – is evoked by Venuti in the following description of their activities:

> Scarce had they begun to dig sideways, before they found some beautiful statues, among which was a marble one of Hercules, and another one which was imagined to represent Cleopatra. Then proceeding on towards the farm of don Antonio Brancaccio, the diggers met with several wrought columns of alabaster, which appeared to them to be a temple of round form, ornamented on the outside with twenty-four of those columns.[12]

In common with the emerging eighteenth-century view of the sense of the past, the value of the discoveries was not called into question. As Winckelmann noted, the 'study of antiquities … [was] of greatest consequence in elucidating history', and Herculaneum was 'as if reserved by the Omnipotent Disposer of all things, for the instruction and improvement of the present century'.[13] The search for the past consisted of galleries scooped out with much labour, but they also made it apparent that there were 'no hopes of moderns ever being able to discover all, that the mountain has overwhelmed'.[14] Winckelmann goes on to describe the process of excavation in more detail: this included the digging of a principal trench on either side of which chambers are

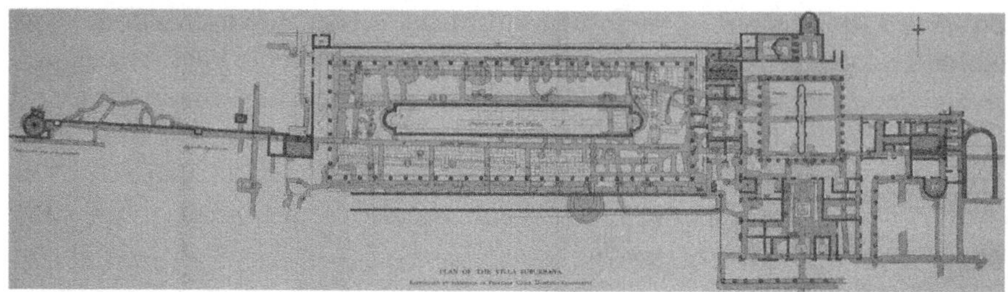

16 Domenico Comparetti, 'Ground plan of the Villa of the Papyri, Herculaneum', from *La villa ercolanese dei Pisoni: I suoi monumenti e la sua biblioteca*, plate 24, 1883

hollowed out, each measuring six *palmi* in length, breadth and height. The diggers removed the rubbish as they proceeded from every chamber to the chamber opposite it that was left hollowed out. This process reduced expense and helped to support the earth above.[15] The effect of this method of excavation was to allow visitors only fleeting glimpses of the 'Immoveable Discoveries';[16] as the rubbish was not completely removed, it was not possible to see the inside of the whole subterranean city of Herculaneum.

Unlike most other archaeological sites, the Villa was experienced principally by touch rather than by sight. When the Villa was seen it was in fragmentary glimpses of its spaces and architectural details revealed by the subterranean excavations which were carefully recorded by Karl Weber, a Swiss military engineer.[17] The notion of blindness is common to many of the contemporary descriptions of this method of exploration. The darkness in which these discoveries were made and the lack of vision is vividly evoked by Charles de Brosses in a letter dated 1 June 1749 describing the process of excavations:

> *Tout ce qu'on y a trouvé dans ce genre, en foüllant à l'aveugle, peut faire juger de ce que produiroit une recherché méthodique.*[18]

It is also important to remember that the 'real' or 'actual' spaces of the Villa were not known or experienced. Instead, the spaces of the Villa were explored through the rooms carved out by the excavators as they groped blindly through the disorientating network of tunnels that zig-zagged down into the earth. Indeed, these tunnels and 'rooms' sometimes cut through the actual walls of the Villa itself. And it is the method of drawing that is of interest here. The visualisation of the Villa in the plan produced by Karl Weber (*c.*1758) remains our means of understanding the spaces of the Villa; it was republished, for example, with Weber's notes in the late nineteenth century (Figure 16). The haptic nature of its production is germane to our consideration of the act of drawing as being one of blindness and how our preconceived ideas and bodily experience of architecture inflect on our knowledge and description of space.

The bodily line

This brings me finally to the plan of the Villa produced by Karl Weber for the Kingdom of Naples. The image of the Villa combines the memory of the experience of the subterranean spaces and the memory trace of the literary descriptions of luxury villas found in writers such as Pliny, which helped provide some kind of orientation to the architecture buried in the darkness underground. The Villa is represented in plan only, so its spaces are flattened into two dimensions. In addition, the access tunnels used by those who explored the subterranean villa are shown as a network of shaded, thick lines and circles, and the spaces that were opened and then filled by the excavators are indicated by a series of thin lines in a honeycomb pattern that spreads out from them. The tunnels that we assume remain and the spaces that were made and then lost in the process of exploration convey a sense of bodily time. We see in the plan something that we know is there but defined only by the spaces made to access it that provide some kind of spatial/tangible reality to the image. This calls into question what we are looking at when we view the plan of the Villa produced by Weber. I would argue that the combination of memory and blindness produces an archivisation of the Villa through the graphic techniques or in other words the recording and ekphrasis of it.[19] And this helps us to understand how forms of knowledge become visible and how architecture is described and historicised visually.

This brings me back to the gap between the subject and the way in which it is represented, specifically here the way in which representation makes us blind to its subject. The distance in the act of drawing or recording can be explained in Derridean terms as the kind of blindness that is implicit in every act of drawing, as the process of looking at that which is to be drawn results in an absence of sight – blindness.[20] It is here in the gap – the moment of blindness – between looking at and recording images, and seeing images and interpreting, where the imagination comes into play. My question here is what the Weber plan can tell us about how knowledge about architecture is made visible. The fact the Villa was never seen is significant here as it elucidates how graphic conventions help make images from the imagined.

The system of architectural drawings using perspective views, orthogonal elevation, details and working drawings is not merely imitative. Instead, buildings are disembodied and dissected, order imposed on chaos – marks on paper evoke the built fabric. But the act of drawing is blind – the building is not in the sightline of the draughtsman when it is being recorded. Instead, an image is held in his imagination and it is the rhetorical devices of architectural draughtsmanship that determine how it is drawn. Weber used some of these conventions of drawing, as he depicted the building in plan he also included the notion of a symmetrical design to help with a notional spatial arrangement.

Although he had seen parts of the Villa as he was excavating it, Weber never saw it in its entirety. Nevertheless, he was able to produce a plausible image of it that has endured to the present day and still informs our thoughts and knowledge of the Villa.[21] As with any architectural drawing it is not merely a representation of the building, instead the graphic conventions make the spaces intelligible. It is not a realistic representation, but as with orthogonal perspective, details and so forth, we accept it as real. Weber makes knowledge visible using a set of graphic conventions that allow thought to be transformed into image. These graphic conventions are based on the human body, and in the case of the Villa of the Papyri these are held in the mind and inform the visualisation of the building. The status of the Weber plan or drawing of the Villa is that it operates like part of the layering of the Freudian mind; it is the ego that negotiates between the id and the superego using recognised 'societal' graphic conventions. By this I mean that the invisible, subterranean villa can in some ways be seen as the id, and that is negotiated into a 'socially acceptable' presence (superego) by means of the graphic conventions of architectural drawing, which here perform the function of the ego. And, we should not forget, drawing is produced at the speed of the body.

The relationship between knowledge and images held in the mind and the ways in which this was made visible is not unique to the Weber plan or, indeed, the subterranean site of the Villa of the Papyri. As with other sites being excavated under the aegis of the Kingdom of Naples, sketching in situ was difficult if not forbidden, and this was remarked on for instance by Goethe[22] and by the French visitors Cochin and Bellicard. This restriction did not, however, prevent the latter two from publishing a book that included illustrations of object found at Herculaneum, albeit that in the frontispiece it was noted the images were drawn from memory. 'The plates that he has added to his explanation, in order to increase their clarity, have been engraved after designs made from memory.'[23] As Derrida has shown us, these notions of memory and the haptic experience of space [*sic* architecture] are concerns which persist to the present day.[24]

In Chapter 1 I talked about our phenomenological, bodily sense of space. Imagine, for instance, the lights failing in a room and we have to negotiate the space through touch, crawling along feeling the floor, walls and doorframe in order to move our bodies in space. Cognitive scientists accept that the body shapes the embodied mind and that this is shaped by the experiences of the body. But the experiential world is more than just a physical place. We experience the world within a certain social and cultural milieu that conditions our view of it and imposes a kind of performativity on us as regards our occupation of that space.[25] Returning to Winckelmann's description of the process of excavation we might note that the 'rooms' that were carved out of the earth were 6 *palmi* square. Like the circle and square of the *Vitruvian Man*, this is a measurement based on the male body: the width of a hand. At this point, returning to the *Vitruvian Woman*, the feminised line, and the wanton chase of history, I will leave you with a question: would the Villa of the Papyri have been experienced and drawn differently by a woman?

Notes

1 Deleuze and Guattari, *A Thousand Plateaus*, p. 293.
2 Locke, *An Essay Concerning Human Understanding*, see book 2, chapter 9.
3 This is known as Molyneux's Question or Problem. It was originally posed to John Locke in a letter from the philosopher William Molyneux.
4 George Berkeley, 'The Theory of Vision Vindicated and Explained', in A. A. Luce and T. E. Jessop (eds), George Berkeley, *The Works of George Berkeley, Bishop of Cloyne*, 9 vols (Edinburgh: Thomas Nelson and Sons, 1948), pp. 241–79. See section 110, p. 248.
5 Jacques Derrida, *Memoirs of the Blind: The Self-Portrait and Other Ruins*, trans. Pascale-Anne Brault and Michael Naas (Chicago: The University of Chicago Press, 1993), p. 3.
6 Ibid., p. 45.
7 Ibid.
8 Michael Newman, 'The Traces and Marks of Drawing', in Catherine de Zegher (ed.), *The Stage of Drawing: Gesture and Act* (London, Tate Publishing; New York, The Drawing Centre, 2003), pp. 93–108.
9 Michael Newman, 'Sticking to the World: Drawing as Contact', in Catherine de Zegher (ed.), *Giuseppe Penone: The Imprint of Drawing* (New York: The Drawing Center, 2004), p. 107. For more in depth readings of Derrida by Newman see, for instance, 'Derrida and the Scene of Drawing', *Research in Phenomenology*, 24 (1994), pp. 218–34.
10 The excavations are discussed in Christopher Parslow, *Rediscovering Antiquity: Karl Weber and the Excavation of Herculaneum, Pompeii, and Stabiae* (Cambridge: Cambridge University Press, 1995).
11 The process of excavation and recording of the villa by Karl Weber, a Swiss military engineer who supervised the excavations Herculaneum, Pompeii, and Stabiae, is discussed at length in Parslow, *Rediscovering Antiquity*. See also Dana Arnold, 'En Foüllant à l'Aveugle: Discovering the Villa of the Papyri in the 18th century', in Mantha Zarmakoupi (ed.), *The Villa of the Papyri at Herculaneum: Archaeology, Reception, and Digital Reconstruction*. Sozomena: Studies in the Recovery of Ancient Texts. Edited on behalf of the Herculaneum Society, vol. 1 (Berlin and Boston: De Gruyter, 2010), pp. 139–54.
12 Marquis Don Marcello di Venuti, *A description of the first discoveries of the antient [sic] city of Heraclea, found near Portici, a country palace belonging to the king of the Two Sicilies. In two parts ... Done into English from the original Italian of the Marquis Don Marcello di Venuti. By Wickes Skurray. To which are added some letters that passed between the learned Jo. Matthia Gesner..., Cardinal Quirini, and Hermannus Samuel Reimarus... concerning these discoveries.* Variant title: *Description of the first discoveries of the ancient city of Heraclea*, 8 vols (London: Printed for R. Baldwin, jun. at the Rose in Pater-Noster-Row, 1750), p. 50.

13 Johann Joachim Winckelmann, *Sendschreiben von den herculanischen Entdeckungen* (Dresden, 1762) was translated into French, *Lettre de M. l'Abbé Winckelmann ... à M. le Comte de Brühl ... sur les découvertes d'Herculanum* (Paris, 1764). This finally appeared in English as *A Critical Account of the Situation and Destruction by the First Eruptions of Mount Vesuvius of Herculaneum, Pompeii, and Stabiae* (London: Printed for T. Carnan and F. Newbery, 1771). All quotations are from the English version (1771 Eng. transl., ii). The use of images including artefacts in the discovery of the past is discussed for instance by Francis Haskell in his wide-ranging book *History and Its Images: Art and the Interpretation of the Past* (New Haven and London: Yale University Press, 1995). Haskell outlines the many ways that historians have used images and how they became available or were discovered through excavation, the creation of private collections and public museums, as well as the increased popularity and ease of travel.

14 Winckelmann, *Sendschreiben*, p. 19.

15 Ibid., p. 24.

16 Ibid., Part IV, p. 27.

17 Parslow, *Rediscovering Antiquity*, pp. 85–103.

18 'Everything found by this method, of excavating blindly, makes it possible to judge what might be produced by a methodical search' (trans. Dana Arnold). Charles de Brosses, Letter dated 1 June 1749 in *Lettres sur l'état actuel de la Ville Souterraine d'Herculée* (Dijon: François Desventes, 1750), p. 11.

19 Jacques Derrida, *Archive Fever: A Freudian Impression*, trans. Eric Prenowitz (Chicago: The University of Chicago Press, 1996), p. 16.

20 Derrida, *Memoirs of the Blind*.

21 Antonio de Simone's recent excavations of the villa confirm that Weber's plan of it is basically correct, albeit with minor adjustments. See for instance Antonio de Simone, 'Rediscovering the Villa of the Papyri', in Mantha Zarmakoupi (ed.), *The Villa of the Papyri at Herculaneum: Archaeology, Reception, and Digital Reconstruction*. Sozomena: Studies in the Recovery of Ancient Texts. Edited on behalf of the Herculaneum Society, vol. 1 (Berlin and Boston: De Gruyter, 2010), pp. 1–20.

22 Johann Wolfgang von Goethe, *The Italian Journey*, trans. W. H. Auden and Elizabeth Mayer (New York: Pantheon Books, 1962), p. 202.

23 C N Cochin et JC Bellicard, *Observations sur les antiquités de la ville de Herculanum*, Paris 1754 repr. Geneva, 1972, p. 30.

24 Derrida, *Memoirs of the Blind*, p.3.

25 This kind of phenomenological notion of space is not solely the preoccupation of cognitive scientists. Kant had posed similar questions over two centuries earlier believing that space was a form imposed by our minds on the world.

Part III: Printing time

I am interested in the notion that if graphic representation is about memory then surely it is also about time. Here the work of Henri Bergson, a radical philosopher whose work addressed the notions of time, memory and duration is helpful for our enquiry.[1] In his *Matter and Memory*, 1896, Bergson describes matter in terms of 'images', the production of images that exist somewhere in between representation and thing – the brain is an image that can facilitate or slow down communication.[2] Importantly for us, Deleuze picks up on this when he remarks:

> The past and the present do not denote two successive moments, but two elements which co-exist: one is the present, which does not cease to pass, and the other is the past, which does not cease to be but through which all presents pass.[3]

The Deleuzian-Bergsonian theory of duration/memory relates not only to contemporary life with the ever-growing sophistication of media and communication technology, but also to the technologies of the print. Both of these visual media collapse the boundaries between present and past. The fluidity between past and present is evident in the moment of pressing the print, which is the moment the image has been made and it becomes the past. Another pressing produces another image, and as we have seen, the second (or third or fourth) image will be subtly different from the first one. Prints can then produce different times, histories and effects. It is in this way, at the moment of its becoming, that the print spatialises time.[4] Albeit anachronistically, we can compare this affect of the print to the snap of the camera as the shutter opens momentarily to record an image. Roland Barthes claims the photograph immobilizes time through 'the stasis of an arrest', where time is held in the past.[5]

Returning to our eighteenth-century Grand Tourists, we can begin to think about how antiquarians seek to both distance and appropriate the past. An antiquarian sensibility makes one's own culture 'other' and time is seen as concomitant with a loss of understanding so the distance of time is key here. This loss can be overcome through the awakening of objects and of narrative. The antiquarian looks for material evidence of the past and at the same time seeks an intrinsic relationship between it and the present. This relationship is only made possible by the disruption of past and present and it is here that we find the intersection between time and the rhetoric of the image. Textual and visual descriptions offer narratives at different speeds that manipulate the reader/viewer through space and time. We must remember, however, that drawing is produced at the speed of the body – the time the hand takes to move over the page, or in the case of the Villa of the Papyri for the draughtsman to crawl through a building. By contrast, prints are produced through mechanical means – what affect does this have on the image and does mass reproduction alter this state and the time the reader may spend 'reading'?

As we have seen, the production of graphic images and their printed counterparts comprises complex processes each of which adds to the temporal disruptions of the narrative. In terms of the images themselves, we can begin with some basic temporal co-ordinates: the time it takes to make the image and the time it takes to look at it and, quite obviously, these may be at variance. But an image can also encapsulate temporality, as it may offer a narration of a building over the passage of time.[6] For instance, in the case of Piranesi's image of the Temple of Neptune at Paestum (Figure 13) we see it simultaneously as an ancient temple and as a ruin in the eighteenth-century.

We have already noted how the addition of text in the form of captions or representations of inscriptions lodges language in the medium of the visual image.[7] This adds another temporal dimension to the graphic image; the time taken to compose the caption may well be far longer than the time it takes us to read it. What I am getting at here is the difference between the speed of writing and reading and the speed of drawing and looking. We read at a certain speed; conversely, images can narrate different times and speed. The important point here for us is that a verbal description does not have this simultaneity, as its syntactical construction relies on sequence. In other words, the reader cannot change the time of a written description – it cannot be made to move faster or more slowly when it is a text. The experience of the past is quite different in the visual realm of the graphic image, as the mode of reproduction transforms the subject. Where the viewer cannot change the time of the description or ekphrasis the subject is the agent of tradition, for instance when we are reading an account of an ancient temple. Conversely, where the image is reproduced the viewer can move the image through space and time as the subject (i.e. temple) is performed or constituted through the mode of its reproduction/description. In this way the notion of linear time is challenged, as there are different modes of temporality. It is hierarchical and differentiated and works to form boundaries, and we experience time and these boundaries through the visual language of the graphic image which organises our spatial experience of architecture in its temporal context.

The temporal dimensions of visual ekphrases are crucial for an understanding of the relationship between past and present in our period. There is no doubt that the belief that ancient cultures hold lessons for the present day continues to endure. But the definition of culture, and what might be learned from it, remains in flux. For instance, the newly discovered material remains of the past unearthed in the excavations at Pompeii and Herculaneum, and the images that sprung from them, undoubtedly produced a new interest in Roman civic life. Similarly, the visual descriptions of the architecture of ancient Greece as encountered at Paestum or in Athens itself encouraged an engagement with the cultural values as expressed in the architectural aesthetics of the ancient Hellenic world. In this way the reconstructions of the past from its material traces become objects of nostalgia for the modern world. The liberation of the image from the text both encourages and enhances the engagement with and visualisation of the past. And here we see how the imagination can affect notions of truth and authenticity. As we have seen in the Prolegomenon, images of the antique attempt to replace the actual past with an imagined past. In this way prints made this vision of the past readily available for present-day consumption, and this temporal resonance evokes nostalgia.[8] The temporality of the original becomes, then, ambiguous, as it is both an object from the past and a representation in the present. In this way the problematic relationship between the present and its pasts or, if you will, the wanton chase of history is revealed through the medium of printed time.

Notes

1 Gilles Deleuze, *Bergsonism* [French edition 1966] trans. Hugh Tomlinson and Barbara Habberjam (New York: Zone Books, 1991).

2 On this point see, for instance, Elizabeth Grosz, *The Nick of Time: Politics, Evolution and the Untimely* (Durham, North Carolina and London: Duke University Press, 2004) and Suzanne Guerlac, *Thinking in Time: An Introduction to Henri Bergson* (Ithaca, New York: Cornell University Press, 2006).

3 Deleuze, *Bergsonism*, p. 59.

4 On this point see Yve Lomax, *Writing the Image: An Adventure with Art and Theory* (London and New York: I.B. Tauris, 2000), p. 123 esp. Here she is reworking Bergson.

5 Roland Barthes, *Camera Lucida: Reflections on Photography*, trans. Richard Howard (London: Vintage, 1993), p. 91 (originally published in French as '*La chambre claire: note sur la photographie*' (Paris: Editions Seuil, 1980). See also chapter 36, pp. 85–9.

6 Michel Butor, *Inventory*, trans. Richard Howard (New York: Simon & Schuster, 1969) for a discussion of time in relation to literary work.

7 See above, Chapter 2, Part I, regarding Walter Benjamin's assertion of the crucial relationship between images, captions and inscriptions. '[T]he linguistic word', he writes, 'lodges in the medium of the language of painting.' 'Painting, or Sign and Mark', in *Walter Benjamin: Selected Writings, Volume 1, 1913–1926*, ed. Marcus Bullock and Michael W. Jennings (Cambridge, Massachusetts: Harvard University Press, 1996), p. 86.

8 On this point see, for instance, Stewart, *On Longing* and Pearce, *On Collecting*.

3 Space

Part I: The spaces of the page

In thinking about space in relation to visual descriptions of architecture we should begin with the spaces where we encounter these images. The literal space where we first see graphic representations of architecture is that of the paper on which it is printed or drawn. The sheet of paper or page is not a neutral surface; rather, it is a physical site that engages with the image it contains. It is a space in its own right that has defined borders that enclose the image. And in the case of prints these are in addition to the edges of the impression of the press itself. The page also offers a conceptual reference to the space alluded to in the image it contains, as it is a window through which we see this. The blankness of the page, where the line is not, can also connote architectural space or the space beyond or through the building that is being represented. The ambiguities between the mark or line and the blankness of the page are noted by Avis Newman and Catherine de Zegher:

> in drawing the surface maintains its separate existence. There is an ambivalence of status between the mark and its support. … marking thoughts, which by definition are open-ended, in a state of flux, [is] suggestive of a perpetual potentiality.[1]

We have seen how prints and sometimes drawings became part of a bound collection. But more importantly, our period also witnessed the rise of the printed book – an assemblage of images with supporting text that offered a detailed description of the architectural site under review. These were costly endeavours requiring subscribers to support production and publication. In return these volumes offered a shared experience of an antique building or site that could be progressed through page by page in a kind of virtual tour. We have already noted how this miniaturisation of the past and its inclusion in a collection creates a souvenir that becomes an experience that can manipulate desire.[2] And this is evident, for instance, in the works of both Stuart and Revett and Le Roy where ancient Athens becomes both knowable and memorialised. Similarly, the enterprises of Kip and Knyff and Colen Campbell show us how this technique of shared experience and memory is used to commodify architecture to project a national identity within the spaces of the page.[3]

My starting point here is to consider what happens to images when they become part of a book or bound volume. Most obviously the pages, whilst retaining their individual nature, also become part of an interrelated sequence that leads us through the space of the book. The binding of the book, its exterior surface, becomes a signifier of this through the depth of its spine and the dimensions of its front and back covers. Indeed, bindings were an important part of the book on many levels, as not only did they signal the physical volume of the bound volume but they were also part of the marketing strategy (to use present-day parlance). We know, for example, that the choices Stuart and Revett made for the binding of *The Antiquities of Athens* were influential for Robert Adam when he published his *Ruins of the Palace of the Emperor Diocletian at Spalatro* (1764).

How, then, do we encounter images of antique architecture within the spaces of a book or bound volume? It is above all a bodily experience that has both a tactile and a performative quality. We need to turn the pages to progress through the sequence and in doing so we touch and feel the paper. Moreover, we see how the shape of each page changes and how the light and shadow cast as it moves challenges the two-dimensionality of the linear graphic images.[4] In turn, an image or a series of images take us through the spaces of a building, as we have seen for instance in Stuart and Revett's *The Antiquities of Athens* (Figures 10, 11 and 12). The building and its spaces are miniaturised and memorialised within the space of the page. And we have a variety of spatial contexts for the image of the building. *Vedute* place the structure in its actual or imagined surroundings, giving a sense of scale and depth. By contrast, plans and elevations deny any spatial context for the building; it is instead isolated and the only spatial co-ordinates are supplied by the mode of description.

The bodily experience of the spaces of the book is made more complex through the miniaturisation of a building on the space of the page. Its monumentality and scale are reduced and its presence is compressed from three dimensions into two, and the viewer understands this through the body. As we have seen, space is experienced and described using the human body, for instance through the haptic encounter of building or page of a book; in the use of Vitruvian proportions in the techniques of architectural representation and reconstruction; or, indeed, in the physical act of drawing or printing. At this point it is helpful to remember Alberti's observation that

> the function of a painter is this: to describe with lines and to tint with colour … observed planes of any body so that at a certain distance and in a certain position from the centre they appear in relief, seem to have mass and to be lifelike.[5]

We have already noted that this is important when thinking about the line; here it is the emphasis on how the line becomes a descriptor of space that is of significance.[6] In his treatise *On Painting*, Alberti claimed the invention of the grid method of representing the space and distance often referred to as the *costruzione legittima* – a horizontal grid comprising orthogonal and transverse lines.[7] This geometric technique of creating the illusion of depth and volume, like other methods of experiencing space, is also based on the body, especially the masculine body. The spacing of the lines of the *costruzione legittima* is governed by one *braccio*, which is a Florentine unit of measurement equal to one third of the height of a man (taken to be approximately 23 in or 58.4 cm). These individual *braccio* divisions, joined to the perspective focus to give the orthogonals, thus create a kind of V shape. The overall effect is a grid comprising squares each of which is based on the measurement of the male body. Importantly, for this perspectival construction to work there needs to be a single viewpoint.

These ideas soon spread across the Alps and were promoted, for instance, by Albrecht Dürer in his *Painter's Manual*, the first edition of which appeared in 1525.[8] This, in common with many other artists' handbooks or treatises on how to make a perspectival drawing, concentrated on the practicalities rather than optical theory and assumed a fixed viewpoint without question.

> There is yet another method of copying an object and of rendering it larger or smaller according to one's wish, and it is more practical than using a glass pane because it is less restricted. In this method one uses a frame with a grid of strong black thread. The spaces or quadrangles should be about two fingers wide. For scanning one must prepare a pointer whose height should be adjustable to be at eye level, which is marked 'o'. Then place the object to be drawn a good distance away. Move it or bend it as you like, and view it from level 'o' to ascertain that it is in the proper position, so as to please you. Then place the grid or frame between the object and the pointer. If you prefer to use fewer spaces of the grid, move it closer to the object. Check how many spaces of the grid will be utilized to accommodate the width and height of the object and then draw a grid, larger or small on a sheet of paper or a panel on which you wish to draw. Now begin to scan the object with your eye – point 'o' – placed above the pointer, and where it points on the grid in the frame, mark it off on the grid on your sheet of paper. It will be good, and it will be correct. But if you prefer to drill a small hole into your scanner, it will serve the same purpose equally well. I have drawn this method below.[9]

Dürer illustrated this method and in Figure 17 we see him demonstrating how to draw a nude female body using a grid based on male proportions. There is a great deal more I would like to say about this way of viewing and describing a female nude on the part of the artist in the image and the viewer of the print itself, but this, together with the idea of the *Vitruvian Woman* discussed earlier in this book are, perhaps issues that I have begun to address elsewhere

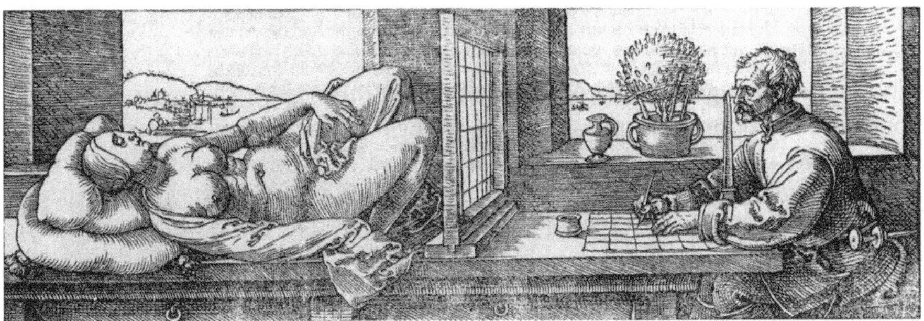

Albrecht Dürer, 'Draughtsman making a perspective drawing of a reclining woman', woodcut, *c.*1525 **17**

and will continue to develop.[10] What is relevant here, albeit that it remains unchallenged, is that it is a visual syntax based on masculine predicates that governs the representation and construction of architectural space. I would like now to return to the importance of the *costruzione legittima* for the notion of an image as being a window onto space. As Panofsky remarks:

> The window definition is a planar cross section through the 'visual pyramid'; the apex of the pyramid is the eye which is connected with various points within the space to be represented.[11]

My interest here is in the effect this has on the viewer whose single eye is the apex of a pyramid constructed on masculine proportions. This mode of viewing endures, as Damisch remarks whilst referring to the apparent end of scientific perspective in the late nineteenth century:

> That does not prevent us from referring back, if not to Ghiberti, at least to Leonardo da Vinci, from finding in his *Treatise on Painting* – the first critical edition of which dates from the end of the nineteenth century – the premonitory symptoms of a critical trope that has scarcely changed since that time, one that holds that *costruzione legittima* reduces the viewing subject to a kind of Cyclops, and obliges the eye to remain at one fixed, indivisible point in other words, obliges it to adopt a stance that has nothing in common with the effective conditions of perception, any more than it does with the goals of painting, as properly understood.[12]

The use of a scale of measurement or perspectival representation augments the viewer's experience of the image. Together these systems of description combine to unlock the spaces of antique architecture from the confines of the page. The process of miniaturising an antique building transforms it into something personal and private. The public nature of the architecture, whether that be its original function as a temple or as a popular site for curious Grand

Tourists, is transformed into a private view for an individual. The notion of time also comes into play here as the image becomes private, as only the viewer who turns the pages of the book in their own time sees it. It is clear, then, that space in all its complexities is there within the pages of a book. Walter Benjamin has already shown us that a book lies flat and its pages are read rather than looked at by the reader/viewer.[13] This is important here as it highlights the gap between seeing and seeing what is meant – that is to say understanding the representation of architecture and its spaces once the modes of visual description move from the pictorial – *veduta* – to the analytical – elevations and sections, for example. At the outset of this enquiry, I highlighted that one of the fundamental questions about descriptions of architecture is how a three-dimensional object is represented in only two dimensions. And beyond this, I questioned how the experience of the space that architecture contains is described. The ground plan and orthogonal elevation – two standard methods of representing a building both present space in two dimensions. The former shows the footprint of a structure, which can be a kind of spatial map that we travel across with our eye. The latter flattens the building pressing it against the surface of the page. But what we see, that is to say the lines on the page, is not the three-dimensional space that we know to be there.

I would like to pause to think about the relationships between resemblance and representation and description and ekphrasis.[14] I begin with the somewhat obvious observation that an image is an artificial likeness or picture of an object that requires our senses, usually sight, to be perceived. In turn this percept relies on and is sustained by a mental picture held in the memory that gives us indirect knowledge of that which is represented. For us this means that a print or drawing, if it is to represent architecture, must be a symbol or referent for it. Nelson Goodman identifies the connection between the visual and linguistic process of description: 'A picture that represents – like a passage that describes – an object refers to and, more particularly, *denotes* it.' He goes on to elucidate:

> If the relationship between a picture and what it represents is this assimilated to the relation between a predicate and what it applies to, we must examine the characteristic of representation as a special kind of denotation. What does pictorial denotation have in common with, and how does it differ from, verbal or diagrammatic denotation? One not implausible answer is that resemblance, while no sufficient condition for representation, is just the feature that distinguishes representation from denotation of other kinds.[15]

Goodman then discusses how reference is a precondition of description or depiction, whereas resemblance is not. In this way depiction and description operate as ways of classifying and codifying the world as 'they interact with each other and with perception and knowledge'.[16]

This conundrum is extended into the realm of the three-dimensional built environment by Robin Evans:

> a work of architecture is more than the sum of its representations. … pictures and words are always less than what they refer to. Referential art is, by its very nature, reduced from its referents.[17]

Here Evans raises the essential questions: What is representation? Is it in fact resemblance? Can something only represent if it resembles? He continues:

> Thus to say that a building is more than its pictures is not to say that it is more art-like than its pictures. It does suggest that it is more difficult to make a building *art-like* than a picture because perceptions of a building are more in themselves but less manageable, *less* capable of full orchestration.[18]

And herein lies a problem: objects can resemble each other without necessarily representing each other. A drawing might represent a building, as we have seen for instance in the Tower of the Winds, but the Tower does not represent the drawing.

Indeed, there is a close link between the drawing and the building but there is only one version of the building whereas there may be many representations of it both visual and textual. The original and its descriptions remain linked but one is not a copy of the other. Returning to the graphic representations of architecture encountered by our armchair Grand Tourists we see that they frequently combined text and image. Ground plans and orthogonal elevation, made up of lines and angles, often include measurements in words and figures that provide a notion of accuracy, albeit predicated on a masculine system of measurement. But these descriptions do not evoke the texture and patina of the building itself, which might be closer to the physical experience of the building on site.

Notes

1 Newman, Avis and Catherine de Zegher, *The Stage of Drawing: Gesture and Act* (London, Tate Publishing; New York, The Drawing Center, 2003), p. 169.
2 See Prolegomenon p. 8 and Stewart, *On Longing*.
3 Johannes Kip and Leonard Knyff, *Britannia Illustrata* (1707) and *Nouveau théâtre de la Grande Bretagne* (1708–13) and Colen Campbell, *Vitruvius Britannicus*, 3 vols (1715–25) were funded by subscription. The former celebrated the houses and landed estates of the owners/subscribers, whilst Campbell presented a digest of classical architecture in Britain since the time of Inigo Jones. See also pp. 99–100 and Figure 18, and p. 115 and Figure 22 of this chapter.
4 On this point see Marian Macken, *Binding Space: The Book as Spatial Practice* (Abingdon: Routledge, 2018), p. 33.
5 Alberti, *On Painting*, Part III, p. 89.

6 Notably here, Alberti had a different opinion of perspective in his *On the Art of Building*, published in 1485, he noted that it had a distorting influence on architecture. However, the form and content of this work did borrow heavily from Vitruvius.
7 Cecil Grayson, 'L.B. Alberti's 'Costruzione Legittima', *Italian Studies*, 19:1 (1964), pp. 14–27 explores the differences between the Italian and Latin versions of the text and issues of translation. See also a response to Grayson by Samuel Y. Edgerton Jr., 'Alberti's Perspective: A New Discovery and a New Evaluation', *The Art Bulletin*, 48:3–4 (1966), pp. 367–78.
8 Albrecht Dürer, *The Painter's Manual: A Manual of Measurement of Lines, Areas, and Solids by Means of Compass and Ruler Assembled by Albrecht Dürer for the Use of All Lovers of Art with Appropriate Illustrations Arranged to be Printed in the Year MDXXV*, 2nd edn [1538] trans. Walter L. Strauss (New York: Abaris, 1977).
9 Ibid., p. 435.
10 See for instance, Dana Arnold, '(Auto)Biographies and Space' in Dana Arnold and Joanna Sofaer Derevenski (eds), *Biographies and Space: Placing the Subject in Art and Architecture* (London: Routledge, 2007 and 2015), pp. 6–16.
11 Erwin Panofsky, *Perspective as Symbolic Form*, trans. Christopher S. Wood (New York: Zone Books, 1991), p. 28.
12 Hubert Damisch, *The Origin of Perspective*, trans. John Goodman, (Cambridge Massachusetts: MIT, 1994), p35. In the footnote to this passage Damisch refers to Martin Kemp, 'Leonardo and the Visual Pyramid', *Journal of the Warburg and Courtauld Institutes*, 11 (1977), pp. 128–49.
13 Walter Benjamin, 'Painting and the Graphic Arts', p. 219.
14 There is a very broad literature addressing these questions from a range of disciplinary perspectives. See for instance Richard Wollheim, 'On Pictorial Representation, *Journal of Aesthetics and Art Criticism*, 56:3 (1998), pp. 217–26 and Svetlana Alpers, 'Interpretation without Representation, or, The Viewing of *Las Meninas*', *Representations*, 1:1 (1983), pp. 30–42.
15 Nelson Goodman, *Languages of Art: An Approach to a Theory of Symbols* (New York: The Bobbs-Merrill Company, 1968), pp. 5–6.
16 Ibid., p. 40.
17 Robin Evans, *The Projective Cast: Architecture and Its Three Geometries* (Cambridge, Massachusetts: MIT Press, 1995), pbk 2000, p. xxi.
18 Ibid. p. xxi [emphasis in original].

Part II: Seeing and knowing

The notion of vision and our various understandings of it and the relationship between vision and knowledge are central to the concerns of this book. In western culture the acts of seeing and knowing are linguistically and metaphorically intertwined. This is evident, for instance, in the many figures of speech that link the two: we 'see what is meant' when we understand something, perhaps more importantly for us here, the metaphor of 'putting things in perspective' is used when we stand back from a situation in order to form a more 'reasoned' opinion and perhaps prioritise the issues as stake. Moreover, the relationship between seeing and knowing goes deeper into our verbal language. The word idea comes from the Greek 'idea' which in turn is derived from the verb *idein* – to see; imagination where we see with the mind's eye stems from the Latin verb *imaginare* – to picture oneself. My purpose in reiterating these metaphors and in exploring their etymology is to help to explain why sight has been characterised so often as the least bodily of the senses. This Aristotelian notion of a sensory hierarchy prioritised sight, as this was the human potential for knowledge and reason whereas touch was the most primordial sense that we share with animals. Yet, we should remember that books and within them the printed page are both experienced with sight and touch.

Perhaps more relevant to my theme is that the conflation of optics with perspective and representations of space with modes of perception can also be traced back to classical antiquity. The powerful combination of classical, Arabic and medieval thinking established optics, and within this *perspectiva*, as the means to understand the natural world. Here we find Euclid's *Optica*, *c.*300 BCE the first text on geometrical optics, followed by Ptolemy's *Optica*, *c.*140 CE, and Galen's *De usu partium*, *c.*175 CE, These works were drawn together in Alhazen's *Perspectiva*, *c.*1000 CE, and this in turn influenced Roger Bacon who was also familiar with most of the newly translated work from Greek, Jewish, and Islamic philosophy and science. Bacon's *Opus Majus*, *c.*1270 CE, included a section on optics, and established the field of *perspectiva* – the study of light and vision. Indeed, Bacon's text was instrumental in defining this scientific discipline in the West for the next 350 years.[1]

Perspective was taken from the verb *perspicere*, which means to survey or scrutinize, to investigate thoroughly, or to 'see through'. In some senses we could think about the geometrical abstraction that formed the basis of perspectival construction of images as akin to an X-ray that permits us to see the underlying structure of the world around us. In this way, it goes beyond the visual. As W. J. T. Mitchell has remarked, albeit with particular reference to modernity, ocularcentrism or the 'notion of vision as hegemonic or non-hegemonic is simply too blunt an instrument to produce much in the way of historical or critical differentiation'.[2] What I am interested in here is first of all the relationship between seeing, knowing and perception; following on from this I think about strategies for the representation of space in our period. We can then see how these influence the experience and understanding of the spaces both of the past and the present.

Vision and knowledge: in the mind's eye

The special status of prints and their concomitant authority as bearers of knowledge was recognised at the very beginning of the eighteenth century by Roger de Piles in his 'Of the Usefulness and Use of Prints'.[3] Piles expressed admiration for prints as displays of skill in their own right but also as mental aids to memory and understanding. Importantly, we must remember that de Piles also recognises the ability of prints to 'represent absent and distant things, as if they were before our eyes … we see countries, towns, and all the considerable places that we have read of in history, or have seen in our travels' and that these may replace travel for those 'who have no strength, leisure or convenience to travel'.[4] Indeed, we have seen this with our armchair Grand Tourists who flicked through volumes such as Stuart and Revett's *The Antiquities of Athens*. Perhaps paradoxically, prints also came to represent what was not visible. This was ably articulated by John Locke in his *An Essay Concerning Human Understanding*.[5] Locke notes that

> the materials of all our knowledge, are suggested and furnished to the mind only by sensation and reflection. When the understanding is once stored [the mind] has the power to repeat, compare, and unite them … and so can make … new and complex ideas.[6]

Here, I want to consider the theories of vision that were current in our period and then map these onto the visual descriptions of architecture and the knowledge these images impart. My discussion centres on Bishop Berkeley, especially his *Essay on a New Theory of Vision* (1709), which expresses many of the key concerns of subsequent thinkers and theorists some of whom we encounter later in this chapter and elsewhere in this enquiry.[7] Berkeley's *Essay* is principally a study of visual perception with a particular interest in how we perceive the distance and size of objects and their spatial relation to other objects. He suggests that sight and the processes of mimesis or recording that follow on from it are part of a subjective gaze of an ethereal field. This signalled a profound shift in conceptions of vision and the act of viewing as the power and potency of non-verbal expression was recognised. The relationship between vision and cognition had currency in the eighteenth century. But at the same time this recognition prompted the wish to confine these images within an established Cartesian rationalist linguistic system of visual signs predicated on the male body, which worked to separate the physiological from the psychological.

Berkeley also discusses the relationship and interaction of vision and language. He denies the existence of material substance and instead argues that objects are only ideas in the minds of perceivers and, as a result, cannot exist without being perceived. Significantly for us, Berkeley considers visual distance, magnitude, position, and problems of sight and touch all of which have resonance with the concerns in this volume. Berkeley argues that there are two classes of objects necessary for human visual perception: the primary objects of sight, according to Berkeley, are light and colour, whilst the secondary objects of sight are the primary objects of touch: distance, figure, magnitude, and situation. To this end, vision is a secondary source of spatial information that would otherwise come only from touch. 'The visible object, which being immediately perceived by sight, is connected with that other which is tangible and placed at a distance.'[8]

Early on in his *Essay*, Berkeley summarises one of his principal concerns thus: 'it is plain that distance is in its own nature imperceptible, and yet it is perceived by sight'.[9] Indeed, Berkeley's ideas about the relationship between the visible and the spatial are crucial here. For Berkeley, visual experience of spatial features is perceptual – we do not see spatial features, as he believes visible features are in fact signs or marks of spatial features. It is the spatial significance of visible features that enables us to see distance, figure, magnitude, and situation.

> [I]t remains that we inquire, what ideas or sensations there be that attend vision, unto which we may suppose the ideas of distance [and other spatial features] are connected, and by which they are introduced into the mind.[10]

I am thinking here of how these ideas map onto representations of space as witnessed in architectural prints and drawings, particularly here in relation to different kinds of perspective. Consider, for example, the work of Leonard Knyff (1650–1722), born in the Netherlands but active in London from *c.*1681. Knyff is notable for his paintings and drawings of grand houses as seen when set in their landscape surroundings. His use of a bird's eye viewpoint or aerial perspective was both novel and innovative. This representation afforded the most complete view of a house, giving the plan of the building as well as making its elevations legible. We also have an excellent sense of the topography and the layout of the grounds. This form of architectural representation is very easily readable, especially when compared to the complexity of other ways of representation space, as we shall see. In 1707, Knyff published *Britannia Illustrata*, a volume comprising 80 engravings of palaces and country houses, and their grounds. The project was funded by subscriptions from the house owners, and many of the images contain future building plans as well as extant architecture. Knyff made numerous drawings, which were then engraved by Johannes Kip (1652/3–1722) to form large, intricately detailed, folio plates. The celebration of architecture and landscape in *Britannia Illustrata* was reprinted in

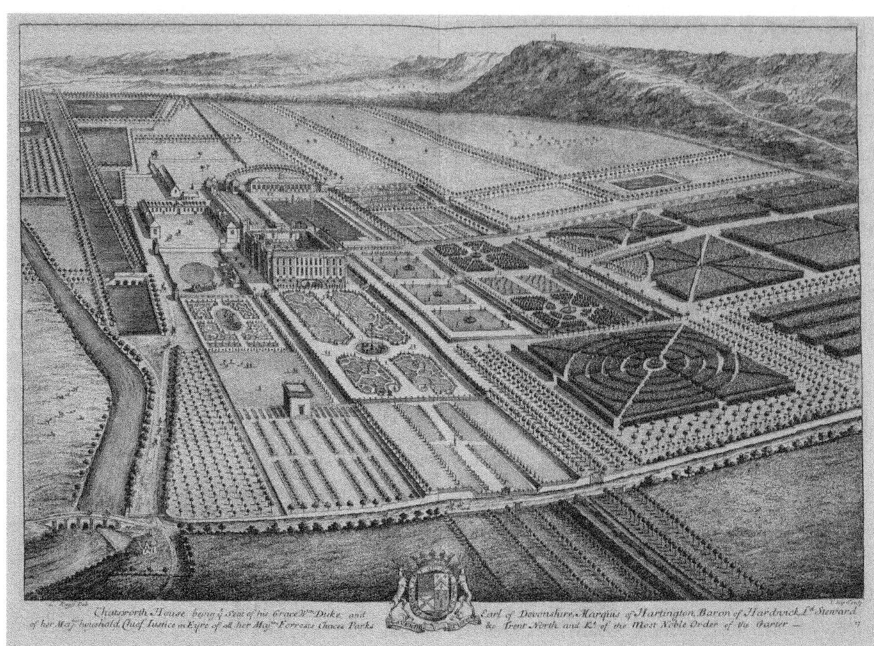

18 After Leonard Knyff, 'View of Chatsworth House', in *Nouveau théâtre de la Grande Bretagne: ou description exacte des palais de la reine et des maisons les plus considerables des seigneurs et des gentilshommes de la Grande Bretagne ...*, 1708

1708–13 with additional engravings in two volumes under the title *Nouveau théâtre de la Grande Bretagne*.[11] What fascinates me is the leap of imagination between what Knyff saw when he was making preparatory sketches on site and what is described in the finished drawings and thence the plates of his book. And we see this vividly in the image of Chatsworth House, the residence of the Dukes of Devonshire (Figure 18). Here, I wonder what image Knyff held in his mind in the moment of blindness when a draughtsman makes a mark on a page?

This brings us back to Berkeley who, to explain his ideas, posits the notion that there is in fact a language of vision, which comes naturally to most of us and is independent of verbal language. This language is predicated on the visual experience through which we anticipate and navigate our spatial environment. Importantly, Berkeley also recognises that there are those who must learn the language of vision in contrast to those for whom it is an innate talent. And here we find ourselves being asked to think about the relationship between images and language very much at a pre-Saussurean moment. Moreover, the similarities and differences between Berkeley and Maurice Merleau-Ponty as regards the subject-object relationship have been noted and ably discussed elsewhere.[12] Not least here is Merleau-Ponty's view of the bodily experience of space, as he argued that parallel lines do not converge in Euclidean space. Instead tactile considerations, derived from bodily spatiality, remain more important than purely visual information – a point to which I shall return.[13] And, arguably, Nelson Goodman, shares Berkeley's interest in how unavoidably existent things rest within the mind.[14] I do not want to rehearse these debates here, rather my point in referring to them is to flag that the kind of reasoning that Berkeley was presenting is not solely the preoccupation of recent philosophical thought. Indeed, we also find echoes of Derrida's concerns in his *Memoirs of the Blind* when, as we have seen, in the final part of his *Essay*, Berkeley considers the difference between perception by sight and by touch and of whether we ever perceive the same thing by both faculties.[15]

> Hence it follows that a man born blind and afterwards, when grown up, made to see, would not in the first act of vision parcel out the ideas of sight into the same distinct collections that others do, who have experienced which do regularly coexist and are proper to be bundled up together under one name. … all these ideas offered at once to his view, he would not distribute into sundry distinct combinations till such time as … he comes to know which are to be separated and which to be collected together.[16]

Berkeley's preoccupations, as with those of John Locke who preceded him, show us that in the eighteenth century the relationship between sight and touch, mind and perception were current. Our Grand Tourists, collectors and antiquarians were part of an educated elite that was sensitised to these issues. And this helps us to understand the visual historicising of the spaces of the visual past. Furthermore, we can see how these images stand distinct from texts and offer different experiences of the past.

Berkeley argues that the geometric theory of spatial representation is used as part of the language of understanding and perceiving depth. In this way, our capacity for understanding uses what is given to the eye, together with geometric information about the angles that subtend the eye, to form judgements about spatial features, which would otherwise be given only by touch. Vision thus becomes a secondary source of spatial information. Visual and tactile features are inter-derivable by a common geometry, supplemented by information about optical angles. Distance, depth, figure and other spatial features are judged rather than seen. These judgements are conclusions of mathematical deductions performed, quietly and quickly, by the understanding.[17]

In many ways the use of perspectival representation in architectural prints and drawings reverses the processes outlined by Berkeley. Visual descriptions portray a depth of field using perspective, but this is in fact a system of subordination where significance is simultaneously assigned and denied. It is important here to think about the question of viewpoint, as this helps us to understand the processes of subjugation as well as the way in which images of architecture acted as descriptions. The relationship between these descriptions and the viewer/reader is also of relevance. We must remember that ambiguity is a tool used by language to create depth of field – the multifocal aspects of a sign lend depth and significance with a multiple set of contexts. This also relates to different kinds of experience and descriptions of space, specifically here the mathematical versus the psycho-physiological.

Seeing through space

Alberti, Leonardo and Dürer speak of a picture being a window into a space. The window or frame through which we look is a planar cross section through the 'visual pyramid'; the apex of the pyramid is the eye, which is connected with various points within the space to be represented.[18] This kind of central perspective makes two assumptions in order to guarantee a fully rational, infinite, unchanging and homogeneous space. Firstly that we see with a single immobile eye and secondly that the planar cross section can pass for an adequate reproduction of our optical image. But in fact these two notions are abstractions from reality, as this kind of unchanging mathematically constructed space is quite different from psycho-physiological space. Indeed, as Ernst Cassirer noted:

> Perception does not know the concept of infinity; from the very outset it is confined within certain spatial limits imposed by our faculty of perception. And in connection with perceptual space we can no more speak of homogeneity than of infinity. [...] Hence homogeneous space is never given space, but space produced by construction. [...] Visual space and tactical space (*Tastraum*) are both anisotropic [my definition: varying in magnitude according to the direction of measurement] and unhomogeneous in contrast to the metric space of Euclidean geometry.[19]

A key issue with single fixed-point perspective is that we in fact see with two moving eyes. Moreover, our field of vision is not a square window (or indeed an oblong-shaped page) through which we see space; it is spheroid in shape, and our retinal image is projected onto a concave surface, not the flat space of the page. Here we find an important differentiation between the constructed mathematical space, and the psycho-physiologically conditioned visual image (i.e. artwork), and the retinal image, which is the world we experience through our eyes. For our purposes this is important, as we are principally concerned with the representation/description of architecture. Here, the discrepancy between a retinal image and a perspectival representation is significant. The orthogonals of a building, which in normal perspectival construction appear straight, would, if they were to respond to the factual retinal image, have to be drawn as curves (as indeed would any verticals). So our conception of space in terms of strict linear perspective is at variance with our own spheroidal optical world. In this way, we can see the invention of linear perspective as a disruption to the visual representation or description of our world and specifically here architecture. In antiquity, theories of optics and of art acknowledged that straight lines are seen as curved and vice versa. Particularly relevant here is that columns, especially in Doric temples, should be subjected to entasis so that they did not appear bent; epistyle and stylobate should be built curved to avoid the impression of sagging.[20] But this form of perspective

> is … the expression of a specific and fundamentally un-modern view of space … . Antique perspective is further more the expression of an equally specific and equally un-modern conception of the world.[21]

Curiously, Vitruvius who, as we have seen, influenced the writings of Alberti and Leonardo amongst others, says very little about perspective, other than the rather enigmatic comment that it is the method of sketching a front with the sides withdrawing into the background, where the lines converge in the centre of a circle.[22] But perhaps this, combined with the references he makes to both Greek and Roman stage design, indicates that he had some notion of the idea of a vanishing point and the various methods available to give the appearance of space and depth.

What matters here is the use of perspective for the creation of the illusion of space – a fiction, if you will, rather than the means by which space is perceived /seen. And here, in this regard, we find a crossover between stage design and architectural drawing. The paradox is that the converging lines of fixed-point perspective that help us to understand and experience the actual world can at the same time create or invent space that is not actually there. And I would like to suggest that perspective could make us think differently about architecture. Perspective is a mode of description (ekphrasis) of the real and the fictive world, and the systems of the construction of perspective are a kind of language (in the Berkeleian sense). The different kinds of perspective – linear, single point, aerial, orthogonal and so forth – operate as if they were syntactical modes that shape the description. They also shape our ways of conceiving of architecture and the spaces it contains. Here, I contest, we find the slippage between verbal and the visual ekphrases where the ambiguities of text and images create visual and intellectual depth.

Blurring space

When, then, do we start to see and think about architecture differently as a result of the way it is being described? Robin Evans addresses the relationship between architecture and its referents thus:

> This is not about claiming architecture is in some way superior or attains a status that cannot be achieved by painting, drawing or photographs, or indeed writings about it. Moreover, if we turn this on its head it is possible to say that a building does not so easily operate as an artwork as the perceptions of a building are not as manipulable. What happens when the artwork and the building collide?[23]

Evans extends this point to consider how the techniques and processes of drawing inflect on the architect's imagination:

> Architectural drawing affects what might be called the architect's field of visibility. It makes it possible to see some things more clearly by suppressing other things; something gained, something lost. Its power to represent is always partial, always more or less abstract. It never gives, nor can it give, a total picture of a project, so in consequence it tends to provide a range of subject-matter that is made visible in the drawing, as opposed to all other possible subject-matter that is left out of the drawing or not so apparent from it.[24]

Evans goes on to discuss the relationship between the architectural drawing and its subject

> Now it may be that some architects can see beyond this field of visibility provided by their own drawings .... But whether it is the direct sponsor of the imaginative effort ... or whether it is a counterpoint to the architect's vision... we have to understand the architectural drawing as something that defines the thing it transmits.... It does not necessarily dominate but always interacts with what it represents.
>
> [...]
>
> How or where does this interaction operate?[25]

But for Evans, as we have seen, there is a distinction between a building and a drawing made of it or a design made for it. Whereas the image may represent the extant structure or the architect's intentions, and is therefore connected to the building as a definition of it, the building has no such relationship to the drawing.

My focus here is different, as I would like to think about instances where the blurring of real and fictitious space reveals the relationship between drawing and building. Moreover, my instances create a link between the Renaissance theories of perspective and eighteenth-century ideas of perception and vision. The first of these is the work of Francesco Borromini much of which can be seen as the architectural realisation of the perspectival theories developed in the Renaissance. His innovative designs, especially in the cramped urban environment of Rome, draw on geometry and optics to create the illusion of movement and space. In buildings such as San Carlo alle Quattro

Fontane (1634) and St Ivo alla Sapienza (1640–50) the plans are governed by systems of interlocking geometrical shapes to the point that a visitor can almost hear the compasses Borromini used to draw them moving across the surface of the paper. Geometry and perspective combine in his work at the Palazzo Spada 1652–53 (Figure 19). Here, working with the Augustinian mathematician Fra Giovanni Maria Bitonti, Borromini designed the perspective corridor and garden. The effect is like a three-dimensional realisation of the theories of the *costruzione legittima* as seen in the treatises of Alberti and Dürer. Accelerated or forced perspective creates the impression that the corridor and garden extended to almost five times its actual depth. This is achieved through diminishing rows of columns and rising floor of the arcaded courtyard. Together the converging lines create the optical illusion of a gallery 37 metres long when it is in fact only eight metres. The sculpture at the end of the vista appears to be life-size but it is actually less than half that. A specific standpoint is essential to fully appreciate this essay in optics. This perspectival sleight of hand, rooted in a single viewpoint, on the part of Borromini makes me think of Merleau-Ponty's ideas about bodily spatial experience that we have already encountered in relation to Berkeley, albeit that in both instances it is an anachronistic juxtaposition.

> Parallel lines did not converge in Euclidean space, where tactile considerations, derived from bodily spatiality, were still more important than purely visual information.[26]

Borromini's plans to publish a treatise working with the French printer Domenico Barrière and Fioravante Martinelli, who had published on Rome both ancient and modern, came to nothing in his lifetime. But his work remained of interest in our period and engravers such as Giovanni Battista Falda, whom we have already come across, made efforts to publish his work. Finally, Sebastiano Giannini published *Opus architectonicum* in 1725, which was based loosely on Borromini's work especially at the Oratory of Saint Phillip Neri.[27] My point in narrating this story is to show the sustained interest into the eighteenth century and beyond in what I might term the three-dimensional perspective of Borromini's designs.

The Italian painter, architect and stage designer, Andrea Pozzo (1642–1709), who was also a Jesuit brother, is probably best known for his frescoes using a method of creating the illusion of three-dimensional space known as *quadratura*. Here, the images of space, instead of being of a two-dimensional construction that was typical of the Renaissance, became a field of representation that merged with the three-dimensionality of the architectural space itself. To achieve this effect, images of architectural features are painted onto the flat surface of a wall or ceiling so that they appear to extend the tangible architecture into an imaginary space that exists beyond the confines of the physical

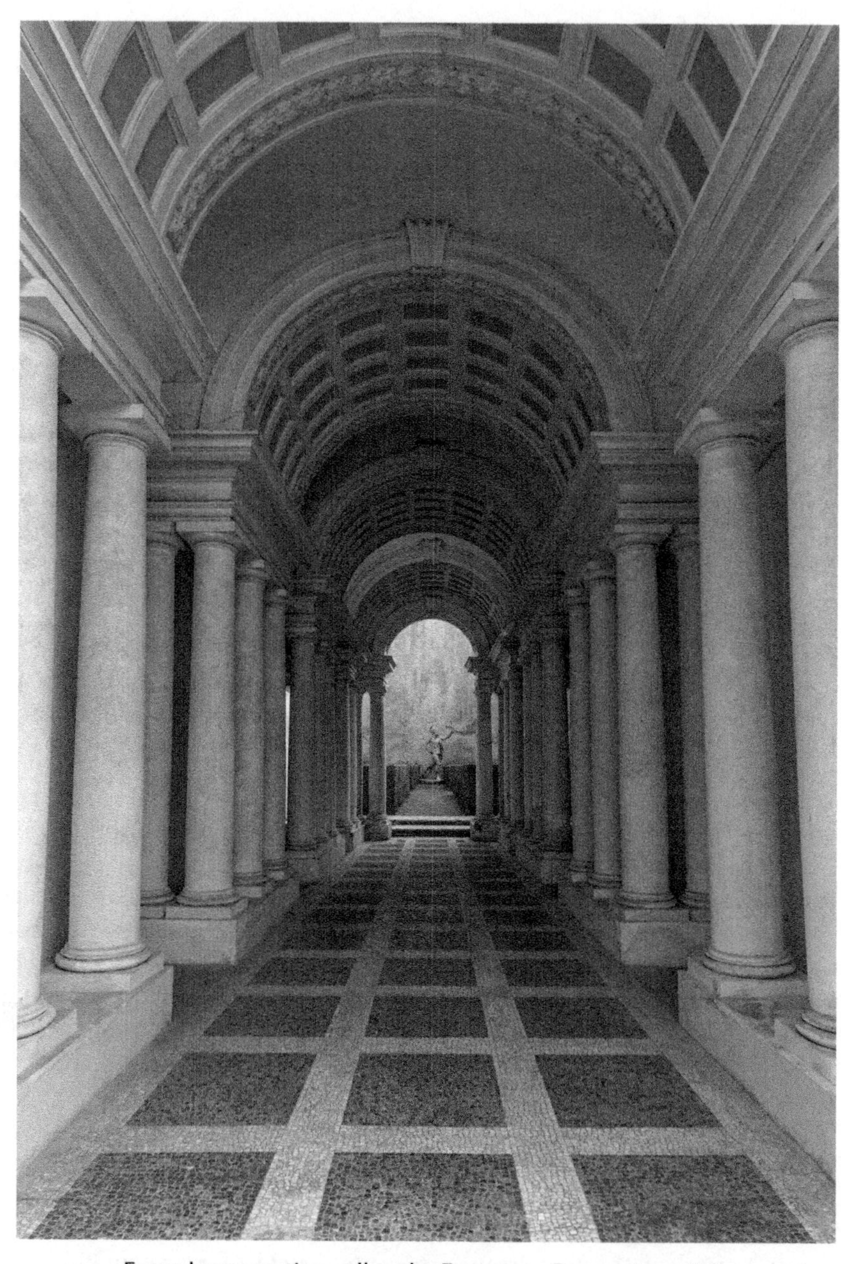

19 Forced perspective gallery by Francesco Borromini, 1653, Palazzo Spada Museum, Rome

area itself. Pozzo's technique is perhaps best exemplified in his nave ceiling of the Church of Sant'Ignazio in Rome (1685–94) where factual and fictional space merge seamlessly when seen from a single point that is marked on the floor of the nave. *Quadratura* is inextricably linked to seventeenth-century theories of perspective and the representation of architectural space. This is important for our purposes, as *quadratura* subjected the three-dimensionality of architectural space to the laws of geometry, so forming a crucial link between the actual space that we inhabit and the geometric space of perspectival representation.[28] The slippage between real and represented space permits the assumption that a perspectival image can be an actual depiction of architectural space. If we accept this premise, it means that the qualitative spatiality of our existence is identical to the objectified space of perspective. As a consequence, it is possible to design in perspective. Pozzo published his theories about perspective in *Perspectiva pictorum et architectorum*, which appeared in 1693 and then 1698.[29] Part treatise, part manual and illustrated with 118 engravings, Pozzo's publication, which was divided into two parts, explained how to produce architectural perspectives and stage sets. Through these images, each of which is accompanied by a brief explanatory text in Latin and Italian, Pozzo demonstrated how through his method of projection, using a plan and an elevation, it is possible to produce a perspective drawing that establishes the absolute proportional relationship of those elements seen in perspective. In this way, the two-dimensionality of plan and section is transformed into three. We can see this, for instance, in plate XV from the second part of the Treatise, 'Tribuna d'Architettura ornata' which shows an architectural tribune – a dais or slightly raised stage – that is sometimes part of an ecclesiastical building, embellished with applied sculptural decoration and two free-standing sculptural figures on plinths in the foreground (Figure 20). The illusion of space and depth is extended in the view through the central arch of the structure, where we see a sequence of archways flanked by engaged columns of ever-diminishing size. In some ways, this is reminiscent of the technique used by Borromoni at the Palazzo Spada. Pozzo notes that this image is a fine example through which to learn how to render architecture in perspective. The structure is shown in part plan, section and in perspectival elevation. Pozzo shows how the various converging lines that create the illusion of space relate to the two-dimensional plan and section. In the text Pozzo explains that the line horizontal and diagonal lines of the ground plan converge on the line EG whilst the line EGLH that runs through the spine of the section, and the ground plan is the cross section of all the lines of perspective in the drawing. Indeed, it was such a valuable resource that it ran to many editions right up to the late nineteenth century and its influence in Europe and beyond was assured through its almost instant translation into French, German, English and Chinese through Pozzo's Jesuit missionary connections.

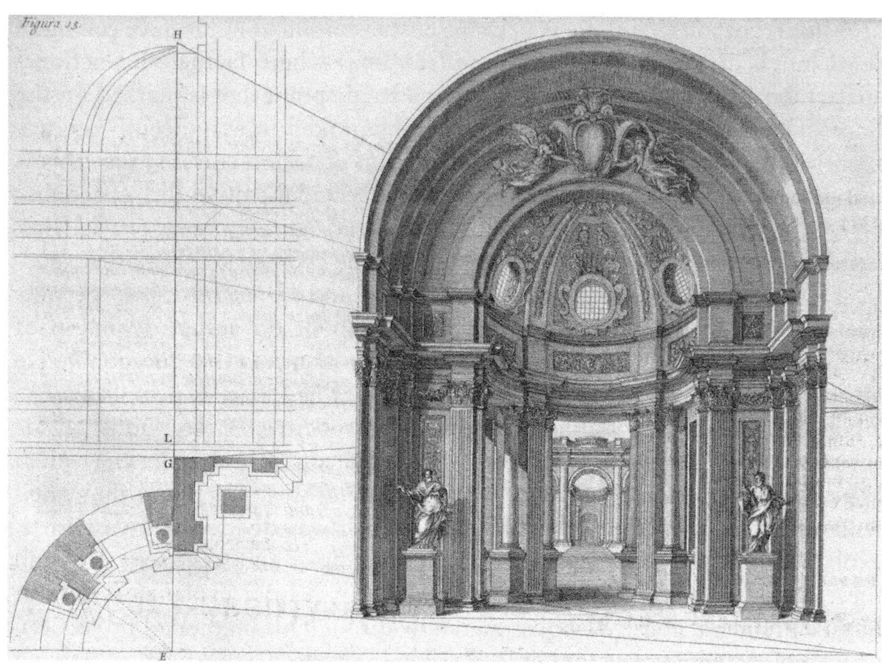

20 Andrea Pozzo, 'Tribuna d'Architettura ornata', in *Perspectiva pictorum et architectorum*, vol. 2, figure 15, 1698

The fusion of geometry and architecture as a means of blurring real and fictitious space is germane to the theory and practice of Borromini and Pozzo. The thinking in perspective and the imaginative leaps exemplified in their work have resonance with the practices and purposes of architectural drawing as a method of representation as well as a process of design in our period, and, more broadly, with the nature of perception.

Notes

1 *Roger Bacon and the Origins of* Perspectiva *in the Middle Ages: A Critical Edition and English Translation*, with Introduction and Notes by David C. Lindberg (Oxford: Oxford University Press, 1996). There were other treatises on optics produced in the Middle Ages that remained influential during the Renaissance, for instance, John Pecham, *Perspectiva communis*, *c.*1270 CE, and Blasius of Parma's *Quaestiones perspectivae*, *c.*1390 CE, which was a popular adaptation of the works of both Bacon and Pecham.

2 W. J. T. Mitchell, 'Showing Seeing: A Critique of Visual Culture', *Journal of Visual Culture*, 1:2 (2002), pp. 165–81.

3 Roger de Piles, 'De l'utilité des Estampes, et de leur usage', in *Abrégé de la vie des peintres, avec des réflexions sur leurs ouvrages* (Paris, 1699), translated as 'Of the

Usefulness and Use of Prints', in *The Art of Painting, with the Lives and Characters … of the Most Eminent Painters* (London: Printed for T. Payne, 1754).

4 Ibid., pp. 56, 58.

5 John Locke, *An Essay Concerning Human Understanding* (London, 1706). Abridged and edited by J. W. Yolton (London and Melbourne: Dent, 1976), book 2, chapter 2.

6 Ibid., p. 45.

7 George Berkeley, *An Essay Towards a New Theory of Vision* (Dublin: Printed by Aaron Rhames, for Jeremy Pepyat, 1709). I am using the original section numbers. The essay was reprinted in Desmond M. Clarke (ed.), George Berkeley, *Philosophical Writings* (Cambridge: Cambridge University Press, 2008), pp. 1–66. On this work see, for instance, Philip D. Cummins, 'On the Status of Visuals in Berkeley's *New Theory of Vision*', in Ernest Sosa (ed.), *Essays on the Philosophy of George Berkeley* (Dordrecht: D. Reidel Publishing Co., 1987), pp. 165–94; Rick Grush, 'Berkeley and the Spatiality of Vision', *Journal of the History of Philosophy*, 45:3 (2007), pp. 413–42.

8 Berkeley, *An Essay Towards a New Theory of Vision*, section 56.

9 Ibid., section 11.

10 Ibid., section 16.

11 For a history of the various editions see Bernard Adams, *London Illustrated 1604–1850: A Survey and Index of Topographical Books and Their Plates* (London: Library Association, 1983), p. 37.

12 See for instance André Moreau, 'Merleau-Ponty et Berkeley', *Dialogue*, 5:3 (1966), pp. 418–24.

13 See Maurice Merleau-Ponty, *Phenomenology of Perception* (London: Routledge & Kegan Paul, 1978), Part I, chapters 1–3.

14 Goodman, *Languages of Art*.

15 Derrida, *Memoirs of the Blind*.

16 Berkeley, *Dialogue*, section 110; and see Chapter 2, Part II.

17 Ibid., section 24.

18 On this point see Panofsky, *Perspective as Symbolic Form*.

19 Ernst Cassirer, *Philosophy of Symbolic Forms, Volume 2: Mythical Thought*, trans. Ralph Manheim (New Haven: Yale University Press, 1955), pp. 83–4.

20 For a very full discussion of this see Panofsky, *Perspective as Symbolic Form*, p. 35 and esp. footnote 12, pp. 87–92.

21 Ibid., p. 43.

22 Vitruvius, *The Ten Books on Architecture*.

23 Robin Evans, *The Projective Cast*, pbk 2000 p. xxi.

24 Robin Evans, 'The Developed Surface: An Enquiry into the Brief Life of an Eighteenth-Century Drawing Technique', in Robin Evans (ed.), *Translations from Drawing to Building*, (Cambridge, Massachusetts, MIT Press, 1997), p. 199.

25 Ibid.

26 Merleau-Ponty, *Phenomenology of Perception*.

27 An augmented edition of the *Opus architectonicum* containing the original drawings and Borromini's first publications and publishing plans of his later years was edited by Joseph Connors. The introduction to this volume traces the history of the

engravings illustrating the different works by Borromini. Francesco Borromini, *Opus architectonicum*, ed. Joseph Connors, 2nd edn (Milan: Il Polifilo, Trattati di architectura, 1998).

28 For a discussion of geometry and perspective in the seventeenth century see Olaf Recktenwald, 'Vredeman de Vries: Geometry and Freedom', *North Street Review*, 17 (2014), pp. 75–84. The links between the Renaissance and our period are discussed in Alberto Pérez-Goméz and Louise Pelletier, 'Architectural Representation Beyond Perspectivism', *Perspecta*, 27 (1991), pp. 21–39 and more broadly in Alberto Pérez-Goméz and Louise Pelletier, *Architectural Representation and the Perspective Hinge* (Cambridge, Massachusetts: MIT Press, 2000).

29 Andrea Pozzo, *Perspectiva pictorum et architectorum, with engravings by Vincenzo Mariotti* (Rome: Joannis Jacobi Komarek, 1693). See also, Rodney Palmer, '"All is very plain, upon inspection of the figure": The Visual Method of Andrea Pozzo's *Perspectiva pictorum et architectorum*', in Rodney Palmer and Thomas Frangenberg (eds), *The Rise of the Image: Essays on the History of the Illustrated Art Book* (Abingdon: Routledge, 2003), pp. 157–213.

Part III: Parallel perspectives

The theory and practice of perspective in our period stood distinct from Renaissance and classical predecessors. Perhaps in response to the increased interest in the philosophical theories of vision and perception, and in mathematical concepts of the rendering of space, artistic thinking became at once more detailed about the 'how to' and more abstract as regards the 'why'? These trains of thought were common across Europe and published works were frequently translated, which points to a common currency of ideas similar to that enabled through the exchange of prints and drawings of the architecture of antiquity. My focus here is on examples in English that are indexical of shared interests and concerns that crossed borders and linguistic divides.

My starting point is Dr Brook Taylor who first published *Linear Perspective or, a New Method of Representing Justly All Manner of Objects* in 1715.[1] In response to criticism a revised, expanded version came only four years later entitled *New Principles of Linear Perspective*.[2] The latter text became a benchmark for the study of perspective. It was referred to as the Taylorian method, and was especially popular in the latter half of the century. Taylor's influence spread beyond the Anglophone world during this period when a French translation appeared in 1755, followed by two Italian versions in 1757 and 1782. Little is known of Taylor's life, but it does appear that he was a landscape painter and a mathematician and it may well be that this combination of talents fuelled his interest in perspective. Indeed, as Taylor remarks in his *New Principles*:

> Considering how few, and how simple the Principles are, upon which the whole Art of PERSPECTIVE depends, and withal how useful, nay how absolutely necessary this Art is to all sorts of Designing, I have often wonder'd, that is has still been left in so low a degree of Perfection, as it is found to be, in the Books that have been hitherto wrote upon it.[3]

The key aspect of Taylor's approach is that the principles of geometry must be understood in order to understand perspective. This is not necessarily a new idea in itself as perspective had been discussed as part of geometry in earlier texts on the subject including texts with which we are already familiar such as Alberti's *De pictura* (1435). More recently, an English translation of the expanded second edition of Jean Dubreuil's *La perspective pratique* of 1671 (first published 1651) appeared in 1672 which included 150 illustrations; this version ran to several editions.[4] We must also remember that an English edition of Leonardo da Vinci's writings on perspective was published in 1721 together with English translations of more contemporary works including Willem Jacob 's Gravesande's *Essai de perspective* in 1724. Taylor is important, as he asserts that knowledge of perspective is an essential part of a painter's training.

> I would first have him learn the most common Effections of Practical Geometry, and the first Elements of Plain Geometry, and common Arithmetic. When he is sufficiently perfect in these, I would have him learn *Perspective* [...] Nothing ought to be more familiar to the Student than Perspective, for it is the only thing that can make the Judgment correct, and will help the Fancy to invent with ten times the case that it could do without it.[5]

Taylor's reference to the imagination is important here and I will return to this later.

Of equal significance for our enquiry is Taylor's linking of incorrect perspectival representation as not representing the object but something else – in other words it is an inaccurate description. Conversely, he asserts that the viewer should not be able to distinguish between the original object and its representation. In this way the viewer's visual experience of both object and image should be identical.[6] Moreover, Taylor makes an analogy between visual and verbal representations:

> A Figure in a Picture, which is not drawn according to the Rules of *Perspective*, does not represent what is intended, but something else. So that is seems to me, that a Picture which is faulty in this particular, is a blameable, or more so, than any Composition in Writing, which is faulty in point of Orthography, or Grammar.[7]

Despite the slight unintended irony in his reference to orthography in the period before the publication of Dr Johnson's *A Dictionary of the English Language* in 1755, the link between verbal and visual descriptions is of note. This is especially so as alongside being a set of conventions for writing a language, including norms of spelling and punctuation, orthography is also a method of projection in which an object is depicted using parallel lines to project its outline on to a plane.

Taylor's texts are then very much a part of this growing interest in perspective across Europe. That said, his influence was seen mostly after his death in 1731 as his work became a benchmark or starting point for subsequent studies. For instance, John Hamilton's *Stereography, or, a Compleat Body of Perspective*, 1738, largely follows Taylor and the author acknowledges this in his complimentary remark:

> Dr. Brook Taylor [whose] two small Treatises and this Subject published some Years since, in which that learned Gentleman has, in a few Pages, made more Advances towards perfecting the Science than all the Writers who went before him.[8]

Hamilton's work leans more towards science than art and he used Taylor as a means of furthering knowledge on the nature of projections encompassing the work of continental mathematicians, including Philippe de la Hire on conic sections.

Perhaps more pertinent for this enquiry are the numerous texts that appeared which were aimed at practitioners in the latter part of the eighteenth century. Here again, Taylor was important, as following his lead these works aimed to bridge the gap between theory and practice. Manuals or handbooks on perspective for artists were devoid of theory and had largely concentrated on explaining how to construct the representation of space. If artists wished to know more or explore further the optical, mathematical and philosophical underpinning of perspectival drawing they had to consult a broad range of literature. Taylor had made the first steps in combining doing with understanding and therefore thinking about the nature of representation, description and perception. And, as if to prove the saying 'great minds think alike', two English artists John Joshua Kirby and Joseph Highmore were working simultaneously but independently on treatises that linked theory and practice and drew on the work of Taylor. In 1754, in a pamphlet 'A Critical Examination …', Highmore announced he had been working on his book for some time.[9] However, in the same year, Kirby published his *Dr. Brook Taylor's Method of Perspective Made Easy, both in Theory and Practice*. This work proved very popular and was reprinted at least three times – the first edition being dedicated to the artist William Hogarth who provided a frontispiece. Kirby followed this successful publication in 1761 with *The Perspective of Architecture Deduced from the Principles of Dr. Brook Taylor*. Highmore's volume *The Practice of Perspective, On the Principles of Dr. Brook Taylor* finally appeared in 1763. In the first part of his volume, Highmore briefly covers the established methods of drawing in perspective, which he considers will inevitably lead to errors, even in the work of well-known theorists such as Andrea Pozzo. Highmore champions Taylor's method in the second part of his survey, arguing that it is simpler to use and the results more intelligible. In his rendering of an octahedron, a Platonic solid that duals with a cube, Highmore demonstrates orthographic and ichnographic (i.e. a ground plan) methods of describing and representing space (Figure 21). And, as we have seen, these modes of visual ekphrasis form a kind of visual syntax.[10] Taylor's theory of perspective enjoyed national and international currency and renown amongst artists, theorists and scientists, and, as we have seen, in the latter half of the century several translated versions appeared in Italian and French. The significance of Taylor's thinking is perhaps summed up by S. N. Michel in his *Traité de perspective linéaire* (1771) where he is credited with the invention of linear perspective.[11] A more unexpected recognition of Taylor's treatise can be found in the work of the polymath Joseph Priestley who taught himself perspective using Taylor in order to illustrate his treatises on the natural sciences including electricity and oxygen. In Priestley's *A Familiar Introduction to the Theory and Practice of Perspective* (1770) he remarks:

> As in all the other branches of mathematical knowledge the progress of this art [perspective] has been slow, but sure; and the English writers (particularly Dr. Brooke Taylor) seem to have carried it to a degree of perfection we can hardly conceive it possible to be exceeded.[12]

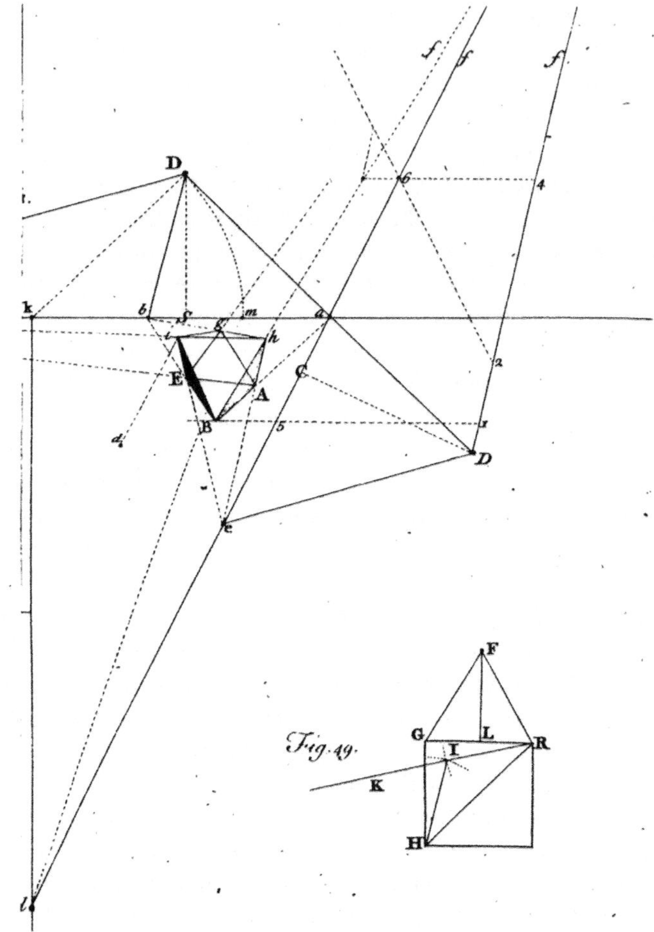

21 Joseph Highmore, *The Practice of Perspective, On the Principles of Dr. Brook Taylor…*, plate XXIII, 1763

The interest in Renaissance treatises on perspective did not abate despite the growing number of contemporary publications, which were frequently translated to ensure their currency across Europe. In 1756 Isaac Ware published his translation of Lorenzo Sirigatti's *La practica di prospettiva* (1596), a text which probably drew on Vignola's *Le due regole della prospettiva pratica* (1582), and is best known for its clear demonstration of an intersection method for geometrical bodies.[13] This challenge to the supremacy of Taylor prompted Kirby to publish a pamphlet, *Dr. Brook Taylor's Method of Perspective, Compared with the Examples Lately Publish'd on This Subject as Sirigatti's by Issac Ware, Esq.* (1757). Whatever the motives behind Ware and Kirby's publications, they, together

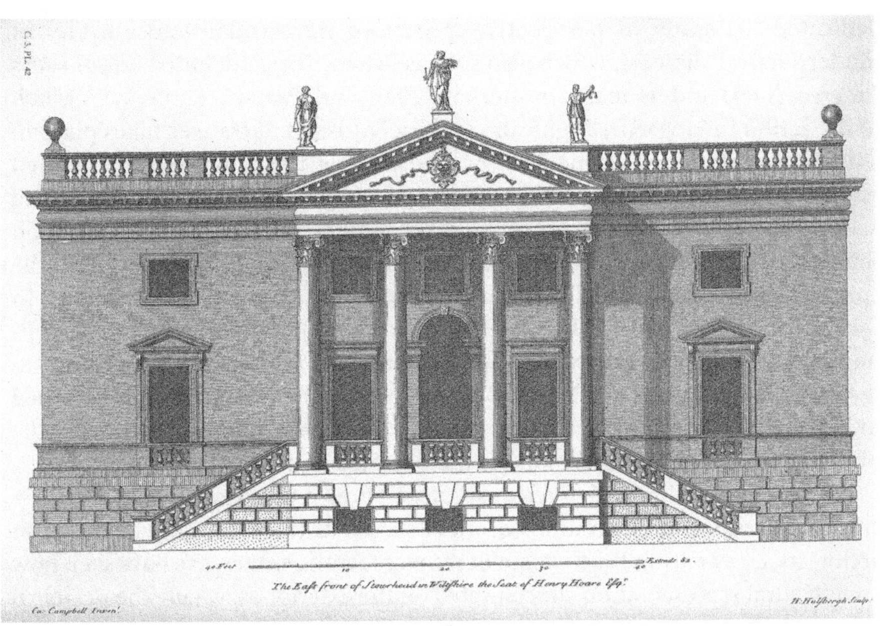

Colen Campbell, 'The East Front of Stourhead in Wiltshire, seat of Henry Hoare Esqr', *Vitruvius Britannicus*, vol. 3, plate 42, 1725 22

with the array of similar volumes, are indicative of the active interest in vision and space in our period.[14]

The concerns and focus of the treatises, whether from the sixteenth, seventeenth or eighteenth century, remained largely the same but the philosophical debates about space gave them a new significance. And there is no doubt that even though he may have drawn on the work of earlier writers, Taylor is key in his abstract theories about linear perspective and vanishing points and his guidance for their use in the rendition of space.[15] But first, I would like to make a conjecture about why the description of space was becoming so important at this time.

Here we are about to re-encounter a number of familiar names. Earlier in this book I outlined the rise of the epistolary novel as a way of introducing and exploring the notion of the conscious and subconscious mind. Samuel Richardson's *Pamela; or, Virtue Rewarded* (1740) and his later novel *Clarissa* (1747–48) are excellent examples of this new literary genre. Highmore illustrated *Pamela* in 12 paintings made between 1741 and 1743, and painted one scene from *Clarissa* between 1745 and 1747. On 16 February 1744 he advertised that ten of the pictures from *Pamela* were ready to be viewed at his studio, the other two became available in May the same year, and that he was taking subscriptions for a set of twelve engravings after the novel.[16] Similarly, William Hogarth, whose *Analysis of Beauty* we have already encountered and to whom Kirby dedicated his study of perspective, produced numerous picture cycles of modern moral subjects, which also sold as prints. These included *The Harlot's Progress* (1731) and its male counterpart *The Rake's Progress* (1733–35).[17] Much of the action in Hogarth, Highmore and Richardson's narratives takes place in a domestic interior; it is enclosed by the space of the room and the painted scenes of it reflect this. Both these forms of verbal and visual descriptions of action and thought were new, and required a different kind of engagement on the part of the reader or viewer. Not least here is that, as already noted, the epistolary novel was a pre-Freudian evocation of the human subconscious. In this way the perception of the spaces of the room ran in parallel to the perception of the thoughts of the various characters. And perhaps here we return to the concerns explored by George Berkeley, where the imagination is required to perceive the physical space that is being represented and by extension the physio-psychological dimensions of the narrated actions.

The preoccupation with interior space and how it was described and experienced in novels and illustrations of them stands distinct from the concerns of architects, especially in the first half of the eighteenth century. We have seen how architectural representation concentrated on the exterior especially the principal elevation of a building that was generally shown in orthogonal perspective with its three-dimensionality also being expressed ichnographically through the use of ground plans. This is evident for instance in the work of Palladio and early eighteenth-century derivatives of the format he established in his *Four Books* such as Colen Campbell's *Vitruvius Britannicus*, where there are very few plates showing interiors. The customary way of representing both the exterior and interior of a building was to compress it into two dimensions and show it in orthogonal section, with the use of shading to give some impression of spatial recession on what is otherwise a flat surface with only one wall of a three-dimensional space in view (Figure 22). There was little attention to interior detail, especially when compared to the articulation of the principal facade. As we have noted, there was a significant growth in the interest in the pictorial representation of the interior in the middle years of the eighteenth century as witnessed in the work of Hogarth and Highmore. And I have argued that this is connected to the rise in the interest in the perspectival representation of space and of our physio-psychological experience of it. The many treatises on perspective that circulated across Europe were both artists' handbooks and theoretical texts on mathematical geometry that met the new needs of a broad spectrum of readers.

I would like to conclude with a juxtaposition of two distinctive descriptions of space. One was intended to speak to an audience of artists and academicians, the other to the landed elite. Perhaps one of the most innovative interpretations of Brook Taylor's work is Thomas Malton's *A Compleat Treatise on Perspective, in Theory and Practice; on the True Principles of Dr. Brook Taylor* (1775). Malton was neither a mathematician nor an architect, but instead kept an upholsterer's shop on the Strand in London. How he made the leap from this to exhibiting architectural drawings at the Incorporated Society of Artists in 1766 and 1768 and to submitting work to the Royal Academy in 1772 remains a mystery.[18] Perhaps as a result of these endeavours Malton developed expertise in geometry resulting in the publication of *The Royal Road to Geometry; or an easy and familiar Introduction to the Mathematics* in 1774. This was a schoolbook intended as an improvement on Euclid's *Elements*, usually seen as the standard introduction to mathematics, and especially geometry. Indeed, the title was inspired by the anecdote about Ptolemy I, King of Egypt when asking Euclid if there really existed no simpler way for learning geometry than to read all of his Elements, to which the mathematician's response was 'There is no royal road to geometry!' An expanded edition appeared in 1793 and *The Monthly Review or Literary Journal*, whilst remarking that it is much improved, note that although Malton criticises the prolix nature of other authors, it is not advice he heeds himself.[19]

Quite how this work on mathematics and geometry morphed into the highly original *A Compleat Treatise on Perspective, in Theory and Practice; on the Principles of Dr. Brook Taylor* that appeared in 1775 is not clear.[20] Malton's debt to Taylor is recognised on the first page of the Preface:

> the Principles, on which he has founded his System are the most simple and perfect that can possibly be conceived.[21]

There is no doubt that Malton's work provides one of the most thorough studies of perspective in our period that addresses the interests of both artists and architects, as well as mathematicians. It was the first substantial book on perspective published after the founding of the Royal Academy in December 1768. Malton personally dedicated a copy to the President and Members of the Academy, and this is not without significance, as Article XII of the Instrument of Foundation of the Academy specifically provides for the teaching of perspective.[22] In recognition of this, many of the Academicians supported Malton's endeavour by subscribing. Indeed, there is a section in the list of Subscribers dedicated to 'Royal Academicians and other Artists, &c.'. Arguably, *The Compleat Treatise* became the standard English work on linear perspective.[23]

My interest here is not so much in the comprehensive coverage of perspective provided by Malton but more in his innovative techniques of describing space through tactile, bodily experience. *The Compleat Treatise* is the earliest known commercially produced pop-up book (Figure 23). It contains three-dimensional paper mechanisms some of which are activated by pulling a string to form geometric shapes intended to assist the reader, or indeed viewer, in understanding the concept of perspective. As a book, *The Compleat Treatise* must lie flat on a table for the paper contrivances to operate. The reader/viewer has to touch the string to operate the device that creates a representation of space and must bend to the level of the surface on which the book rests to

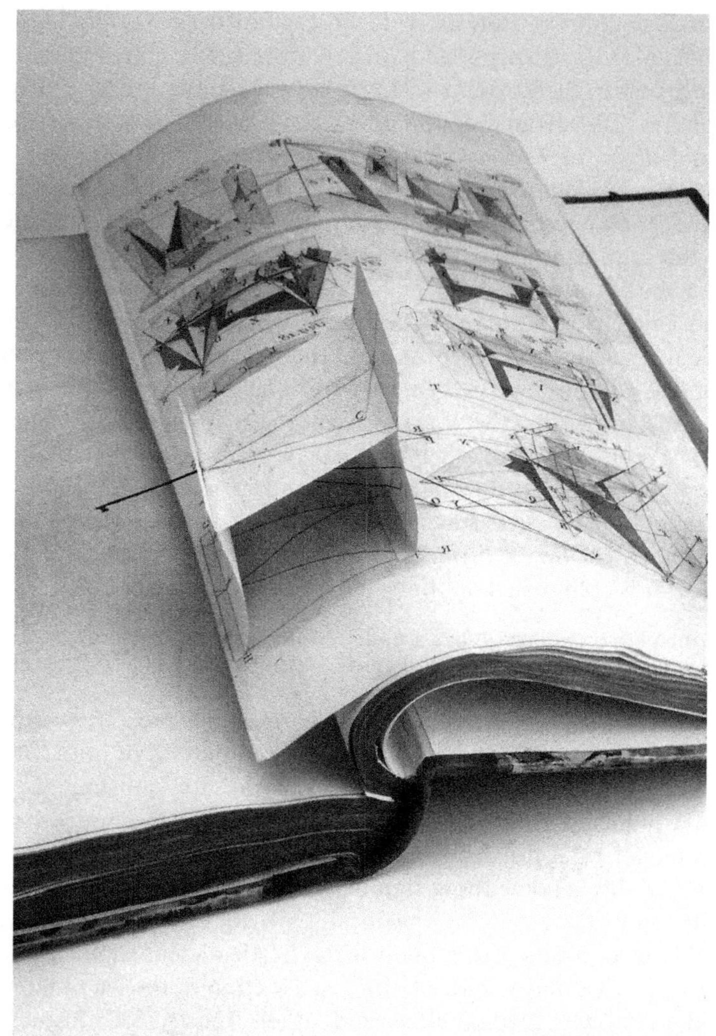

23 Thomas Malton the Elder, pop-up from *A Compleat Treatise on Perspective, in Theory and Practice; on the Principles of Dr. Brook Taylor…*, 1775

achieve the correct viewpoint to see this space. It is a kind of Berkeleian moment that addresses questions of viewpoint and perception, and this helps us to understand the processes of subjugation as well as the way in which images of architecture acted as descriptions. *The Compleat Treatise* gives us three-dimensional spaces that only have a single viewpoint. And paradoxically these pop-up spaces serve to show how three dimensions can be represented in only two. The relationship between these descriptions and the viewer/reader is also of relevance. We must remember that ambiguity is a tool used by language to create depth of field – the multifocal aspects of a sign lend depth and significance with a multiple set of contexts. I wonder if in Malton we find the intersection between the different kinds of description of space that have been explored in this enquiry. Specifically here I am thinking of the conjuncture of the mathematical nature of the geometry of linear perspective and the psycho-physiological experience of the spaces of the page. Moreover, we see how the haptic bodily experience of space informs the making of visual ekphrases.

My second example offers a kind of antithesis to Malton's three-dimensional artifice. In the latter part of the century there was a change in the way architects rendered interior spaces, but this was arguably for different purposes and with markedly different affect from Malton. Geometry is, however, still germane to this form of description. Robin Evans has named this the '*developed surface interior*';[24] by which he refers to the process in geometry where a three-dimension object is folded out so that all its surfaces can be shown laid out flat adjacent to each other on a single sheet of paper. Evans argues that this technique became a way of turning architecture inside out so that interior elevations were privileged over external facades. This conception of space was not necessarily new – it had been used to represent open spaces that were defined by borders such as town squares or formal gardens, but here the technique was turned on the enclosed spaces of the architectural interior. This means of communicating designs for interiors to clients was adopted by Robert and James Adam as part of their lucrative business of providing opulent designs for the most wealthy of the elite. Indeed, Horace Walpole remarked, for instance, that at Syon House, one of Adam's grandest commissions where he worked from 1762–68, 'Adam has displayed great taste and the Earl matches it with magnificence.'[25] We see the design route to this magnificence in the plan and laid out wall elevations in pen and wash for the entrance hall at Syon House (Figure 24), where a minimal ground plan was surrounded by the four walls that are folded out around it. This was presented to the client, the Earl of Northumberland, in 1761 and accepted and executed with some minor alterations. Here the space of the entrance hall is completely flattened so denying any sense of spatial volume – but the decorative scheme is made very clear. It was not unusual for commissions such as these to be an addition to an existing building or a re-design of a suite of rooms. But this form of interior rendering was common across the Adam's practice. Evans has argued that it signalled the growing importance of the individuality of rooms rather than their place in an hierarchical layout that has been the hallmark of established modes of spatial planning.[26] And it offered a complete articulation of a discrete space.

My concerns here are rather different. Many of the Adam brothers' clientele were Grand Tourists and antiquarians who may well have poured over the kinds of images of antiquity drawn in perspective we have encountered in this book. But when it came to commissioning a personal space they needed a different route into

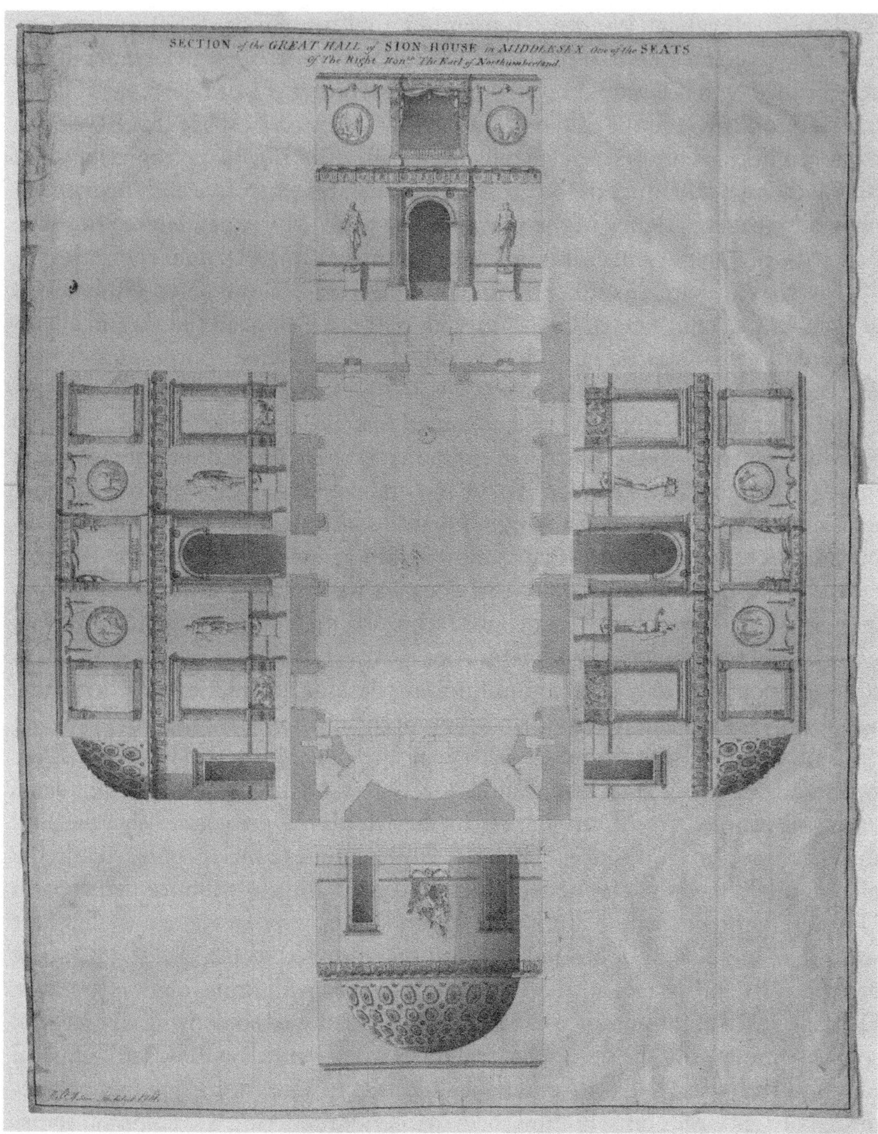

24 Robert Adam, 'Plan and wall elevations for the entrance hall at Syon House', pen and wash, 1761. SM Adam vol. 39/3

understanding how it would be experienced. In the design for Syon House there is a disruption between the space of the ground plan and each of the four walls. Unlike Highmore's octahedron, the ichnographic and the orthographic representations remain separate and we have no sense of spatial volume. We almost need Malton's strings to pull the two-dimensional flat surfaces into a three-dimensional space.

I wonder if this is a kind of 'seeing in' or 'twofoldness' where the physicality of the object – a drawing, and its content – a three-dimensional space, are seen simultaneously.[27] The difference here is that what is described and the means of its description are discrete. In this way the space of the page has its own phenomenology. We perceive the surface, and in this surface we see something else. As a result, the folded-out geometry of the developed surface denies the Euclidean geometry of perspectival space and becomes, then, a very different mode of ekphrasis.

Notes

1 On this point see, for instance, P. S. Jones, 'Brook Taylor and the Mathematical Theory of Linear Perspective', *The American Mathematical Monthly*, 58:9 (1951), pp. 597–606 and Kirsti Andersen, *The Geometry of an Art: The History of the Mathematical Theory of Perspective from Alberti to Monge* (New York: Springer, 2007).

2 Brook Taylor, *Linear Perspective or, a New Method of Representing Justly All Manner of Objects as They Appear to the Eye in All Situations* (London: Printed for R. Knaplock, 1715) and *New Principles of Linear Perspective* (London: Printed for R. Knaplock, 1719). Both editions were printed for R. Knaplock at the Bishop's Head in St Paul's Churchyard. See also Kirsti Andersen, *Brook Taylor's Work on Linear Perspective* (New York: Springer, 1992). This is a facsimile edition of both of Taylor's works on perspective accompanied by an introductory essay.

3 Taylor, *Linear Perspective*, p. iii.

4 Jean Dubreuil, *La perspective* pratique. Seconde édition … augmentée (Paris: A. Dezallier, 1671) translated as *Perspective practical. Or, a plain and easie method of true and lively representing all things to the eye at a distance, by the exact rules of art … Very useful and necessary for all Painters … By a Religious Person of the Society of Jesus, a Parisien* [J. Dubreuil]. *Faithfully translated out of French, and illustrated with 150 copper cuts. Set forth in English by R. Pricke for the Lovers of Art* (London: Printed by H. Lloyd, and sold by Robert Pricke…, 1672).

5 Taylor, *Linear Perspective*, pp. xii–xiii.

6 Ibid., p. 1.

7 Ibid., p. ix.

8 John Hamilton, *Stereography, or, a Compleat Body of Perspective* (London: Printed for the author by W. Bowyer, 1738), p.a. 4.

9 Joseph Highmore, *A Critical Examination of those two paintings on the cieling* [*sic*] *of the banqueting-house at Whitehall: in which architecture is introduced, so far as relates to the perspective …* (London: J. Nourse, 1754).

10 Joseph Highmore, *The Practice of Perspective on the Principles of Dr. Brook Taylor* (London: Printed for A. Millar and J. Nourse, 1763), pp. 56–60.

11 S. N. Michel's *Traité de perspective linéaire: avec une planche en taille-douce* (Paris: Lottin, 1771), p. 6.

12 Joseph Priestley, *A Familiar Introduction to the Theory and Practice of Perspective* (London: Printed for J. Johnson and J. Payne, 1770), pp. v–vi.

13 Issac Ware, *The Practice of Perspective, from the original Italian of Lorenzo Sirigatti. With the figures engraved by Isaac Ware, Esq* (London: Printed for the Author, and sold by T. Osborne, and J. Shipton, in Gray's-Inn; J. Hodges, near London-Bridge;

L. Davis, in Fleet-Street; J. Ward, in Cornhill; and R. Baldwin, in Paternoster-Row., 1756). This is discussed in, for instance, Harris and Savage, *British Architectural Books and Writers*, p. 828.

14 Some publications attempted to amalgamate three centuries of perspectival thinking. For instance, James Malton's *Young Painter's Maulstick; being a practical treatise on perspective* (London: V. Griffiths, 1800) is an attempt to combine the perspectival methods of Sirigatti and Vignola with those of Taylor.

15 On this point see for instance Jones, 'Brook Taylor' and Andersen, *Brook Taylor's Work on Linear Perpective.*

16 On this point see Thomas Keymer and Peter Sabor, *'Pamela' in the Marketplace: Literary Controversy and Print Culture in Eighteenth-Century Britain and Ireland* (Cambridge: Cambridge University Press, 2005), p. 222.

17 There is a broad literature on William Hogarth's picture cycles, see for instance Paulson, *Hogarth's Graphic Works* and *Hogarth*, 3 vols.

18 Information from *Dictionary of National Biography* (London: Smith, Elder & Co., 1885–1900).

19 *The Monthly Review or Literary Journal*, (second series) vol. 14 (1794), pp. 226–7 which also refers to its review of the Malton's original publication in (first series) vol. lii (1775), p. 359.

20 A second edition was published in 1778 after a fire had destroyed the stock of the first edition and was reissued in 1779 with minor editorial adjustments.

21 Thomas Malton, *A Compleat Treatise on Perspective in Theory and Practice, on the Principles of Dr. Brook Taylor* (London: Printed for the Author by Cox and Bigg, and sold by Messrs. Robson, Dodsley, Becket, Taylor, and Richardson & Urquhart, 1775), p. i.

22 By 1802 the Academy's library contained sixteen books on perspective, including editions of the classic treatises by Vignola, Bosse, Niceron, Pozzo and Sirigatti, together with works by more recent writers on the subject such as Cowley, Fournier, Hamilton, Kirby, and Thomas Malton the Elder's son, James Malton.

23 See Nicholas Savage *et al.*, *Early Printed Books 1478–1840*, 3 vols (London: RIBA, 1999), III, pp. 1066–7. Also, Martin Kemp discusses Malton in his book *The Science of Art: Optical Themes in Western Art from Brunelleschi to Seurat* (New Haven and London: Yale University Press, 1990), pp. 154–6.

24 Evans, *Translations from Drawing*, p. 202.

25 As quoted in Arthur T. Bolton, *The Architecture of Robert and James Adam (1758–1794)*, 2 vols (London: *Country Life*, 1922; reprinted 1984), p. 356. Bolton's text gives an historical outline of the role of drawing in the Adam brothers' practice.

26 Evans, *The Developed Surface*, p. 209. This hierarchical system of planning interior layouts is discussed by Mark Girouard in *Life in the English Country House: A Social and Architectural History* (New Haven and London: Yale University Press, 1978), chapter 5, pp. 119–62 esp.

27 On this point see Richard Wollheim, *Art and its Objects*, 2nd edn (Cambridge: Cambridge University Press, 1980) and *Painting as an Art* (London: Thames & Hudson, 1987).

Part IV: Fissures

If I have one residual concern, it is that in concentrating on graphic descriptions of architecture, I have widened the perceived gaps between architectural and artistic practice, not least as regards the interest in the representation of space. This gap is a preoccupation of twentieth-century historians, theorists and artists. We see this clearly in Hubert Damisch's remark:

> I will take a single example, one that is now rather commonplace: the idea that perspective has become archaic, that its time has passed (painters' perspective, not that of architects and geometers, which is another story entirely), that the life cycle of classic representation has run its course. This is not a new idea. But it is significant that those artists and critics who were among the first to propose it based their argument on the cubist experiment and its immediate antecedents. I emphasize again that one of the basic tenets of the prevailing artistic discourse, and a commonplace of criticism, holds that the lesson of Cezanne (that of Seurat usually being passed over in silence) signalled the end of so-called scientific perspective and at the same time of an age, many would say the age par excellence, of representation.[1]

Albeit perhaps unintentionally, Damisch's perceived difference between the painter's perspective and that of architects and geometers identifies a fissure between the interests of histories of painting and architecture that reach beyond twentieth-century concerns. The archive of this enquiry points to a rather different historical interpretation.

We have already noted the rise of academies of art and the hierarchies they imposed on both the subject matter and mediums of art.[2] Here, I would like to concentrate on the instance of the Royal Academy, founded in London in 1768 by Sir Joshua Reynolds. Alongside the President, of whom Reynolds was the first, several professorships were established, the post holders being drawn from the founding membership. The inaugural professorships included painting (Edward Penny, 1768–82), architecture (Thomas Sandby, 1768–98) and perspective (Samuel Wale, 1768–86). My interest here is in the Professorship of Perspective. The post holder was expected to 'read annually six public lectures in the Royal Academy, in which the most useful propositions of geometry, together with the principles of linear and aerial perspective, shall be fully and clearly illustrated' to an audience comprising both colleagues and students of painting, sculpture and architecture.[3] For students, regular attendance to these and the other lectures was rewarded by eligibility for the gold 'Premium' medal. Wale's tenure was followed by that of Edward Edwards who, as an Associate member, had delivered a series of private lectures since Wale's death in 1786 under the title of 'Teacher of Perspective'. Edwards's appointment was not without controversy. At the General Assembly of 10 February 1790,

Reynolds had supported the election and thus appointment to the professorship of the Italian architect Giuseppe Bonomi. Sir William Chambers and William Tyler led the objections to the appointment of Bonomi as he was not even an Associate of the Academy – and a foreigner. Consequently, Reynolds resigned on 22 February, albeit he was reinstated some three weeks later.[4] My point in relating this episode is to demonstrate the, although perhaps obliquely, intertwined nature of artistic and architectural practices and the importance of perspective and, I would add, drawing to each. This relationship is perhaps underscored with the appointment of J. M. W. Turner as Professor of Perspective (1807–37), whom we might not at first associate with an interest in pictorial depth. Indeed, we would more readily think of Turner an artist principally concerned with colour and light – or to use Duchamp anachronistically: the retinal art that was only intended to please the eye, rather than service the mind.[5] Nevertheless, perhaps prompted by a lack of other candidates, Turner stepped forward to offer his services, driven by his hope to be

> useful to an institution to which I owe everything. For I cannot look back but with pride and pleasure to that time, the Halcyon perhaps of my days, when I received instruction within these walls; and listened, I hope I did, with a just sense and respect.[6]

And, although he freely admitted that he might not be ideally suited for the post, there is no doubt that he had a sound knowledge of the subject. In the 1780s Turner had been apprenticed to Thomas Malton the Elder from whom he learned the practical skills of drawing in perspective. Moreover, his employment as a draughtsman to architects including Thomas Hardwick and James Wyatt provided Turner with the powerful combination of the interrelationship of two-dimensional and three-dimensional thinking in relation to drawing as a predicate to artistic and architectural thinking and practice. There are many detailed studies of Turner's life and work, and my purpose here is not to add to this substantial body of knowledge.[7] It is rather to focus on the lectures he delivered, especially the drawings or diagrams that Turner produced to illustrate them and to question how they operate as visual ekphrases of architecture and its spaces.

As with the other professors, Turner was expected to deliver an annual lecture series for which he created about 170 diagrams to help illustrate the theories and procedures covering a broad range of subjects related to both linear and atmospheric perspective that he addressed in his lectures, as well as producing copious notes.[8] Around half of this material was prepared in advance of his lectures, which began in 1811. After which, until the late 1820s, Turner added new diagrams as he reworked and re-ordered the sequence of his lectures, annotating the texts with comments and additions. His illegible handwriting and frequent grammatical inaccuracies can make his notes difficult to follow.[9] Turner befriended John Soane, who had been appointed Professor of Architecture in 1806. The two professors prepared their lectures in consultation.[10] Indeed, their collaboration spilled over into architectural practice, as in 1813 Turner, guided by his friend Soane, designed and built a small villa, Sandycombe Lodge, near the Thames at Twickenham.

Turner's texts and illustrations for his lectures drew on a wide range of historic treatises and more common eighteenth-century sources, some of which we have encountered. These included, for instance, Pozzo's *Perspectiva pictorum et architectorum* (1693) and Dubreuil's *La perspective pratique* (1671) together with Kirby's *Dr. Brook Taylor's Method of Perspective Made Easy, both in Theory and Practice* (1765). Turner also turned to his mentor Thomas Malton the Elder's *A Compleat Treatise on Perspective, in Theory and Practice; on the True Principles of Dr. Brook Taylor* (1775); as we have seen, Malton had personally dedicated a copy to the President and Members of the Academy many of whom were subscribers. Alongside his own book collection, it is likely that Turner also consulted Soane's extensive library and collection of architectural prints, drawings and models. These included works we have already encountered such as studies by James 'Athenian' Stuart of the Temple of Jupiter Olympus in *The Antiquities of Athens* (1762).[11] In addition, Piranesi's drawings and posthumous engravings of the Temples at Paestum 1777–78, which may have been the basis for his lecture diagram of the Temple of Neptune with dramatically slanting shadows (Figure 25). This lecture diagram typifies Turner's opinion that perspective was the 'colouring of architecture', a telling phrase that points to it not only as a technical depiction but also as mode of describing our sensory experience of architectural space. Perspective can, then, combine two apparently discrete modes of ekphrasis, and in Turner we see that the result can be very powerful.

The majority of Turner's lecture diagrams are more simply constructed but no less evocative.[12] These were executed, usually freehand or sometimes using a straight edge, in bold strokes of red and black watercolour over pencil. As we have seen, Turner relied on several well-known authors for the technical processes of perspectival construction and he usually acknowledge these by identifying his source above or below diagram. In Lecture 2, for example, Turner aimed to equip his audience with definitions of the terminology required for a verbal description of perspective. This was followed by an exposition on the theory of rectilinear perspective based on Book II of Thomas Malton the Elder's *A Compleat Treatise on Perspective, in Theory and Practice; on the True Principles of Dr. Brook Taylor* (1775). Lecture Diagram 17, 'Principles of Rectilinear Perspective' (after Thomas Malton Senior) *c.*1810, is, as the title indicates, based on Malton's treatise (Figure 26).[13] And Turner refers to Malton in the lecture text itself when he states that his intention is 'to divest the partiality practitioners entertain for the horizontal line' and to turn their attention to

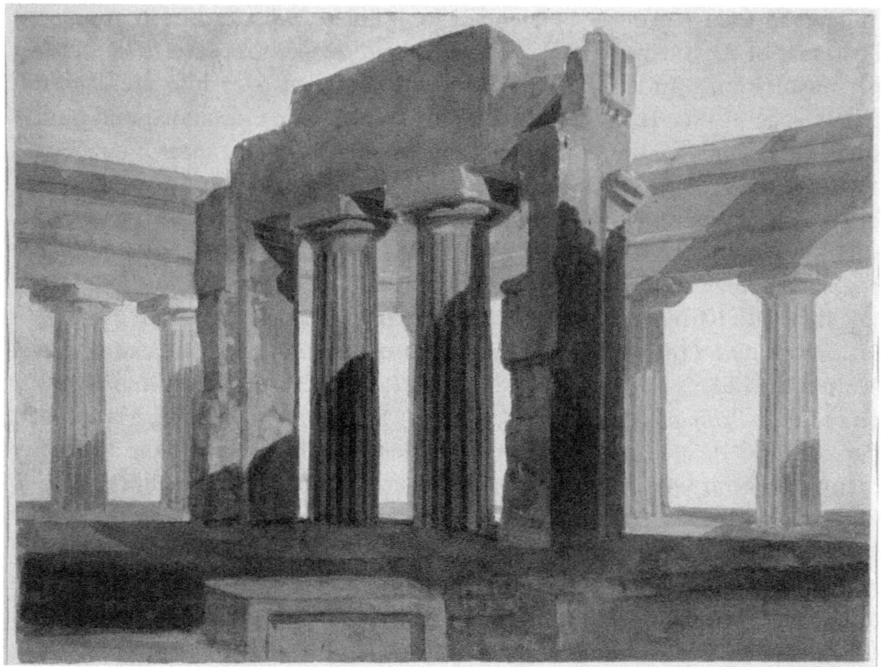

25 J. M. W. Turner, 'Lecture Diagram 52*: The Temple of Neptune at Paestum' (?after Giovanni Battista Piranesi), pencil and watercolour, *c.* 1810

vanishing lines. Although Turner acknowledges that the diagram 'may appear rather intricate', it is in reality 'analyzable'.[14] This diagram is complemented by Lecture Diagram 18, which also has Malton as its source.[15] This pair of diagrams was used by Turner to explain that despite the apparent off-putting complexities, 'the shortest way to perspective is through theory to practice, the loss of time (if any) will never be regretted'. We can see how the two techniques of representing space demonstrated in Lecture Diagrams 52* and 17 combine in Lecture Diagram 48, which shows the Pedestal of the Column of Antoninus Pius, *c.*1810 (Figure 27). Here the guiding lines for the correct perspectival construction of the image are visible in red and black watercolour and the illusion of volume is enhanced by the colouring of the pedestal itself and the use of shadow, as we have seen in the Temple of Neptune. We can see how Turner's diagrams are the inheritors of the modes of visual ekphrasis that I have outlined in this enquiry. As images they are both seductive and powerful, and, especially in the case of examples such as Lecture Diagram 17, display an atemporal quality that speaks to the preoccupations with the rendering of space we might expect to find in the work of the Cubists. Perhaps, then, Turner fulfils

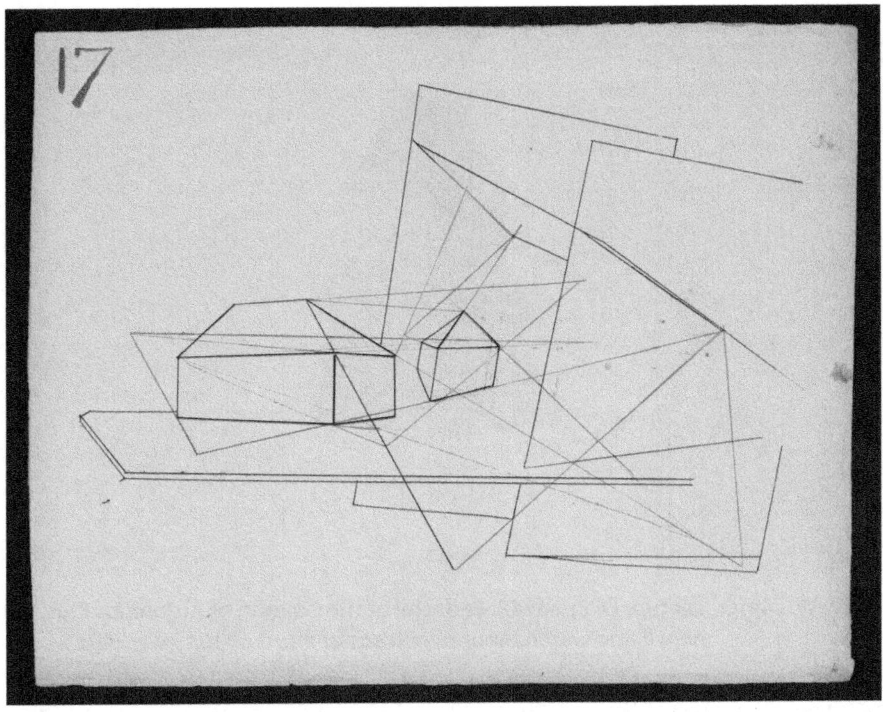

J. M. W. Turner, 'Lecture Diagram 17: Principles of Rectilinear Perspective' (after Thomas Malton Senior), pen and ink, *c.* 1810 26

Duchamp's need for retinal art, rather than negating it. But perhaps the most potent of these images is the *Column of Antoninus Pius*. Here we find a visual ekphrasis of the architecture of antiquity that is held in time and space through a vortex of perspectival lines.

It is important to remember that Turner's lecture diagrams had performative qualities, not only in the embodied movement of the artist as their means of production, but also in the manner in which they were viewed. Professorial lectures took place in the Great Room at Somerset House, which was home to the Academy between 1780 and 1836. The Great Room was better suited as a venue for the exhibiting of pictures, although some improvements to seating and lighting were made at the suggestion of Turner and Soane in 1809.[16] Turner delivered his lectures from a stage and his diagrams were carried on and off by assistants as he spoke. This offered a very different kind of experience from the turning of the pages of a book or the pulling of one of Malton's strings, which could be done at the speed of the viewer's body. Instead the drawings themselves were part of a performance where the viewers remained passively seated whilst the images passed in front of them at the speed that was not of their choosing.

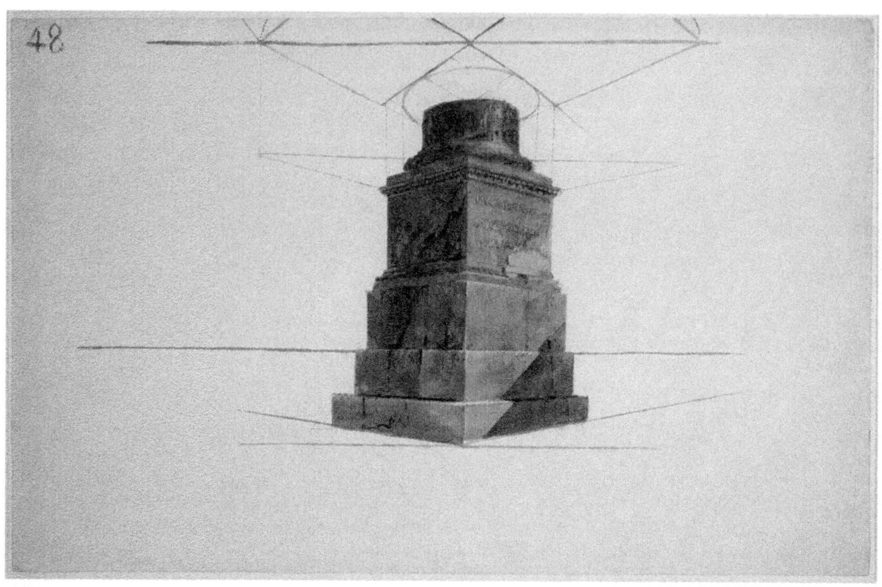

27 J. M. W. Turner, 'Lecture Diagram 48: Pedestal of the Column of Antoninus Pius', pencil and watercolour over transfer ink, *c.* 1810

The distance between viewer and drawing meant that the diagrams had to be large, typically 64–98 cm, in order to be visible. But there was no sense of texture or touch.

My focus in this enquiry has been on the resonance between text and image where the visual and tactile senses have been privileged. And we have already noted the dissonance between Turner's lecture notes and his diagrams. But I do, however, also wonder what the past sounded like, and Turner's lectures provide a rare excursion into the aurality of architectural discourse. Turner was a poor orator and an awkward, if not chaotic, public speaker, for which he received much criticism. We also have insights into Turner's own diction, which was condemned for its vulgarity. In this vivid account, published in *The New Monthly Magazine*, we can almost hear Turner as he stumbles to pronounce mathematics as 'mithematics' and spheroids as 'sphearides' or to say 'haiving' or 'towaards'.[17] A comment in the *Annals of the Fine Arts* is less harsh and perhaps typifies the reaction to Turner as he 'delivered his usual course to the students, distinguished for its usual inanity, want of connection, bad delivery and beautiful drawing.'[18] But it is the mismatch between the shambolic nature of Turner's words, whether written or spoken and the power of his drawings that interests me here. The notes for his lectures remain enigmatic through their incompleteness and untidiness and, as we have noted, still wait to be edited and published as a corpus. Yet, Turner's lecture diagrams speak cogently of the principles of perspective that he wished to explain. The illustrations, as we have seen, are the inheritors of the rich tradition of visual architectural ekphrasis that I have explored throughout this enquiry. As such, the diagrams describe architecture in its spatial and temporal dimensions through a visual language that transcends the verbal counterpoint of the lecture texts. Perhaps here also, given the audience of painters and architects, there is a kind of rapprochement between the three-dimensional spaces of the building and the two-dimensional spaces of the page or the canvas.

Notes

1 Hubert Damisch, trans. John Goodman, *The Origin of Perspective* (Cambridge, Massachusetts: MIT Press, 1994), chapter 2, p. 35.
2 Chapter, 1, Part II, p. 33. For the history of the Royal Academy of Arts in London see Holger Hoock, *The King's Artists: The Royal Academy of Arts and the Politics of British Culture 1760–1840* (Oxford: Oxford University Press, 2003).
3 *Abstract of the Constitution and Laws of the Royal Academy of Arts in London: Established December 10, 1768* (London: Printed By B. McMillan, Bow-Street, Covent-Garden, Printer To The Royal Academy, 1815), pp. 18–19.
4 Royal Academy of Arts Archive REY/3/67–94.
5 For a discussion of the reactions to Turner and the retrospective creation of him as a forward-looking artist who prefigured modern painting, see Sam Smiles, *J. M. W. Turner: The Making of a Modern Artist* (Manchester: Manchester University Press, 2007).
6 J. M. W. Turner, 'Royal Academy Lectures', circa 1807–38, Department of Western Manuscripts, British Library, London, ADD MS C folio 3.
7 See for instance: Andrew Wilton, *Turner in his Time*, London: Thames & Hudson, 2006; Christine Riding and Richard Johns (eds), *Turner and the Sea* (London: Thames & Hudson; National Maritime Museum, 2013); David Blayney Brown, *J. M. W. Turner: Watercolours* (London: Tate Publishing, 2019).
8 On this point see Jerrold Ziff, '"Backgrounds, Introduction of Architecture and Landscape": A Lecture by J. M. W. Turner'. *Journal of the Warburg and Courtauld Institutes* 26:1/2 (1963) pp. 124–47. This remains the only lecture that has been fully published. It was translated into French as 'Arrière-plans, introduction de l'architecture et du paysage, par J. M. W. Turner', by Pierre Wat in his *Turner, Menteur magnifique* (Paris, Hazan, 2010). See also Maurice Davies, *Turner as Professor: The Artist and Linear Perspective* (London: Tate Publishing, 1993) and Hélène Ibata, 'J. M. W. Turner and the Dynamics of Perspective', *European Romantic Review*, 19:4 (2008), pp. 351–63.
9 Turner's lecture texts survive in manuscript form in the Department of Western Manuscripts, British Library, London: ADD MS 46151. Three more are now in a private collection.
10 See Gillian Darley's contribution in Margaret Richardson and MaryAnne Stevens (eds), *John Soane Architect: Master of Space and Light*, exhibition catalogue (Royal Academy of Arts, London 1999), p. 24.

11 James Stuart and Nicolas Revett, *The Antiquities of Athens*, London, 1762, vol. I, chapter V, plates II and IV and Lecture Diagrams 8/1, 8/2 and 8/3. Tate D17140, D17141 and D17142; Turner Bequest CXCV 169, 170, 171.

12 The lecture drawings, catalogued by John Ruskin, are held at Tate Britain. See Andrea Fredericksen, *Vanishing Point: The Perspective Drawings of J. M. W. Turner* (London: Tate Publishing, 2004).

13 See plate VI, figure 23 in Thomas Malton the Elder, *A Compleat Treatise on Perspective, In Theory and Practice, on the True Principles of Dr. Brook Taylor* (London, 1775).

14 Turner, 'Royal Academy Lectures', Department of Western Manuscripts, British Library, London, ADD MS 46151 L folio 6 verso.

15 See Malton, *A Compleat Treatise*, Fig.15. Lecture Diagram 18 is part of the Turner Bequest at Tate Britain, Tate D17031; Turner Bequest CXCV 61.

16 Royal Academy Council Minutes, 15 December 1809.

17 *The New Monthly Magazine*, 1 February 1816.

18 *Annals of the Fine Arts*, vol. 4, London 1820, p. 98.

Epilogue

My concern in this volume has been to examine visual ekphrases of the architecture of antiquity, to question what these images can articulate that words cannot, and in turn to explore the interaction between these images and the imagination. The themes of the perceived neutrality of the authorial voice and of embodiment have run in parallel to these lines of enquiry as a means of challenging the masculinist norms through which the past is described. These canonical structures are manifest in the systems of proportion used to represent and reconstruct antique buildings, the physical processes of producing a print or drawing and in the nature of human perception, where the usually perceived binaries of 'visual' or 'tactile' are seen to elide. In this way, my enquiry has moved beyond the established boundaries of ekphrasis and artistic production in Europe, to consider how the phenomenological experience of descriptions of architecture in terms of how they are both created and read inflect on our understanding. A substantial evidence base, including familiar theorists and artists, lesser-known eighteenth-century figures as well as parallel developments in cognate fields such as fiction writing, has been refracted through the paradigmatic lenses of the notions of the Past, Time and Space. This approach has enabled me to situate both texts and images within the personal and cultural context of their creators. And throughout this book contemporary critical discourse provided an effective tool with which to tease out historical meanings and interpretations that might not otherwise have been apparent.

We can now see, then, that the past is not a neutral place. Indeed, the trend in our period towards an increasing interest in the accurate representation of the antique past and the adoption of a mode of visual ekphrasis which claims to be 'neutral' is highly questionable. As a consequence, we have also begun to see that such a claim to neutrality must inevitably carry its own political freight. Turning once again to a scientific language of neutral observation, we see how Palladio establishes a set of masculine predicates that he employs in reducing, abstracting, and restructuring Rome and the Veneto to conform to these imposed norms. These conventions are rooted in the architectural ekphrases from antiquity and remain the established method of describing the past in our period. In this way, for instance, Colen Campbell uses a similar technique with his survey of British architecture, *Vitruvius Britannicus.* We also experience a bifocal vision of the past in works such as Stuart and Revett's *The Antiquities of Athens*, which also draws on the European conventions of picturesque aesthetics. Both the use of the picturesque to commodify and appropriate the past, and the language of scientific neutrality are familiar devices. This kind of approach of double viewing constructs an ancient culture, which is at once exotically separate from and yet comfortingly supportive of the visual account of it in the modern world. However, this 'neutral' style adopted in these attempts to bring the architecture of antiquity to a broader public should not necessarily be associated with Walter Benjamin's assumption that mass-production and dissemination inevitably leads to democratisation. The very abstraction and reduction involved in the scientific language of Palladio, Campbell, and Stuart and Revett could ultimately exclude all but an educated minority: that is, the cultural competence required to read such images inevitably becomes a demonstration not simply of taste but, in Bourdieu's terms, of taste as means of legitimating social difference.[1] Thus, whilst the move towards accuracy and fidelity and the adoption of formal qualities which claim neutrality would seem to imply an address to Habermas's broad public of rational individuals, such democratisation can be resisted even in the very codes of representation an image adopts.

The structure of this book has also explored how space and time operate as dimensional frameworks in which we construct experience. They are built into the perceiving process, and we cannot but think in terms of space and time. But can we really see space and time as binary forces? Surely theory, whether masculinist or not, has called into question this notion. Temporal gaps and the spaces in between make cohesion impossible; instead, space and time can be seen as being two oppositional elements vulnerable to deconstruction, so space cannot be a unified subject or object. I am thinking here of Jacques Derrida's essay '*Ousia* and *Grammē*',[2] where he argues that to differentiate in absolute terms between time and space would demolish them both and undermine the basic theoretical tenet that it is possible to define something by that which it is not; that is to say its opposite. Instead, we are left with the spaces in between – with differences that give the illusion of presence. Space becomes, then, in Derrida's argument no longer represented as a subject or object distinct from temporal events. It is instead 'the rhetoric of temporality',[3] where

> an interval must separate the present time from what it is not in order for the present to be itself … . In constituting itself, in dividing itself dynamically, this interval is what might be called spacing, the becoming-space of time or the becoming-time of space (temporization).[4]

If we return to the visual representation of architecture and its spaces, we can see how its temporisation means that it is neither a unified subject nor object.

This surely helps to inform our theorisation of representations of space as its formulation is transformed over time. Visual descriptions of architecture become both subject and object and their status remains volatile and fluid within its space/time location.

Gender has remained a predominant theme throughout this enquiry. My aim has not been simply to try to write women into this discourse by finding examples of female travellers or women's drawings of ancient architecture. Had I have done so would have been to ignore feminist thinking and its questioning of theoretical and historiographic norms through the act of *differencing*.[5] I wanted instead to use my archive to reveal the female absence and her implicit presence in order to understand what these two states may bring and take away from the visual ekphrases, and ultimately our understanding of description's antique architecture. Locating the female absence and presence uncovers paradoxes. We find these for instance in the phenomenological experience of space; the proportional system or syntax used in architectural drawing; in the line that creates images; and in the bodily processes through which prints and drawings are produced. In this way, I have located in the actions (by which I mean gestures and marks) that create visual ekphrases, and in the spaces and surfaces that these images inhabit, a reading of categories of production and historical analysis that *differs* from canonical norms.

My principal focus has been on examples from the long eighteenth century, which is undoubtedly a crucial moment in the account of description as a theory and practice. But the themes I explore and questions I raise are not unique to this period and enable us to address issues from a much broader historical sweep. Most urgent here is perhaps the present-day shift to digital imagery and writing and the concomitant loss of the printed page. Our phenomenological, perceptual experience, and engagement with this new medium requires a re-thinking of description in all its complexities.

Notes

1 On this point see Pierre Bourdieu, *Distinction: A Social Critique of the Judgement of Taste*, trans. Richard Nice (London: Routledge & Kegan Paul, 1984).

2 Jacques Derrida, '*Ousia* and *Grammē*: Note on a Note from *Being and Time*', in *Margins of Philosophy*, trans. Alan Bass (Chicago: University of Chicago Press, 1982), pp. 29–67.

3 I borrow this phrase from Paul de Man, 'The Rhetoric of Temporality', in *Blindness and Insight*, 2nd edn (Minneapolis: University of Minnesota Press, 1989).

4 Jacques Derrida, *Margins of Philosophy*, p. 13.

5 On this point see Griselda Pollock, *Differencing the Canon: Feminist Desire and the Writing of Art's Histories* (London: Routledge 1999).

Select bibliography

Primary sources

Abstract of the Constitution and Laws of the Royal Academy of Arts in London: Established December 10, 1768 (London: Printed By B. McMillan, Bow-Street, Covent-Garden, Printer To The Royal Academy, 1815).

Adam, Robert, *Ruins of the Palace of the Emperor Diocletian at Spalatro* (London: Printed for the author, 1764).

Addison, Joseph, 'The Pleasures of the Imagination', *The Spectator*, nos. 411–21 (London, 1712).

Annals of the Fine Arts, vol. 4 (London, 1820).

Berkeley, George, *An Essay Towards a New Theory of Vision* (Dublin: Printed by Aaron Rhames, for Jeremy Pepyat, 1709).

de Blainville, *Travels Through Holland, Germany, Switzerland, and other parts of Europe; but especially Italy*, trans. Turnbull, Guthrie and Lockman (London: John and Joseph Noon, 1757).

Bosse, Abraham, *Traité des manières de graver en taille-douce sur l'airain, par le moyen des eaux-fortes & des vernis durs & mols: Ensemble de la façon d'en imprimer les planches, & de construire la presse* (Paris, 1645).

Boyle, John, Earl of Corke and Orrery, *Letters from Italy, in the Years 1754 and 1755* (London: B. White, 1773).

de Brosses, Charles, *Lettres sur l'état actuel de la Ville Souterraine d'Herculée* (Dijon: François Desventes, 1750).

Burke, Edmund, *Philosophical Enquiry into the Origin of the Sublime and the Beautiful* (London: Printed for R. and J. Dodsley, 1757).

Campbell, Colen, *Vitruvius Britannicus or The British Architect, containing The Plans, Elevations, and Sections of the Regular Buildings, both Publick and Private, in Great Britain,...* 3 vols (London: Printed and sold by the author, Andrew Bell, W. Taylor, Henry Clements, and Jos. Smith, 1715–25).

Cochin, Charles Nicolas and Jérôme Charles Bellicard, *Observations sur les antiquités de la ville d'Herculanum avec quelques reflexions sur la Peinture & la Sculpture des Anciens; & une courte description de quelques Antiquités des environs de Naples* (Paris: Charles Antoine Jombert, 1754).

Diderot, Denis and Jean le Rond d'Alembert (eds), *Encyclopédie, ou dictionnaire raisonné des sciences, des arts, et des métiers* (Paris: Briason, 1751–65).

Dubreuil, Jean, *Perspective practical. Or, a plain and easie method of true and lively representing all things to the eye at a distance, by the exact rules of art … Very useful and necessary for all Painters … By a Religious Person of the Society of Jesus, a Parisien* [J. Dubreuil]. *Faithfully translated out of French, and illustrated with 150 copper cuts. Set forth in English by R. Pricke for the Lovers of Art* (London: H. Lloyd, and sold by R. Pricke, 1672).

Dubreuil, Jean, *La perspective pratique*. Seconde édition … augmentée (Paris: A. Dezallier, 1671).

Fuseli, Henry, *Reflections on the Painting and Sculpture of the Greeks: with Instructions for the Connoisseur, and An Essay on Grace in Works of Art* (London: Printed for the Translator, and Sold by A. Millar in the Strand, 1765).

'ʼs Gravesande, Willem Jacob, *Essai de perspective* (London: Printed for J. Senex; W. Taylor; W. and J. Innys; J. Osbourne; and E. Symon, 1724).

Hamilton, John, *Stereography, or, a Compleat Body of Perspective, in all its Branches. Teaching to describe, by mathematical rules, the appearance of lines, plain figures, and solid bodies… Together with their projections or shadows and their reflections by polished planes* (London: W. Bowyer, 1738).

Highmore, Joseph, *The Practice of Perspective, On the Principles of Dr. Brook Taylor: in a series of examples, from the most simple and, and easy, to the most complicated, and difficult cases. In the course of which, his method is compared with those of some of the most celebrated writers before him, on the subject. Written many years since, but now first published* (London: Printed for A. Millar, and J. Nourse, 1763).

Highmore, Joseph, *A Critical Examination of those two paintings on the cieling [sic] of the banqueting-house at Whitehall: in which architecture is introduced, so far as relates to the perspective* (London: J. Nourse, 1754).

Hogarth, William, *The Analysis of Beauty* (London: Printed by John Reeves for the Author, 1753).

Home, Henry, Lord Kames, *Elements of Criticism* (Edinburgh: Printed for A. Miller, London; and A. Kincaid & J. Bell, Edinburgh, 1762).

Hugues, Pierre-François, called Baron d'Hancarville, *Antiquités étrusques, grecques et romaines, tirées du cabinet de M. William Hamilton* (Naples: François Morelli, 1766–1767 [correct date c. 1776]).

Hume, David, *An Enquiry Concerning the Human Understanding* (London: Printed for A. Miller, 1748).

Johnson, Samuel, *A Dictionary of the English Language: in which the words are deduced from their originals, explained in their different meanings and authorized by the means of the writers in whose works they are found*, 6th edn, 2 vols (London: Printed for A. Millar, 1766).

Kip, Johannes and Leonard Knyff, *Nouveau théâtre de la Grande Bretagne: ou description exacte des palais de la reine et des maisons les plus considerables des seigneurs et des gentilshommes de la Grande Bretagne…* (London, 1708–13).

Kip, Johannes and Leonard Knyff, *Britannia Illustrata or Views of several of the Queen's Palaces as also of the principal Seats of the Nobility and Gentry of Great Britain, curiously engraven on 80 copper plates* (London: D. Mortier, 1707).

Kirby, John Joshua, *The Perspective of Architecture … a work entirely new, deduced from the principles of Dr. Brook Taylor…* (London: R. Francklin, 1761).

Kirby, John Joshua, *Dr. Brook Taylor's Method of Perspective Made Easy, both in Theory and Practice*, 2nd edn, 2 vols (London: R. Francklin, 1755).

Lassels, Richard, *The Voyage of Italy, or, A compleat journey through Italy: in two parts: with the characters of the people, and the description of the chief towns, churches, monasteries, tombs, libraries, pallaces, villas, gardens, pictures, statues, and antiquities: as also of the interest, government, riches, force, &c. of all the princes: with instructions concerning travel / by Richard Lassels, Gent. who travelled through Italy five times as tutor to several of the English nobility and gentry; never before extant* (Paris: V. du Moutier; London: J. Starkey, 1670).

Leoni, Giacomo, *The Architecture of A. Palladio in Four Books containing a Short Treatise on the Five Orders*, 4 vols (London: Printed by John Watts, for the Author, 1715–20).

Major, Thomas, *The Ruins of Paestum, Otherwise Posidonia, in Magna Grecia* (London: Published by T. Major, in St. Martin's Lane. Printed by James Dixwell, 1768).

Malton, James, *The Young Painter's Maulstick; Being a Practical Treatise on Perspective; Containing Rules and Principles for Delineation on Planes, Treated so as to render the Art of Drawing correctly, easy of Attainment even to common Capacities; and entertaining at the same Time, from its Truth and Facility. Founded on the clear mechanical Process of Vignola and Sirigatti; United with the Theoretical Principles of the Celebrated Dr. Brook Taylor. Addressed to Students in Drawing. By James Malton, Architect And Draftsman* (London: V. Griffiths, 1800).

Malton, Thomas, *A Compleat Treatise on Perspective, in Theory and Practice; on the Principles of Dr. Brook Taylor* (London: Printed for the Author by Cox and Bigg, and sold by Messrs. Robson, Dodsley, Becket, Taylor and Richardson & Urqhart, 1775).

Malton, Thomas, *The Royal Road to Geometry; or an easy and familiar Introduction to the Mathematics* (London, 1774).

Michel, S. N., *Traité de perspective linéaire: avec une planche en taille-douce* (Paris: Lottin, 1771).

de Montfaucon, Bernard, *L'antiquité expliquée et représentée en figures*, 15 vols (Paris, 1719–24).

de Montfaucon, Bernard, *Antiquity Explained and Represented in Diagrams*, trans. David Humphreys (London: J. Tonson & J. Watts, 1721–22).

Palladio, Andrea, *I quattro libri dell'architettura* (Venice: Dominico de' Franceschi, 1570).

de Piles, Roger, 'Of the Usefulness and Use of Prints', in *The Art of Painting, with the Lives and Characters … of the Most Eminent Painters* (London: Printed for T. Payne, 1754).

de Piles, Roger, 'De l'utilité des Estampes, et de leur usage', in *Abrégé de la vie des peintres, avec des réflexions sur leurs ouvrages* (Paris: François Muguet, 1699).

Piranesi, Giovanni Battista, *Differentes vues de quelques restes de trois grands edifices qui subsistent encore dans le milieu de l'ancienne ville de Pesto autrement Posidonia qui est située dans la Luganie* (Rome: 1778).

Piranesi, Giovanni Battista, *Le antichità romane* (Rome: Angelo Rotili, 1756).

Pozzo, Andrea, *Perspective in architecture and painting: an unabridged reprint of the English and Latin edition of the 1693 'Perspectiva pictorum et architectorum'* (New York: Dover Publications, 1989).

Pozzo, Andrea, *Perspectiva pictorum et architectorum, with engravings by Vincenzo Mariotti* (Rome: Joannis Jacobi Komarek, 1693).

Priestley, Joseph, *A Familiar Introduction to the Theory and Practice of Perspective* (London: Printed for J. Johnson and J. Payne, 1770).

Richardson, Samuel, *Pamela; or, Virtue Rewarded. In a series of familiar letters from a beautiful young damsel, to her parents* (London: Printed for C. Rivington and J. Osborn, 1740).

Royal Academy Council Minutes, 15 December 1809.

Russel, James, *Letters from a Young Painter Abroad to his Friends in England* (London: W. Russel, 1750).

Stuart, James and Nicholas Revett, *The Antiquities of Athens: Measured and Delineated by James Stuart, FRS and FSA, and Nicholas Revett, Painters and Architects* (London: Printed by John Haberkorn, 1762).

Taylor, Brook, *New Principles of Linear Perspective* (London: R. Knaplock, 1719).

Taylor, Brook, *Linear Perspective or, a New Method of Representing Justly All Manner of Objects as They Appear to the Eye in All Situations* (London: R. Knaplock, 1715).

The Monthly Review or Literary Journal, vol. 14 (London, 1794).

The New Monthly Magazine (1 February 1816).

Turner, Joseph Mallord William, 'Royal Academy Lectures', Department of Western Manuscripts, British Library, London, ADD MS 46151.

Vasari, Giorgio, *Le Vite de' Piu Eccellenti Pittori, Scultori, e Architettori. Scritte da M. Giorgio Vasari Pittore et Architetto Aretino, Di nuovo dal medesimo riviste et ampliate con i ritratti loro et con l'aggiunta delle vite de' vivi, & de' morti, Dall'anno 1550 infino al 1567. Prima, e Seconda Parte. Con le Tavole in ciascun volume, delle cose piu notabili, de' ritratti, delle vite degli artefici, et de i luoghi dove sono l'opere loro. Con Licenza e Privilegio di N.S. Pio V. et del Duca Di Fiorenza e Siena* (Florence: Giunti, 1568).

di Venuti, M. Don Marcello, *A description of the first discoveries of the antient [sic] city of Heraclea, found near Portici, a country palace belonging to the king of the Two Sicilies. In two parts ... Done into English from the original Italian of the Marquis Don Marcello di Venuti. By Wickes Skurray. To which are added some letters that passed between the learned Jo. Matthia Gesner..., Cardinal Quirini, and Hermannus Samuel Reimarus... concerning these discoveries. Variant Title: Description of the first discoveries of the ancient city of Heraclea* (London, Printed for R. Baldwin jun. at the Rose in Pater-Noster-Row, 1750).

Walpole, Horace and George Montagu, *Correspondence of Horace Walpole, with George Montagu, Esq., [and others]* (London: Henry Colburn, 1837).

Walpole, Horace, *Anecdotes of painting in England: with some account of the principal artists; and incidental notes on other arts; collected by the late Mr. George Vertue; and now digested and published from his original mss. The fourth edition, with additions and portraits. In four volumes* (London: Printed for J. Dodsley, 1786).

Ware, Isaac, *The Practice of Perspective, From The Original Italian of Lorenzo Sirigatti. With the Figures Engraved by Isaac Ware, Esq.* (London: Printed for the Author, 1756).

Winckelmann, Johann Joachim, *A Critical Account of the Situation and Destruction by the First Eruptions of Mount Vesuvius of Herculaneum, Pompeii, and Stabiae* (London: T. Carnan and F. Newbery, 1771).

Winckelmann, Johann Joachim, *Monumenti antichi inediti, spiegati ed illustrati* (Rome, 1767).

Winckelmann, Johann Joachim, *Geschichte der Kunst des Alterthums* (Dresden: Walther, 1764).

Winckelmann, Johann Joachim, *Anmerkungen über die Baukunst der Alten* (Leipzig: Johann Gottfried Dyck, 1762).

Winckelmann, Johann Joachim, *Sendschreiben von den Herculanischen Entdeckungen* (Dresden: Walther, 1762).

Winckelmann, Johann Joachim, *Gedanken über die Nachahmung der griechischen Werke in der Malerei und Bildhauerkunst* (1755).

Wood, Robert, *The Ruins of Balbec, Otherwise Heliopolis in Coelosyria* (London, 1757).

Wood, Robert, *The Ruins of Palmyra, Otherwise Tedmor* (London, 1753).

Wright, Edward, *Some Observations Made in Travelling Through France, Italy &c in the Years 1720, 1721 and 1722* (London: Thomas Ward and E. Wicksteed, 1730).

Secondary sources

Adams, Bernard, *London Illustrated 1604–1850: A Survey and Index of Topographical Books and Their Plates* (London: Library Association, 1983).

Alberti, Leon Battista, *On the Art of Building in Ten Books*, trans. Joseph Rykwert, Neil Leach, and Robert Tavernor (Cambridge, Massachusetts: MIT Press, 1988).

Alberti, Leon Battista, *On Painting*, trans. John R. Spencer, 2nd edn (New Haven and London: Yale University Press, 1966).

Alpers, Svetlana, 'Interpretation without Representation, or, the Viewing of Las Meninas', *Representations*, 1:1 (1983), pp. 122–32.

Alpers, Svetlana Leontief, '*Ekphrasis* and Aesthetic Attitudes in Vasari's *Lives*', *Journal of the Warburg and Courtauld Institutes*, 23:3/4 (1960), pp. 190–215.

Andersen, Kirsti, *The Geometry of an Art: The History of the Mathematical Theory of Perspective from Alberti to Monge* (New York: Springer, 2007).

Andersen, Kirsti, *Brook Taylor's Work on Linear Perspective* (New York: Springer, 1992).

Aristotle, *Poetics*, trans. Malcolm Heath (Harmondsworth: Penguin Classics, 1996).

Aristotle, *Metaphysics*, trans. Hugh Lawson-Tancred, 2nd edn (Harmondsworth: Penguin Classics, 2004).

Armstrong, Christopher Drew, *Julien-David LeRoy and the Making of Architectural History* (London Routledge, 2011).

Arnold, Dana, 'En Foüllant à l'Aveugle: Discovering the Villa of the Papyri in the 18th Century', in Mantha Zarmakoupi (ed.), *The Villa of the Papyri at Herculaneum: Archaeology, Reception, and Digital Reconstruction.* Sozomena: Studies in the Recovery of Ancient Texts. Edited on behalf of the Herculaneum Society, vol. 1 (Berlin and New York: Walter de Gruyter, 2010).

Arnold, Dana and Joanna Sofaer Derevenski (eds), *Biographies and Space: Placing the Subject in Art and Architecture* (London: Routledge, 2007 and 2015).

Arnold, Dana and Stephen Bending (eds), *Tracing Architecture: The Aesthetics of Antiquarianism* (London: Wiley & Sons, 2003).

Arnold, Dana, 'Facts or Fragments? Visual Histories in the Age of Mechanical Reproduction', *Art History*, 25:4 (2002), pp. 450–68.

Bal, Mieke and Norman Bryson, 'Semiotics and Art History', *The Art Bulletin*, 73:2 (1991), pp. 174–208.

Baridon, Michel, 'Hogarth's "Living Machines of Nature" and the Theorisation of Aesthetics', in David Bindman, Frédéric Ogée, and Peter Wagner (eds), *Hogarth: Representing Nature's Machines* (Manchester: Manchester University Press, 2001).

Barkan, Leonard, *Unearthing the Past: Archaeology and Aesthetics in the Making of Renaissance Culture* (New Haven and London: Yale University Press, 1999).

Barthes, Roland, *Camera Lucida: Reflections on Photography*, trans. Richard Howard (London: Vintage, 1993).

Bartsch, Shadi and Jaś Elsner (eds), *Classical Philology*, Special Issue on Ekphrasis, 102:1 (2007).

Baxandall, Michael, *Giotto and the Orators: Humanist Observers of Painting in Italy and the Discovery of Pictorial Composition 1350–1450* (Oxford: Clarendon Press, 1986).

Baxandall, Michael, 'The Language of Art History', *New Literary History*, 10:3 (1979), pp. 453–65.

Benjamin, Walter, *The Work of Art in the Age of Its Technological Reproducibility, and Other Writings on Media*, ed. Michael W. Jennings, Brigid Doherty, and Thomas Y. Levin, trans. E. Jephcott, R. Livingstone, H. Eiland, and others (Cambridge, Massachusetts: The Belknap Press of Harvard University Press, 2008).

Benjamin, Walter, *Walter Benjamin: Selected Writings, Volume 1, 1913–1926*, ed. Marcus Bullock and Michael W. Jennings (Cambridge, Massachusetts: Harvard University Press, 1996).

Benjamin, Walter, 'The Work of Art in the Age of Mechanical Reproduction', in *Illuminations*, ed. Hannah Arendt, trans. Harry Zohn (London: Fontana, 1973).

Bennett, Judith M., 'Feminism and History', *Gender and History*, 1:3 (1989), pp. 251–72.

Berkeley, George, *Philosophical Writings*, ed. Desmond M. Clarke (Cambridge: Cambridge University Press, 2008).

Berkeley, George, 'The Theory of Vision Vindicated and Explained', in A. A. Luce and T. E. Jessop (eds), *The Works of George Berkeley, Bishop of Cloyne*, 9 vols (Edinburgh: Thomas Nelson and Sons, 1948).

Black, Jeremy, *The British Abroad: The Grand Tour in the Eighteenth Century* (Stroud: Alan Sutton, 1992).

Blayney Brown, David, *J. M. W. Turner: Watercolours* (London: Tate Publishing, 2019).

Bloomer, Jennifer, *Architecture and the Text: The (S)crypts of Joyce and Piranesi* (New Haven and London: Yale University Press, 1993).

Bolton, Arthur T., *The Architecture of Robert and James Adam (1758–94)*, 2 vols (London: *Country Life*, 1922).

Borromini, Francesco, *Opus architectonicum*, ed. Joseph Connors, 2nd edn (Milan: Il Polifilo, Trattati di architectura, 1998).

Boschloo, Anton W. A. *et al.* (eds), *Academies of Art between Renaissance and Romanticism, Leids Kunsthistorisch Jaarboek V-VI* (1986–87) ('s Gravenhage: SDU Uitgeverij, 1989).

Bourdieu, Pierre, *Distinction: A Social Critique of the Judgement of Taste*, trans. Richard Nice (London: Routledge & Kegan Paul, 1984).

Brewer, John, *The Pleasures of the Imagination: English Culture in the Eighteenth Century* (London: Harper Collins, 1997).

Bryant, Julius, 'James "Athenian" Stuart: The Architect as Landscape Painter', *V&A online journal*, Issue 1 (2008). www.vam.ac.uk/content/journals/research-journal/issue-01/james-athenian-stuart-the-architect-as-landscape-painter/.

Bryson, Norman, Michael Ann Holly, and Keith Moxey (eds), *Visual Culture: Images and Interpretations* (Middletown, Connecticut: Wesleyan University Press, 1994).

Butor, Michel, *Inventory*, trans. Richard Howard (New York: Simon & Schuster, 1969).

Cameron, Eric, 'The Depictional Semiotic of Alberti's *On Painting*', *Art Journal*, 35:1 (1975), pp. 25–8.

Canning, Katherine, 'Feminist History after the Linguistic Turn: Historicising Discourse and Experience', *Signs*, 19:2 (1994), pp. 368–404.

Cassirer, Ernst, *Philosophy of Symbolic Forms, Volume 2: Mythical Thought*, trans. Ralph Manheim (New Haven: Yale University Press, 1955).

Chard, Chloe, *Pleasure and Guilt on the Grand Tour: Travel Writing and Imaginative Geography 1600–1830* (Manchester: Manchester University Press, 1999).

Clayton, Tim, *The English* Print 1688–1802 (New Haven and London: Yale University Press, 1997).

Cosgrove, Brian, 'Murray Krieger: Ekphrasis as Spatial Form, Ekphrasis as Mimesis', in Jeff Morrison and Florian Krobb (eds), *Text into Image: Image into Text*; Proceedings of the Interdisciplinary Bicentenary Conference Held at St. Patrick's College, Maynooth (the National University of Ireland), September 1995 (Amsterdam: Rodopi, 1997).

Cummins, Philip D., 'On the Status of Visuals in Berkeley's *New Theory of Vision*', in Ernest Sosa (ed.), *Essays on the Philosophy of George Berkeley* (Dordrecht: D. Reidel Publishing Co., 1987).

Damisch, Hubert, *The Origin of Perspective*, trans. John Goodman (Cambridge Massachusetts: MIT Press, 1994).

Davies, Maurice, *Turner as Professor: The Artist and Linear Perspective* (London: Tate Publishing, 1993).

Deleuze, Gilles, *Bergsonism*, trans. Hugh Tomlinson and Barbara Habberjam (New York: Zone Books, 1991).

Deleuze, Gilles and Félix Guattari, *A Thousand Plateaus: Capitalism and Schizophrenia*, trans. Brian Massumi (London: Athlone Press, 1988).

Deleuze, Gilles and Claire Parnet, *Dialogues*, trans. Hugh Tomlinson and Barbara Habberjam (London: Athlone Press, 1987).

Deleuze, Gilles and Félix Guattari, *On the Line*, trans. John Johnston (New York: Semiotext(e), 1983).

de Man, Paul, 'The Rhetoric of Temporality', in *Blindness and Insight*, 2nd edn (Minneapolis: University of Minnesota Press, 1989).

Derrida, Jacques, 'To Unsense the Subjectile', in Jacques Derrida and Paule Thévenin (eds), trans. Mary Ann Caws, *The Secret Art of Antonin Artaud* (Cambridge, Massachusetts: MIT Press, 1998).

Derrida, Jacques, *Of Grammatology*, trans. Gayatri Chakravorty Spivak (Baltimore: Johns Hopkins University Press, 1997).

Derrida, Jacques, *Archive Fever: A Freudian Impression*, trans. Eric Prenowitz (Chicago: The University of Chicago Press, 1996).

Derrida, Jacques, *Memoirs of the Blind: The Self-Portrait and Other Ruins*, trans. Pascale-Anne Brault and Michael Naas (Chicago: The University of Chicago Press, 1993).

Derrida, Jacques, *Margins of Philosophy*, trans. Alan Bass (Chicago: The University of Chicago Press, 1982).

Dictionary of National Biography (London: Smith, Elder & Co., 1885–1900).

Dolan, Brian, *Ladies of the Grand Tour* (London: Harper Collins, 2001).

Dürer, Albrecht, *The Painter's Manual: A Manual of Measurement of Lines, Areas, and Solids by Means of Compass and Ruler Assembled by Albrecht Dürer for the Use of All Lovers of Art with Appropriate Illustrations Arranged to be Printed in the Year MDXXV*, 2nd ed. Published 1538 and trans. Walter L. Strauss (New York: Abaris, 1977).

Edgerton Jr., Samuel Y., 'Alberti's Perspective: A New Discovery and a New Evaluation', *The Art Bulletin*, 48:3–4 (1966), pp. 367–78.

Elkins, James, *On Pictures and the Words that Fail Them* (Cambridge: Cambridge University Press, 1998).

Elkins, James, *The Object Stares Back: On the Nature of Seeing* (London: Routledge, 1996).

Elsner, Jaś, 'Art History as Ekphrasis', *Art History*, 33:1 (2010), pp. 10–27.

Etheridge Moore, Robert, 'The Art of Piranesi: Looking Backward into the Future', in Robert E. Moore and Jean H. Hagstrum (eds), *Changing Taste in Eighteenth-Century Art and Literature* (Los Angeles: William Andrews Clark Memorial Library, 1972).

Etheridge Moore, Robert and Jean H. Hagstrum (eds), *Changing Taste in Eighteenth-Century Art and Literature* (Los Angeles: William Andrews Clark Memorial Library, 1972).

Evans, Robin, *Translations from Drawing to Building and Other Essays* (Cambridge, Massachusetts: MIT Press, 1997).

Evans, Robin, *The Projective Cast: Architecture and Its Three Geometries* (Cambridge, Massachusetts: MIT Press, 1995).

Foucault, Michel, *The Order of Things* (London: Tavistock Publications, 1970).

Fredericksen, Andrea, *Vanishing Point: The Perspective Drawings of J. M. W. Turner* (London: Tate Publishing, 2004).

Freud, Sigmund, *Interpreting Dreams*, trans. J. A. Underwood (Harmondsworth: Penguin, 2006).

Freud, Sigmund, 'Civilization and its Discontents', in A. Dickson (ed.), *Civilization, Society and Religion*, The Penguin Freud Library, vol. 12 (Harmondsworth: Penguin, 1991).

Fyfe, Gordon, *Art, Power, and Modernity: English Art Institutions, 1750–1950* (London and New York: Leicester University Press, 2000).

Gibbon, Edward, *Memoirs of My Life*, ed. Georges A. Bonnard (London: Nelson, 1966).

Gilbert, Creighton E., *Italian Art 1400–1500: Sources and Documents* (Englewood Cliffs, New Jersey: Prentice Hall, 1980).

Gilbert, Creighton E., 'Antique Frameworks for Renaissance Art Theory', *Marsyas*, 3 (1943–45), pp. 87–98.

Girouard, Mark, *Life in the English Country House: A Social and Architectural History* (New Haven and London: Yale University Press, 1978).

Goethe, Johann Wolfgang von, *Collected Works*, ed. V. Lange *et al.* (Princeton, New Jersey: Princeton University Press, 1995).

Goethe, Johann Wolfgang von, *Italian Journey*, (vol 6: Goethe Collected Works) ed. Thomas P. Saine and Jeffrey L. Sammons, trans. Robert R. Heitner (New York: Suhrkamp, 1989; reprint Princeton, New Jersey: Princeton University Press, 1994).

Goethe, Johann Wolfgang von, *The Italian Journey*, trans. W. H. Auden and Elizabeth Mayer (New York: Pantheon Books, 1962).

Goldstein, Carl, *Print Culture* in *Early Modern France: Abraham Bosse and the Purposes of Print* (Cambridge: Cambridge University Press, 2012).

Gombrich, Ernst H., *Tributes: Interpreters of Our Cultural Tradition* (Oxford: Phaidon, 1984).

Gombrich, Ernst H., 'Lessing: Lecture on a Master Mind', *Proceedings of the British Academy*, 43 (1957), pp. 133–56.

Goodman, Nelson, *Languages of Art: An Approach to a Theory of Symbols* (New York: The Bobbs-Merrill Company, 1968).

Grayson, Cecil, 'L. B. Alberti's 'Costruzione Legittima', *Italian Studies*, 19:1 (1964), pp. 14–27.

Griffiths, Antony, *Prints and Printmaking: An Introduction to the History and Techniques* (Berkeley and Los Angeles: University of California Press, 1996).

Griffiths, Antony, 'Print Collecting in Rome, Paris, and London in the Early Eighteenth Century', *Harvard University Art Museums Bulletin*, 2:3 (1994), pp. 37–58.

Grosz, Elizabeth, *The Nick of Time: Politics, Evolution and the Untimely* (Durham, North Carolina and London: Duke University Press, 2004).

Grush, Rick, 'Berkeley and the Spatiality of Vision', *Journal of the History of Philosophy*, 45:3 (2007), pp. 413–22.

Guerlac, Suzanne, *Thinking in Time: An Introduction to Henri Bergson* (Ithaca, New York: Cornell University Press, 2006).

Habermas, Jürgen, *The Structural Transformation of the Public Sphere: An Inquiry into a Category of Bourgeois Society*, trans. Thomas Burger and Frederick Lawrence (Cambridge: Polity Press, 1989).

Hambly, Maya, *Drawing Instruments 1580–1980* (London: Sotheby's Publications, 1988).

Harloe, Katherine, *Winckelmann and the Invention of Antiquity: History and Aesthetics in the Age of Altertumswissenschaft* (Oxford: Oxford University Press, 2013).

Harris, Eileen, assisted by Nicholas Savage, *British Architectural Books and Writers, 1556–1785* (Cambridge: Cambridge University Press, 1990).

Haskell, Francis, *History and Its Images: Art and the Interpretation of the Past* (New Haven and London: Yale University Press, 1995).

Hegel, Georg Wilhelm Friedrich, *Aesthetics: Lectures on Fine Arts*, trans. T. M. Knox (Oxford: Oxford University Press, 1975).

Hogarth, William, *The Analysis of Beauty: With the Rejected Passages from the Manuscript Drafts and Autobiographical Notes*, ed. Joseph Burke (Oxford: Clarendon Press, 1955).

Hoock, Holger, *The King's Artists; The Royal Academy of Arts and the Politics of British Culture 1760–1840* (Oxford: Oxford University Press, 2003).

Ibata, Hélène, 'J. M. W. Turner and the Dynamics of Perspective', *European Romantic Review*, 19:4 (2008), pp. 351–63.

Ingamells, John (ed.), *A Dictionary of British and Irish Travellers to Italy 1701–1800* (London and New Haven: Yale University Press, 1997).

Ingold, Tim, *Lines: A Brief History* (London: Routledge, 2007).

Ingraham, Catherine, *Architecture and the Burdens of Linearity* (New Haven and London: Yale University Press, 1998).

Ivins, Jr., William M., *Prints and Visual Communication* (Cambridge, Massachusetts: MIT Press, 1969).

Jarzombek, Mark, 'The Structural Problematic of Leon Battista Alberti's *De pictura*', *Renaissance Studies*, 4:3 (1990), pp. 273–86.

Jones, Inigo, *Inigo Jones on Palladio, being the notes of Inigo Jones in the copy of I quattro libri dell'architettura di Andrea Palladio, 1601 in the Library of Worcester College, Oxford* (Newcastle: Oriel Press, 1970).

Jones, P. S., 'Brook Taylor and the Mathematical Theory of Linear Perspective', *The American Mathematical Monthly*, 58:9 (1951), pp. 597–606.

Le Roy, Julien-David, *The Ruins of the Most Beautiful Monuments of Greece*, trans. David Britt (Los Angeles: Getty Research Institute, 2004).

Kant, Immanuel, *Critique of Judgment* [1790], trans. W. S. Pluhar (Indianapolis: Hackett, 1987).

Kemp, Martin, *The Science of Art: Optical Themes in Western Art from Brunelleschi to Seurat* (New Haven and London: Yale University Press, 1990).

Kemp, Martin, 'Leonardo and the Visual Pyramid', *Journal of the Warburg and Courtauld Institutes*, 11 (1977), pp. 128–49.

Keymer, Thomas and Peter Sabor, *'Pamela' in the Marketplace: Literary Controversy and Print Culture in Eighteenth-Century Britain and Ireland* (Cambridge: Cambridge University Press, 2005).

Kitson, Michael, 'Hogarth's "Apology for Painters"', *Walpole Society*, 41 (1966/1968), pp. 46–111.

Krieger, Murray, *Ekphrasis: The Illusion of the Natural Sign* (Baltimore: Johns Hopkins University Press, 1992).

Lacan, Jacques, *Ecrits, A Selection*, trans. Alan Sheridan (New York: W.W. Norton, 1977).

Landy, Jacob, 'Stuart and Revett: Pioneer Archaeologists', *Archaeology*, 9:4 (1956), pp. 252–9.

Lang, Suzanne, 'Early Publications of the Temples at Paestum', *Journal of the Warburg and Courtauld Institutes*, 13:1/2 (1950), pp. 48–64.

de Lauretis, Teresa, *Technologies of Gender: Essays on Theory, Film and Fiction* (Macmillan: London, 1987).

Lawrence, Lesley, 'Stuart and Revett: Their Literary and Architectural Careers', *Journal of the Warburg Institute*, 2:2 (1938), pp. 128–46.

Lessing, Gotthold Ephraim, *Laocoön: An Essay on the Limits of Painting and Poetry*, trans. E. A. McCormick (Baltimore: Johns Hopkins University Press, 1984).

Lifschitz, Avi and Michael Squire (eds), *Rethinking Lessing's* Laocoon*: Antiquity, Enlightenment, and the 'Limits' of Painting and Poetry* (Oxford: Oxford University Press, 2017).

Lindberg, David C., *Roger Bacon and the Origins of* Perspectiva *in the Middle Ages: A Critical Edition and English Translation* (Oxford: Oxford University Press, 1996).

Locke, John, *An Essay Concerning Human Understanding*, [London, 1706] ed. and abridged by J. W. Yolton (London and Melbourne: Dent, 1976).

Lolla, Maria Grazia, 'Monuments and Texts: Antiquarianism and the Beauty of Antiquity', in Dana Arnold and Stephen Bending (eds), *Tracing Architecture: The Aesthetics of Antiquarianism. Art History*, Special Issue, 25:4 (2002), pp. 431–49.

Lomax, Yve, *Writing the Image: An Adventure with Art and Theory* (London and New York: I.B. Tauris, 2000).

Macken, Marian, *Binding Space: The Book as Spatial Practice* (Abingdon: Routledge, 2018).

Markey, Lia, 'The Female Printmaker and the Culture of the Reproductive Print', in Rebecca Zorach and Elizabeth Rodin (eds), *Paper Museums: The Reproductive Print in Europe, 1500–1800* (Chicago: The University of Chicago Press, 2005).

Merleau-Ponty, Maurice, *Phenomenology of Perception* (London: Routledge & Kegan Paul, 1978).

Mitchell, W. J. T., *What Do Pictures Want?: The Lives and Loves of Images* (Chicago: The University of Chicago Press, 2006).

Mitchell, W. J. T., 'Showing Seeing: A Critique of Visual Culture', *Journal of Visual Culture*, 1:2 (2002), pp. 165–81.

Mitchell, W. J. T., *Picture Theory: Essays on Verbal and Visual Representation* (Chicago: The University of Chicago Press, 1994).

Mitchell, W. J. T., 'Ekphrasis and the Other', *South Atlantic Quarterly*, 91:3 (1992), pp. 695–719.

Mitchell, W. J. T., *Iconology: Image, Text, Ideology* (Chicago: The University of Chicago Press, 1986).

Mitchell, W. J. T., 'The Politics of Genre: Space and Time in Lessing's *Laocoön*', *Representations*, 6:1 (1984), pp. 98–115.

Mitchell, W. J. T., 'What Is an Image?', *New Literary History*, 15:3 (1984), pp. 503–37.

Mitchell, W. J. T., 'Metamorphoses of the Vortex: Hogarth, Turner and Blake', in Richard Wendorf (ed.), *Articulate Images: Sister Arts from Hogarth to Tennyson* (Minneapolis: University of Minnesota Press, 1983).

Montagu, Mary Wortley, *The Complete Letters of Lady Mary Wortley Montagu*, ed. Robert Halsband, 3 vols (Oxford: Clarendon Press, 1965–67).

Moreau, André, 'Merleau-Ponty et Berkeley', *Dialogue: Canadian Philosophical Review*, 5:3 (1966), pp. 418–24.

Newman, Avis and Catherine de Zegher, *The Stage of Drawing: Gesture and Act* (London, Tate Publishing; New York, The Drawing Center, 2003).

Newman, Michael, 'Sticking to the World: Drawing as Contact', in Catherine de Zegher (ed.), *Giuseppe Penone: The Imprint of Drawing* (New York: The Drawing Center, 2004).

Newman, Michael, 'The Traces and Marks of Drawing', in Catherine de Zegher (ed.), *The Stage of Drawing: Gesture and Act* (London, Tate Publishing; New York, The Drawing Center, 2003).

Newman, Michael, 'Derrida and the Scene of Drawing', *Research in Phenomenology*, 24 (1994), pp. 218–34.

Ogée, Frédéric, 'The Flesh of Theory: The Erotics of Hogarth's Lines', in Bernadette Fort and Angela Rosenthal (eds), *The Other Hogarth: Aesthetics of Difference* (Princeton, New Jersey: Princeton University Press, 2001).

Ong, Walter J., *Orality and Literacy: The Technologizing of the Word* (London and New York: Routledge, 1982).

Palladio, Andrea, *I quattro libri dell'architettura*, 1570, trans. Isaac Ware, ed. Adolf K. Placzek (New York: Dover Publications, 1965).

Palmer, Rodney, '"All is very plain, upon inspection of the figure": The Visual Method of Andrea Pozzo's *Perspectiva pictorum et architectorum*', in Rodney Palmer and Thomas Frangenberg (eds), *The Rise of the Image: Essays on the History of the Illustrated Book* (Abingdon: Routledge, 2003), pp. 157–213.

Panofsky, Erwin, *Perspective as Symbolic Form*, trans. Christopher S. Wood (New York: Zone Books, 1991).

Parslow, Christopher, *Rediscovering Antiquity: Karl Weber and the Excavation of Herculaneum, Pompeii, and Stabiae* (Cambridge: Cambridge University Press, 1995).

Paulson, Ronald, *Hogarth's Harlot: Sacred Parody in Enlightenment England* (Baltimore and London: Johns Hopkins University Press, 2003).

Paulson, Ronald, *Hogarth* (New Brunswick, New Jersey: Rutgers University Press, 1991–93).

Paulson, Ronald, *Hogarth's Graphic Works*, 3rd edn (London: The Print Room, 1989).

Paulson, Ronald, 'The Aesthetics of Modernity: Hogarth', in *Breaking and Making: Aesthetic Practice in England, 1700–1820* (New Brunswick, New Jersey: Rutgers University Press, 1989), pp. 149–202.

Pearce, Susan, *On Collecting: An Investigation into Collecting in the European Tradition* (London and New York: Routledge, 1995).

Penny, Nicholas, *Piranesi* (London: Bloomsbury Books, 1988).

Pérez-Goméz, Alberto and Louise Pelletier, *Architectural Representation and the Perspective Hinge* (Cambridge, Massachusetts: MIT Press, 2000).

Pérez-Goméz, Alberto and Louise Pelletier, 'Architectural Representation Beyond Perspectivism', *Perspecta*, 27 (1991), pp. 21–39.

Petherbridge, Deanna, *The Primacy of Drawing: Histories and Theories of Practice* (New Haven and London: Yale University Press, 2010).

Pollock, Griselda, *Differencing the Canon: Feminist Desire and the Writing of Art's Histories* (London: Routledge, 1999).

Postle, Martin *Sir Joshua Reynolds: The Subject Pictures* (Cambridge: Cambridge University Press, 1995).

Potts, Alex, *Flesh and Ideal: Winckelmann and the Origins of Art History* (New Haven and London, Yale University Press, 1994).

Read, Stanley E., 'Some Observations on William Hogarth's *The Analysis of Beauty:* A Bibliographical Study', *Huntington Library Quarterly*, 5:3 (1941–42), pp. 360–73.

Recktenwald, Olaf, 'Vredeman de Vries: Geometry and Freedom', *North Street Review*, 17 (2014), pp. 75–84.

Redford, Bruce, *Dilettanti: The Antic and the Antique in Eighteenth-Century England* (Los Angeles: Getty Research Institute, 2008).

Redford, Bruce, 'The Measure of Ruins: Dilettanti in the Levant, 1750–1770', *Harvard Library Bulletin*, 13:1 (2002), pp. 5–36.

Reid, Peter H., 'The Decline and Fall of the British Country House Library', *Libraries & Culture*, 36:2 (2001), pp. 345–66.

Reynolds, Joshua, *Discourses on Art*, ed. Robert R. Wark (San Marino, California: Huntington Library, 1959).

Richardson, Margaret and MaryAnne Stevens (eds), *John Soane Architect: Master of Space and Light*, exhibition catalogue (London: Royal Academy of Arts, 1999).

Riding, Christine and Richard Johns (eds), *Turner and the Sea* (London: Thames & Hudson; National Maritime Museum, 2013).

Rifkin, Adrian, 'Addressing Ekphrasis: A Prolegomenon to the Next', *Classical Philology*, 102:1 (2007), pp. 72–82.

Rubin, Patricia, *Giorgio Vasari: Art and History* (New Haven: Yale University Press, 1995).

Salmon, Frank, 'Stuart as Antiquary and Archaeologist in Italy and Greece', in Susan Weber Soros (ed.), *James 'Athenian' Stuart 1713–1788: The Rediscovery of Antiquity* (New Haven and London, Yale University Press, 2006).

de Saussure, Ferdinand, [*Cours de linguistique générale* (1916)], *Course in General Linguistics*, trans. Wade Baskin, ed. Perry Meisel and Haun Saussy (New York: Columbia University Press, 2011).

de Saussure, Ferdinand, *Course in General Linguistics*, ed. Charles Bally and Albert Sechehaye in collaboration with Albert Riedlinger, trans. Wade Baskin (New York: McGraw-Hill, 1966).

Savage, Nicholas, Alison Shell, Paul W. Nash, Gerald Beasley and John Meriton, *Early Printed Books 1478–1840: Catalogue of the British Architectural Library, Early Imprints Collection* (London: Bowker-Saur, 1994–2003).

Scott, Jonathan, *Piranesi* (London: Academy Editions, 1975).

de Simone, Antonio, 'Rediscovering the Villa of the Papyri', in Mantha Zarmakoupi (ed.), *The Villa of the Papyri at Herculaneum: Archaeology, Reception, and Digital Reconstruction*. Sozomena: Studies in the Recovery of Ancient Texts. Edited on behalf of the Herculaneum Society, vol. 1 (Berlin and Boston: De Gruyter, 2010), pp. 1–20.

Smiles, Sam, *J. M. W. Turner: The Making of a Modern Artist* (Manchester: Manchester University Press, 2007).

Spencer, John R., '*Ut rhetorica pictura:* A Study in Quattrocento Theory of Painting', *Journal of the Warburg and Courtauld Institutes*, 20:1/2 (1966), pp. 26–44.

Stewart, Susan, *On Longing: Narratives of the Miniature, the Gigantic, the Souvenir, the Collection* (Durham, North Carolina: Duke University Press, 1992).

Sweet, Rosemary, *Antiquaries: The Discovery of the Past in Eighteenth Century Britain* (London and New York: Hambledon and London, 2004).

Vasari, Giorgio, *The Lives of the Artists*, trans. George Bull (Harmondsworth: Penguin, 1971).

Vitruvius, *The Ten Books on Architecture*, trans. Morris Hicky Morgan (Cambridge, Massachusetts: Harvard, 1914).

Wat, Pierre, *Turner, Menteur magnifique* (Paris: Hazan, 2010).

Weber Soros, Susan (ed.), *James 'Athenian' Stuart 1713–1788: The Rediscovery of Antiquity* (New Haven and London: Yale University Press, 2006).
Wendorf, Richard, 'Piranesi's Double Ruin', *Eighteenth-Century Studies*, 34:2 (2001), pp. 161–80.
Wiebenson, Dora, *Sources of Greek Revival Architecture* (London, A. Zwemmer, 1969).
Wilton-Ely, John, *Piranesi as Architect and Designer* (New Haven, London and New York: Yale University Press and The Pierpont Morgan Library, 1993).
Wilton-Ely, John, *The Mind and Art of Giovanni Battista Piranesi* (London: Thames & Hudson, 1978).
Wilton, Andrew, *Turner in his Time* (London: Thames & Hudson, 2006).
Wilton, Andrew and Ilaria Bignamini, *The Grand Tour, The Lure of Italy in the Eighteenth Century* (London: Tate Gallery, 1996).
Winckelmann, Johann Joachim, *History of the Art of Antiquity*, trans. Harry Frances Malgrave (Los Angeles: Getty Research Institute Texts and Documents, 2006).
Winckelmann, Johann Joachim, *Reflections on the Imitation of Greek Works in Painting and Sculpture*, trans. Elfriede Heyer and Roger C. Norton (London: Open Court Classics, 1986).
Wollheim, Richard, 'On Pictorial Representation, *Journal of Aesthetics and Art Criticism*, 56:3 (1998), pp. 227–33.
Wollheim, Richard, *Painting as an Art* (London: Thames & Hudson, 1987).
Wollheim, Richard, *Art and its Objects* (Cambridge: Cambridge University Press, 1980).
Woodbridge, Kenneth, *Landscape and Antiquity Aspects of English Culture at Stourhead: 1718–1838* (Oxford: Clarendon Press, 1970).
Wright, D. R. E., 'Alberti's *De pictura:* Its Literary Structure and Purpose', *Journal of the Warburg and Courtauld Institutes*, 47 (1984), pp. 52–71.
Young, Iris Marion, *'Throwing Like a Girl' and Other Essays in Feminist Philosophy and Social Theory* (Bloomington: University of Indiana Press, 1990).
Yourcenar, Marguerite, *'The Dark Brain of Piranesi' and Other Essays*, trans. Richard Howard (New York: Farrar, Straus and Giroux, 1984).
Ziff, Jerrold, '"Backgrounds, Introduction of Architecture and Landscape": A Lecture by J. M. W. Turner', *Journal of the Warburg and Courtauld Institutes*, 26:1/2 (1963), pp. 124–47.
Zitin, Abigail, 'Wantonness: Milton, Hogarth, and *The Analysis of Beauty*', *Differences*, 27:1 (2016), pp. 25–47.
Zorach, Rebecca and Elizabeth Rodini (eds), *Paper Museums: The Reproductive Print in Europe, 1500–1800* (Chicago: David and Alfred Smart Museum of Art, University of Chicago, 2005).

Index

Page numbers in *italic* refer to illustrations